The Union Politic

THE UNION POLITIC
The CIO Political Action Committee

James Caldwell Foster

WITHDRAWN

University of Missouri Press, 1975

Library of Congress Cataloging in Publication Data

Foster, James Caldwell, 1943–
    The union politic.

    Bibliography: p.
    Includes index.
    1. Congress of Industrial Organizations. Political
Action Committee.   I. Title.
HD8055.C75F68   1975   322′.2′0973   74–22240
ISBN 0–8262–0171–7

To Gerd Korman and Paul Gates

Acknowledgments

Among the many people who have helped me during the preparation of this work, I would like to single out the following for my especial thanks.

Professor Richard Polenberg at Cornell University first interested me in the Political Action Committee, and his guidance was instrumental in the publication of my first work on the CIO–PAC, an article entitled "1954: A CIO Victory?" that appeared in the Summer, 1971 *Labor History*.

All three men who helped to shape the final work, professors Gerd Korman, Paul W. Gates, and Edward Fox, added immeasurably to the final product. Professor Korman spent many hours working over the first rough drafts, while professors Gates and Fox gave me the benefit of their personal experiences with the PAC of the 1940s.

Of course, the work itself could never have been completed without the cooperation of archivists at Wayne State University's Archives of Labor History and Urban Affairs (particularly Dennis East and Warner Pflug), at the Catholic University of America (headed by Moreau Chambers), at the Wisconsin State Historical Society, and at the Pennsylvania State University Library (particularly Leon Stout). To all of these, I am grateful.

J. C. F.
Tempe, Arizona
October, 1974

Contents

Introduction, 1

1. The Beginning, 3

2. Vainglory or Victory: The CIO in 1944, 16

3. From a Dubious Victory to Taft–Hartley, 49

4. Mr. Murray and the Great Red Menace, 76

5. 1947: "Mistaken Political Tactics," 95

6. PAC Victorious: The 1948 Elections, 108

7. PAC Almost Victorious: 1950, 133

8. Defeat Becomes a Habit: 1952, 155

9. 1954: A CIO Victory?, 176

10. The Dilemma of Partisan Politics, 196

Statistical Appendix, 208

Bibliography, 226

Index, 243

Introduction

July 7, 1943, was a typically hot summer day in Washington, D.C. The city was alive with the unnatural hurrying of a nation's capital in wartime. Yet, as soldiers and civilians scurried from one appointment to another under the heat of the sun, a small group of men quietly gathered in the national headquarters of the Congress of Industrial Organizations. These men, the national officers of the CIO, were meeting to discuss the political future of that young and growing labor federation. When the meeting ended late that afternoon and the officers departed, the CIO had taken a decisive step: Its leaders had voted to enter politics. As the CIO was well aware, however, entering the political arena required more than approving a resolution.

To coordinate the organization's political efforts, the assembled officers had also voted to create what they called the Political Action Committee. Under the able leadership of one of the CIO's founders, President Sidney Hillman of the Amalgamated Clothing Workers of America, the Committee was instructed to leap into the turbulent waters of American presidential politics. The first assignment was to reelect President Franklin D. Roosevelt. This first campaign, the 1944 elections, in the long run would prove to be but the CIO's apprenticeship in the craft of politics. The CIO and the PAC would remain active practitioners of that craft for the next six national elections.

As active politicians, the members of the CIO–PAC would discover that the political waters were turbid as well as turbulent. The CIO executives would find that the optimism and progressive spirit of the 1930s were poor tools with which to shape public opinion in the 1940s and 1950s. The times and issues were changing and, too often, the CIO and the PAC were the last groups to spot the new trends. Communism, corruption, and the Cold War would dominate domestic politics in the next decades. Unfortunately for the PAC, the easygoing attitude of the 1930s toward these issues and the quick dismissal of communism as a threat were no longer answers in a decade of suspicion and fear. Only some adroit political sidestepping by Hillman's successor, Jack Kroll, would save the CIO–PAC from complete disaster. Strangely enough, the same decade that witnessed so many PAC *faux pas* also witnessed the growth of the myth of an invincible PAC.

Political myths have always found some way to germinate in the fertile American public imagination. In the case of the CIO–PAC, the connivance of rival politicians and the CIO's own optimistic rendition of past triumphs combined to produce a mythical PAC. This mythical Committee was a veritable political juggernaut that could crush any politician who would ever venture to limit the labor movement. To its allies, the PAC appeared as the single force that had preserved organized labor from the vicious strictures of reactionary Republicans. To its foes, the PAC was an alien force in American politics, a body that had broken the sacred tenets of Samuel Gompers's voluntarism and was ruthlessly campaigning for that European evil, class legislation.

The real PAC was quite different. It was an active participant in every national election and it did campaign for candidates and legislation favorable to the labor movement. However, both opponents and allies conveniently overlooked the PAC's track record. Far from being a juggernaut, the PAC was often an inadequate and poorly-informed campaign organization. In the twelve years of its existence, the CIO–PAC lost many more elections than it won. The 1930s-thinking of a number of CIO leaders led them to champion the wrong causes in front of the wrong audiences at the wrong times. It was poor judgment, not bravery, that placed the PAC on the wrong side of the Communist issue in the 1946 elections. Yet, despite the defeats and mistakes, the PAC did have its positive side.

It was the CIO–PAC that kindled the first fires of political consciousness in the breasts of most CIO members; it was the PAC that helped transform the CIO's millions into alert and liberal members of the body politic; and it was the PAC that changed those unionist millions into the union politic.

1

The Beginning

The Political Action Committee began without drama. On July 7, 1943, the Executive Board of the Congress of Industrial Organizations met as it had met many times before and as it would meet many times thereafter. The day was not unusual; Washington, D.C., sweltered under a score of such days every summer. Even the principal players were not out of the ordinary. President Philip Murray of the CIO had called the meeting, but compared to John L. Lewis, the former holder of that office, he was a most undramatic figure. Most of the board members had been heroes of varying degrees in the labor clashes of the 1930s, but the smoke of those battles had long cleared. Regardless, that ordinary assembly of July 7 produced something that was remarkable in its own way, something that would be the topic of conversations for years. To some, the creation of that meeting would be merely one in a whole series of reelect Roosevelt committees. To others, that same creation would be the foundation upon which could be laid wholly new American political alignments. To others still, that CIO creation would be the arch violator of Samuel Gompers's sacred apolitical tradition. The creation was the Political Action Committee.

To most of the board members, one of the key considerations in forming a CIO political committee was that it follow the practical maxims which had made both the CIO and the American Federation of Labor successful unions. Hardly theoreticians, the CIO board members wanted something that would work in the political arena as effectively as their labor Congress worked in the economic realm. The key to such success in the past had been found in the fundamental labor philosophy of Samuel Gompers, a philosophy usually called "voluntarism." It was an idea that could apply equally well to the AFL of the 1890s and the CIO of the 1940s.

While Gompers had often condemned "the damning influences of partisan political action," [1] he was not apolitical. Indeed, when the AFL came under political attack, Gompers demanded that the union punish its political foes just as it struck its economic enemies. To quote a 1906 pronouncement of the master himself,

> Let us emphasize the declaration that the toilers and their friends will enforce our watchword; that we will stand by our friends and administer a stinging rebuke to men or parties who are either indifferent, negligent, or hostile. [2]

In practice, voluntarism meant that the Gompers AFL was involved in politics at almost every level. From the 1906 publication of the AFL's Bill of Grievances (presented as a memorial to Congress) to the death of Gompers, the federation found itself playing the political game in virtually every national election. Moreover, AFL politics was not restricted solely to pious pronouncements from the Olympian heights of the *American Federationist*. Gompers sent regular, paid staff members into such states as Maine and Illinois and instructed them to dirty their hands in the practical partisan world of backroom politics. [3] Admittedly, the federation never depended too much upon the cooperation of the established parties, but during the Wil-

1. Samuel Gompers, "Trade Union and Party Politics," *American Federationist*, 3 (August 1896), p. 11.
Gompers said in full, "The industrial field is littered with more corpses of organizations destroyed by the damning influences of partisan political action than from all other causes combined. . . .
"In the light of that experience, the American Federation of Labor has always declared and maintained that the unions of labor are above, and should be beyond, the power and influence of political parties."
2. Samuel Gompers, "Labor Day! Toilers Rejoice and Resolve," *American Federationist*, 13 (September 1906), p. 695.
3. Samuel Gompers to B. N. Tretheway, August 2, 1906; Samuel Gompers to Calvin Wyatt, August 7, 1906, Volume 114, Samuel Gompers Letterbooks (film), Labor Management Documentation Center, Cornell University, Ithaca, N.Y.
See also: Samuel Gompers to Frank Morrison, September 8, 1906; R. Lee Guard to F. S. Soies, August 25, 1906, Vol. 115, Samuel Gompers Letterbooks (film), Labor Management Documentation Center.

son Administration Gompers came dangerously close to such a course.

The key to voluntarism, then, was the nonpartisan nature of the animal. Dirty, practical politics was acceptable as long as the sacred AFL did not drift too close to established political parties, whether the latter were Democrat, Republican, or Labor. In this sense, the PAC of the 1940s and the 1950s was a departure from the Gompersian tradition. However, in other ways the CIO–PAC was very close to the spirit of voluntarism. To understand this link, it is necessary to return to that July meeting of 1943.

In Gompers's own words, a stinging rebuke was in order whenever politicos ignored or opposed the labor line. In 1943, the CIO felt that the time for rebuke was at hand. Although the war years did much to benefit organized labor, they also served to disguise antilabor attitudes under the cloak of patriotism and national expediency. Just as the AFL, when threatened, turned to politics and bills of grievance, so did the CIO, under threat, turn to the political arena. Yet, just what were the threats of 1943?

During that crucial July meeting, four key issues were discussed by the assembled CIO leaders. Each of the four sheds light not only on the grievances of the war years, but also upon the basically voluntaristic nature of the assembly.

The item that topped the list of CIO grievances was the outcome of the 1942 congressional elections. Twenty-five years later, the CIO's secretary–treasurer, James Carey, still would be bemoaning the huge labor losses in that most sparsely supported of all congressional elections. By Carey's count, the CIO lost forty-two allies in the House alone. In the Senate, such long-standing friends of the CIO as Senator George Norris of Nebraska were defeated.[4] Such defeats spelled political trouble for the CIO and, specifically, they threatened the National Labor Relations Act, the foundation of the 1930s labor revival. After such a dismal defeat, it was not surprising that the elections had been a topic of discussion at secret CIO meetings before.

As early as November 14, 1942, CIO President Philip

4. James B. Carey to author, May 5, 1969. Carey expressed what was essentially the CIO line of 1943–1944.

Murray had broached the subject at a CIO Executive Board meeting. He was so concerned by the prospect of an anti-CIO Congress that he asked and received permission from the board to create the special Legislative Committee to examine fully the CIO political position. The problem, according to Murray, was that the CIO almost had abandoned politics after its controversial first president, John L. Lewis, had left the organization with his political toy, Labor's Non-Partisan League, in tow. Uncertain of what course to follow, Murray appointed three of his most politically active subordinates, Nathan Cowan, John Brophy, and J. Raymond Walsh, as Legislative Committee members with the assignment of mapping out a CIO political position. Their final report would be the second major topic of discussion at the July meeting.[5]

Between November 14 and December 30, Nathan Cowan, the CIO's chief congressional lobbyist, John Brophy, director of state CIO councils, and J. Raymond Walsh, head of the union's Research Department, hammered out a position paper outlining possible CIO alternatives from complete withdrawal from politics at all levels to the creation of a labor party. The paper also dealt with such items as the lessons learned from the LNPL of the 1930s, coordination of CIO political action at all levels of the organization, financing of political action, and even possible Democratic presidential candidates in 1944 (the CIO was already leaning toward Henry Wallace). However, the heart of the Cowan–Brophy–Walsh report, submitted to President Murray on December 30, was an analysis of what went wrong in 1942. According to the report, the chief failure in the congressional elections was the CIO's failure to pay attention to the details of political work. With the official removal of the LNPL from CIO jurisdiction, the remaining CIO-controlled LNPL local groups found them-

5. Congress of Industrial Organizations, *Proceedings of the International Executive Board, November 14, 1942,* pp. 264–65. An original typed copy is located in the Office of the President, International Union of Electrical, Radio, and Machine Workers, Washington, D.C. (hereafter cited as IUE).
    Until 1973, there was no other complete record of CIO International Executive Board meetings open to researchers.

selves either insufficiently funded or insufficiently organized for serious political campaigning. In only a few states such as New York were local CIO–LNPL remnants able to pack any political punch. Even in New York, the CIO-sponsored American Labor party was having trouble delivering the votes. The elections of 1942 had proved that something more was needed.[6]

The report next made an inventory of the CIO's political arsenal. In addition to the national Legislative and Industrial Union Council departments, there were a number of state CIO bodies that also studied and publicized congressional candidates. In Ohio, Michigan, and Oregon, for instance, the CIO Industrial Union councils were directly responsible for political work. These councils held regular political conventions, endorsed candidates, and had local organizations capable of some influence over the outcome of the election. In Georgia and other states, the state council had set up autonomous political bodies that were directly responsible to the assembled CIO local unions of the state.[7] In every state, there was some form of CIO political organization, no matter how ragged.

Cowan, Brophy, and Walsh, after reviewing the situation in their report, asked that the national CIO take immediate steps to set up autonomous political bodies in each state. Autonomy was necessary for two reasons. First, if the organizations at least appeared to be autonomous, AFL and independent railroad union members might be expected to join; any organization formally associated with the CIO would alienate such possible members by its association. Only the active aid of the entire labor movement could recoup the kind of losses suffered in 1942. Second, if the political organizations were separate from the CIO, it would save the latter much embarrassment under the Corrupt Practices Act (by that act, any group involved in a national political contest was required to open its books to public

6. Nathan E. Cowan, John Brophy, and J. Raymond Walsh to Philip Murray, December 30, 1942, CIO Political Programs Folder, Box 25, Wayne County AFL–CIO Papers, Archives of Labor History and Urban Affairs, Wayne State University, Detroit, Mich. (hereafter cited as ALH). This letter will be hereafter cited as the Cowan–Brophy–Walsh report.
7. Ibid., pp. 3–8.

investigators). The militant union was afraid that public investigators might hamper some of its organization activities.[8]

The report next moved to the national CIO political organization, which was to be tied much more closely to the CIO than the state political bodies were. Cowan, Brophy, and Walsh suggested that their Legislative Committee be utilized temporarily as a political organization. In the long run, a new body would have to be named by Murray to head a 1944 effort. To head this body, the Legislative Committee suggested either James Carey or the president of any of the large national CIO unions.[9]

Once the political body was formed, it was to take on certain organizational responsibilities that the LNPL had never faced. For instance, there was the sticky question of finances. The LNPL had been largely financed by massive grants from the United Mine Workers of America. With the departure of the UMWA from the CIO that avenue of financing had been closed. Cowan, Brophy, and Walsh suggested a twofold approach to the problem. First, the national unions would be asked to contribute to political action on a regular and fixed basis. Second, local unions would be brought into the effort by paying a per capita tax of a penny per member, the proceeds of which would be used for local political action.[10]

Perhaps the most intriguing part of the report was the section dealing with the operation of the new body. The

8. Ibid., pp. 9–11.

9. Ibid., p. 15.

10. Ibid., pp. 19–20. Labor's Non-Partisan League had been founded by John L. Lewis with United Mine Workers' funds in 1936 to ensure the reelection of Franklin D. Roosevelt and the election of a prolabor Congress. As a CIO auxiliary, it had served—not too effectively—as a proto-PAC in the years 1936–1941. In the states of New York and Michigan it had served as a nucleus for new political parties, the New York American Labor party and the Michigan Non-Partisan League, the latter of which never really got started (it was in the process during 1942–1943).

The chief contribution of the LNPL was its nonpartisan tone. Lewis insisted that AFL leaders be included in the executive offices of the league. See, Labor's Non-Partisan League, *Labor's Non-Partisan League: Its Origins and Growth* (Washington: Labor's Non-Partisan League, 1939). A copy can be found in the Labor Management Documentation Center.

writers emphasized the need to operate inside the Democratic party. Abandoning any pretense of nonpartisanship, they noted that the CIO "should not pretend that there is the slightest possibility of our achieving genuine influence in the Republican Party." Yet, even in endorsing the Democrats, they admitted that in many districts the CIO would have to work with Republicans because the Democratic candidate would have no chance of winning. Moreover, cooperation with either existing party did not preclude "consideration of the possible need of a new labor party later on." Following this almost startling reference to that dreaded European alternative, a labor party, the report concluded with a battle plan for 1944.[11]

After the more detailed sections of the report, the 1944 section was most disappointing. Cowan, Brophy, and Walsh returned to the twin battle cries that had marked labor political action from the time of Gompers. To get workers to vote with the union, they suggested only a strong registration drive and the creation of a rather nebulous program that would place the CIO foursquare behind President Roosevelt and the New Deal. Even the union line was nothing new. Picking up on Roosevelt's cue, the writers suggested that the CIO enter the 1944 campaign with a drive to warn workers of a coming depression if the Hooverite Republicans returned to office. As far back as 1906, the AFL had emphasized registration and the wishbook approach to political programs. Only the names and circumstances of the 1930s made the proposed 1944 CIO program different from the 1908 proposals of the AFL.[12]

The Cowan–Brophy–Walsh recommendations had already been partially adopted by the time of the July meeting. As early as January 8, 1943, Murray had called a special legislative conference of all CIO unions to act upon

11. Cowan–Brophy–Walsh report, p. 21.
12. Ibid., pp. 23–36. The 1908 AFL political program included everything from a national eight-hour day law to massive restrictions upon the use of the antilabor injunction. As the CIO program of 1943–1944, it was less a list of realistic demands than a wishbook of ideal congressional accomplishments. See Marc Karson, *American Labor Unions and Politics, 1900–1918* (Carbondale: Southern Illinois University Press, 1958), pp. 50–60.

the report. A month later, the CIO Executive Board had unanimously adopted an interim plan proposed by Nathan Cowan that would have created a special legislative auxiliary in every national and local CIO union. Before the vote had been taken, Cowan had emphasized the seriousness of the situation. The CIO, he noted, had but 106 congressmen whom it could trust. That meant there were only 106 loyalists standing between the CIO and a veritable flood of antiunion legislation.[13] Nobody missed the significance of his remarks.

From the beginning, many CIO leaders had realized that much of their success depended upon the continued independent operation of the National Labor Relations Board. That independence had been under almost constant threat since the 1938 AFL convention had demanded basic changes in the Wagner Act. On July 20, 1939, congressional conservatives had joined the anti-NLRB brigade with the creation of Howard Smith's Special Committee to Investigate the National Labor Relations Board. From that date until December, 1941, congressional hoppers had been filled with about fifty antiunion bills. So serious had the situation become that the AFL reversed its stand and joined the CIO in a last ditch attempt to defeat the anti-Wagner Act proposals. As it turned out, only the Japanese attack on Pearl Harbor succeeded in putting off congressional criticism. The anti-NLRB Smith Act, passed by the House on December 3, 1941, was buried in America's rush to war.[14] Even so, the warning remained, a warning reiterated by Cowan in February.

As the meeting of July considered its third major topic of discussion, it returned to those warnings of February. The war had derailed congressional action on the Smith bill only temporarily; June, 1943, marked a massive effort in both houses that resulted in the passage of the antilabor Smith–Connally Act, an act rammed past a presidential veto: The CIO was in trouble.

13. CIO, *Proceedings of the International Executive Board, February 5, 1943*, pp. 70–73, IUE.

14. Joel Seidman, *American Labor from Defense to Reconversion* (Chicago: University of Chicago Press, 1953), pp. 67–73. See also, Irving Bernstein, *Turbulent Years* (Boston: Houghton–Mifflin Co., 1971), pp. 666–71.

Coming as they had amidst a series of John L. Lewis-sponsored wartime coal strikes, the Smith and Connally bills to prevent wartime strikes gained more and more support in the spring of 1943. Although most Americans seemed to agree that Lewis and the United Mine Workers needed shackling, the two bills had gone far beyond the apparent mandate. In three major sections, the bills empowered the President to take over any plant or industry in which a halt in production threatened the war effort (if the War Labor Board could not effect reconciliation beforehand); they required both a thirty-day cooling-off period and a NLRB-administered strike vote before strikes could occur in noncritical industries; and they prohibited union contributions to political campaigns. Criminal penalties were also authorized for any individual or group that advocated a strike in those critical industries seized by the President.[15] All in all, the Smith and Connally bills should have had little effect on either the major AFL or the CIO unions except for the political contributions prohibition. That and the bills' implication that all labor was disloyal to the war effort (why else, reasoned CIO leaders, would thirty-day cooling-off periods and strike votes be necessary) transformed a minor anti-Lewis action into an act that transformed CIO headquarters into a scene of panic. Fearing the worst, Murray frantically called together the CIO executives on May 14. All that the assembly could devise was a last-minute telegram campaign aimed at members of Congress and the President himself. In June, all else was dropped while CIO leaders scurried between their Washington offices and Capitol Hill. A last-ditch lobbying effort was launched, but it was too late.[16] By July, the time had come to regroup.

As President Murray opened the July 7 meeting, his remarks were addressed to but one point, the Smith–Connally Act. Quickly skirting the actual provisions of the act, he

15. U.S., *Congressional Record,* 78th Cong., 1st sess., 1943, 89, Part 4, 5382. Almost every CIO union reacted violently to the passage of Smith–Connally. Aside from the Executive Board reaction, a typical comment was the *CIO News'* characterization of the act as the "to Hell with (the) War Bill," *CIO News,* May 10, 1943, p. 3.

16. CIO, *Proceedings . . . , July 7–8, 1943,* pp. 4–8, IUE.

got to the heart of the issue within minutes. Not only did the act make the CIO appear disloyal, he said, but it also revealed a cynical and dangerous alliance between certain congressmen and the AFL. While the CIO had done everything in its power to protect labor's interest in the Smith–Connally fight, the AFL's chief lobbyist, John Frey, had secretly allowed a number of pro-AFL congressmen to vote with the majority in overriding President Roosevelt's veto of the measure. This kind of action made the already serious situation much more dangerous for the CIO. An AFL–conservative alliance might go even further in legislatively controlling the actions of the upstart Congress of Industrial Organizations. In view of this, the CIO must respond politically so that the nascent AFL–conservative alliance could do no more damage. To add emphasis to his presentation, Murray noted in closing that the new alliance was at work again. On July 6, a CIO-sponsored price rollback bill had been defeated by the same congressmen who had enacted Smith–Connally.[17] The CIO must act, and it must act at once.

After the speeches were over and the past defeats had been weighed, those assembled turned to the final and key issue of the meeting. What would the CIO do? As luck would have it, the final debate concerned the creation of a labor party. Would or would not the CIO violate the labor movement's fifty-year pledge to the voluntarist ethic?

As Murray returned to his chair, Samuel Wolchok, president of the Retail, Wholesale, and Department Store Union, asked the question foremost in the minds of all: "How are we going to strike back politically?"[18] The ensuing discussion revealed that Gompersian voluntarism still had some influence on the leaders of labor.

---

17. Ibid., pp. 9–11. Inflation was an important issue to the CIO during the war. CIO executives had always claimed that wages could not keep pace with prices after 1941 because of the Little Steel formula's theoretical fifteen per cent ceiling on wage hikes. The Bureau of Labor Statistics saw wages increase thirty per cent in the same period (1941–1943) that prices increased by only twenty-four per cent. U.S., Bureau of Labor Statistics, *Monthly Labor Review,* 56 (1943), 1179; 57 (1943), 1205.

18. CIO, *Proceedings . . . , July 7–8, 1943,* p. 25.

Some sentiment came out almost immediately for the formation of a labor party. The unionists of Europe had taken such a course with marked success. In the United States, labor had no party that it could call its own; moreover, the Cowan–Brophy–Walsh report had specifically included a labor party as a possible CIO alternative. At this point, Murray and the conservatives reasserted control over the meeting. President Murray was opposed to the labor party idea and he made his opposition clear. Using words similar to those expressed by Samuel Gompers in 1896, he asked the board to keep its options open by backing a nonpartisan labor league, not a party. A labor league had already been tried by the CIO with some degree of success. Not only would a league be following the established course of labor political action (as in the case of Labor's Non-Partisan League), but it would also be following the nonpartisan guideline of the Cowan–Brophy–Wash report. A labor party would merely alienate the AFL and independent unions whose support was desperately needed in the 1944 contest. In due course, even the labor party advocates were won over to temporary acceptance of the Murray view. The board backed the nonpartisan proposal unanimously, just as it had backed Murray's choices for positions of leadership in the new league. These choices also followed the Cowan–Brophy–Walsh guidelines. The presidents of two of the largest CIO unions, Sidney Hillman of the Amalgamated Clothing Workers of America and R. J. Thomas of the United Automobile Workers, were chosen as chairman and secretary of what would be known as the CIO Political Action Committee.[19]

As the sun set over Washington that night, lights were still burning at CIO headquarters. While most of the CIO Executive Board had recessed that afternoon, Hillman and Thomas had called the new Political Action Committee into a special session to prepare a plan of action for the

19. Ibid., pp. 147–49. Other Political Action Committee members were: Van Bittner, assistant to President Murray; Sherman Dalrymple, president of the United Rubber Workers of America; Albert Fitzgerald, president of the United Electrical, Machine, and Radio Workers of America; and David McDonald, the secretary–treasurer of the United Steel Workers of America.

Executive Board on the following day. That report would not be optimistic.

July 8 was another busy day at CIO headquarters. By midmorning, most of the CIO vice presidents and other executives had returned to the Executive Board room, where R. J. Thomas was about to make a preliminary report on the CIO political program. Rising slowly, Thomas addressed his fellows in tones of caution. Unlike 1936, he said, the CIO of 1943 was emotionally unprepared for mass political action. In 1936, the CIO was ready. The membership was ready. John L. Lewis was ready. The result was the successful debut of Labor's Non-Partisan League. Yet, only seven years later, the CIO faced an anti-union Congress and a passive group of union voters. The job for the next few months must be to recoup the losses of the last seven years. The CIO must restore the spirit of 1936 both to itself and to its members. Only then would it have a chance to think seriously of 1944. In the meantime, even the slightest thought of a third party effort was not only unrealistic, but was downright bad for the mother union. Practical political organization must be the sole concern for the next few months.

Thomas then turned the meeting over to John Brophy, who as head of the CIO Industrial Union Council Department was best informed on what was happening in the field.[20] Brophy, too, sounded a note of caution. CIO personnel at the state level, he explained, had been deeply concerned about the political situation for some time. To assuage their fears and get them into the new political organization, he suggested a series of quiet, informal meetings between the new CIO–PAC staff and the various state CIO leaders. Not only would this mesh them into the PAC organization, but it would also give the local leaders an opportunity to give the PAC the benefit of their political savvy, their special understanding of local political issues and personalities. Such meetings should be scheduled as soon as possible. Brophy fully approved of an earlier suggestion made by Thomas that regional political action conferences should begin no later than a planned meeting on July 17 in Chicago.[21] There was no time to waste.

20. Ibid., pp. 223–29.
21. Ibid., pp. 229–30.

The last speaker to address the meeting was Sidney Hillman, the PAC's chairman. Although the third-party issue had been temporarily buried, Hillman revived it by announcing that the coming regional conferences would make the final decision. Yet, even Hillman entered into the compromising spirit of the meeting. All he asked was that New York state leaders be given the option of supporting the CIO-sponsored American Labor party. He did nothing to push the formation of a national labor party.[22] On this note, the meeting adjourned.

As the sun began to set that evening, Hillman and his new associates were already beginning to plan for 1944. The July 17 meeting in Chicago would be of most immediate concern, but ahead of them was the most important test of all: November, 1944.

22. Ibid., p. 232.

2

Vainglory or Victory: The CIO in 1944

It was a boisterous and exuberant crowd that faced Sidney Hillman as he rose to address the November 22, 1944, CIO convention. The mention of Hillman's name had caused union members to break into a jubilant ten-minute demonstration. Elated over Franklin D. Roosevelt's recent and decisive victory, the crowd was eager for the chairman of the famed CIO Political Action Committee to pull out all the rhetorical stops in his description of the CIO part in the glorious triumph. The crowd was not to be disappointed. He began,

> November 7 was our Battle of Britain, our Stalingrad. The loss of that battle would have meant disastrous, irretrievable defeat for the cause of peace and freedom here at home and throughout the world. The bloodless victory which we scored on election day is as significant for the ultimate triumph of that cause as the heroic achievements of our great allies over London and on the Volga . . .
> We of the CIO can take great pride in our contribution to that victory.[1]

When the cheers and applause of the convention died, however, some important questions remained unanswered. What exactly was the CIO's contribution to the Democratic victory? If the November 7 elections were indeed as great a victory as Hillman had declared, how had the CIO Political Action Committee aided the Democratic cause? Indeed, should the self-congratulatory words of Hillman be taken at face value, or should Hillman's rhetoric be looked upon as more vainglorious than deservedly victorious?

1. CIO, *Final Proceedings of the Seventh Constitutional Convention of the Congress of Industrial Organizations, November 20–24, 1944, Chicago, Ill.,* pp. 202–3, 206.

The CIO began to take an active role in the 1944 electoral contest in the summer of 1943. After the July 7 Executive Board meeting that had created the Political Action Committee and its sister organization, the Committee on Congressional Action, the board began to prepare for political action in earnest.[2] It had been almost three years since the CIO had last been involved in a national campaign. Its aging political machine had to be carefully checked, primed for the battle, and cautiously restarted.

Preparation for the 1944 election involved three essential steps. First, the Executive Board and the Political Action Committee needed to devise a long-term strategy for political action. Second, this strategy had to be translated into specific tactics, tactics that could win a prolabor Congress and President in 1944. Finally, the CIO had to deliver its votes on election day. The labor voter was the key to victory.

The CIO's master plan for 1944 was primarily concerned with what a pamphlet published by the Textile Workers Union of America termed membership development of "a new awareness of the world."[3] The CIO worker had to become a CIO voter; he had to become aware of the pressing political issues of the day and the injustices of the existing system. Through the intelligent use of his ballot, he and his fellows would create a better America. Or, as the pamphlet stated,

> Together—textile workers and aircraft workers, farmers and seafarers, miners and clerks, clothing workers and bridge builders, all who do the work of America—we

2. *CIO News,* July 12, 1943, p. 3. The Political Action Committee was formed as a direct result of the series of anti-labor measures considered and enacted by the conservative Congress elected in 1942. The final blow, as far as the CIO was concerned, was the enactment of the Smith–Connally (War Labor Disputes Act) bill over President Roosevelt's veto in late June, 1943. See, *Packinghouse Worker,* July 2, 1943, p. 1. The general work on this is Joseph Gaer, *The First Round* (New York: Duell, Sloan and Pearce, Inc., 1944).

3. "Toward a New Day" presented to the Third Biennial Convention of the Textile Workers Union of America, May 12, 1943, p. 14, Union File, New York State School of Industrial and Labor Relations. (Hereafter cited as "Toward a New Day").

must go forward in our march for a better day. Together
we can establish the dignity of the common man.[4]

Yet, the CIO voter had to be guided by more than rhetoric.
If he were to become a CIO voter, he would have to follow
a CIO political program.

The CIO political program for 1944 was more than a
campaign document that could be discarded after one election. It represented the new CIO drive for CIO voters,
voters who could be depended upon to support the same
type of ideals and candidates supported by the CIO leadership. This call for a new kind of CIO voter was repeated
again and again in Political Action Committee publications
distributed during the 1944 campaign.

Perhaps the first public statement of the new CIO program was the Textile Workers' pamphlet entitled "Toward
a New Day." In early 1943, Emil Rieve, the Textile Workers' president who would later become a charter member
of the CIO Political Action Committee, submitted this
political program to his union's convention. Along with
the inspired rhetoric concerning the new awareness required
of union voters, the document also contained a seven-point
program to guide the prospective CIO citizen. The program
called for an international organization of all nations, a
domestic order designed to strengthen the Bill of Rights
and the Four Freedoms, a guarantee of full employment
at reasonable wages, aid for the farmer, taxation based
upon the ability to pay, and an industrial system controlled
by the "many" (meaning nationalization).[5] This would
serve as a guide for several CIO political statements during
the campaign.

The first official Political Action Committee publication
that embraced the themes of "Toward a New Day" was
the widely circulated PAC pamphlet called "This Is Your
America." This pamphlet, written by PAC Publication
Director Joseph Gaer, reiterated the necessity for a new
political awareness among labor voters. In addition, it
stressed what Gaer called "freedom for all our people." In
essence, the CIO was asking its members to respect and
fight for the civil rights of all races. The CIO–PAC was

4. Ibid.
5. Ibid.

emphasizing its dedication to all the "common people." As the pamphlet stated, it was through the union of the worker and the common people that the CIO–PAC would strive to "create a more perfect union." [6]

The program for this new alliance was spelled out in more detail in another PAC publication. The "People's Program for 1944" was the June, 1944, statement of the CIO's immediate political goals. It set forth proposals in four areas of foreign and domestic policy. Concerning the war, the program called for a peace based upon the Four Freedoms, the Good Neighbor Policy, and the United Nations Declaration. It also urged formation of an international organization open to all nations, donation of long-term credits to industrially-backward countries, extension of the right of asylum to all the world's persecuted minorities, and the rehabilitation of war-ravaged lands through United States financing.[7] The program asked only that the United States redeem its wartime pledges to the people of the world.

The second area to which the program addressed itself was postwar domestic planning. Citing President Roosevelt's January, 1944, call for a new Bill of Rights, the PAC asked that every citizen be guaranteed the right to earn a decent living. This guarantee was to extend to everyone regardless of race, creed, or occupation. Every citizen must also be assured some form of medical care, housing, secondary education, and insurance against sickness, unemployment, and the insecurity of age.[8] The program emphasized that economic security was the basic need of every American.

The third area of concentration was the CIO's answer to the problem of returning servicemen. Anticipating a postwar labor market swollen with returning soldiers, the PAC proposed a three-point program to protect the interests of demobilized veterans and unionized workers.[9]

6. "This Is Your America" in Gaer, pp. 39, 43.
7. "People's Program for 1944" in Gaer, pp. 192–97.
8. Ibid., pp. 199–208.
9. The CIO's concern with the problem of returning servicemen was essentially the same as that of the AFL in the period 1918–1919. The AFL's reconstruction program called for up to one year's wage to be paid by the government to an unemployed veteran. Both AFL workers (in 1917–1918) and

The basic provision was the payment of unemployment benefits to jobless veterans for a period of up to two years. Additionally, the CIO urged the creation of both a government-sponsored program to help returning soldiers complete their academic or vocational training and the payment of a demobilization stipend sufficiently large to allow returning servicemen to make the initial adjustment to civilian life.[10] Here, the PAC was trying to devise a plan to reintroduce veterans into the labor force without penalizing existing jobholders.

The final section of the "People's Program of 1944" dealt with the question of civil rights. After the 1943 Detroit race riot, which occurred in a city where CIO members composed over forty per cent of the electorate, it was not surprising that the CIO–PAC turned its attention to the pressing national race problem.[11] The civil rights plank of the PAC platform began with the statement that "Anti-Negro practices undermine the very foundation of our democracy." [12] To overcome the evils of racial discrimination, the CIO demanded the establishment of a permanent Fair Employment Practices Commission with enough funds and power to operate effectively. Moreover, the program stipulated that the federal government must enact legislation that would prohibit propaganda or activities directed against anyone due to his race, creed, or color. At the same time, the Administration was called upon to end poll taxes, which disfranchised millions.[13]

CIO workers (1941–1944) had benefitted from the draft that had removed millions of workers from industry. To both unions, unplanned reconversion could have been an economic nightmare. Harry A. Millis and Royal E. Montgomery, *Organized Labor,* Vol. 3 (New York: McGraw–Hill Book Co., 1945), pp. 131–43.

10. "People's Program for 1944" in Gaer, pp. 209–10.

11. CIO members, both black and white, comprised about forty-three per cent of the 1944 electorate in Wayne County (Detroit), Mich. See, Appendix B. On the Detroit race riot see Rayford Logan, *The Negro in American Life and Thought* (New York: The Dial Press, 1954).

12. Gaer, p. 211.

13. Ibid., p. 212. The PAC operated on the assumption that many southerners on marginal incomes were disfranchised, since they didn't have money to spend on such luxuries as poll taxes.

The call for civil rights legislation may have represented not only the liberal leanings of CIO leaders, but also their realization that the Negro was becoming an increasingly important factor in their organization. This was especially true in such cities as Detroit, New York, and Chicago.

The "People's Program," "Toward a New Day," and many other CIO–PAC publications all emphasized the basic strategy of the CIO in 1944.[14] The CIO unionist was to become an active and concerned CIO voter, because, it was hoped, of the inspiring nature of the CIO program and platform. Yet, even if such a utopian goal were achieved, three million CIO voters meant nothing without a candidate and party to support. With this in mind, CIO–PAC leaders began to lay plans to trade their support for major Democratic concessions.

Obviously, the Democrats were the only alternative for the CIO. As early as the 1942 Cowan–Brophy–Walsh political action report, the CIO party line had been to follow the Democrats. The key to the report had been the sage advice to abandon false hopes of "achieving genuine influence in the Republican Party."[15] The 1944 Republican hopefuls were unlikely to discredit such advice.

While CIO officials were considering their next move, the Republican contest had already come down to a battle between Governor Thomas Dewey of New York, General Douglas MacArthur, lawyer and business executive Wendell Willkie, and Governor John Bricker of Ohio. Although Willkie fell in the primaries and MacArthur never officially announced his candidacy, none of the four would have

14. Gaer quotes many other CIO–PAC pamphlets that share the same message. Gaer was the author of all the PAC pamphlets cited. The TWUA program, so very similar in thought, was probably the work of Herbert Payne, a TWUA leader. Both the PAC and the TWUA were influenced by the thinking of their founders, who were in both cases Sidney Hillman and Emil Rieve. See, Martha L. Saenger, "Labor Political Action at Mid-Twentieth Century: A Case Study of the CIO–PAC Campaign of 1944 and the Textile Workers Union of America," Ph.D. dissertation, Ohio State University, 1959, pp. 318–20, 372–75.

15. Nathan E. Cowan, John Brophy, and J. Raymond Walsh to Philip Murray, December 30, 1942, p. 21, CIO Political Programs Folder, Box 25, Wayne County AFL–CIO Papers, ALH.

been satisfactory to the CIO's political leaders.[16] None had the liberal record of the incumbent Roosevelt and none were likely to barter their souls for a few labor votes. With this in mind, Sidney Hillman opened the delicate negotiations with Roosevelt in mid-1943.

Before the public had even been given the full details on the new CIO–PAC, Hillman wrote a long, personal letter to Roosevelt asking for an appointment to explain the CIO's new political program. Emphasizing that the sole purpose of the CIO–PAC was to elect congressmen who "support you" (referring to the President), Hillman intimated that the CIO and the Democratic party could become complementary political tools.[17] With this appointment, the PAC–Democratic negotiations began.

With Hillman and Roosevelt closeted in intense political negotiations, the CIO–PAC, as an organization, found itself an infant in the adult world of big-time politics. Hillman could promise to deliver the labor vote to both Roosevelt and pro-Roosevelt congressmen, but his organization, at least in 1943, was not capable of delivering those votes. The Political Action Committee had to close the gap between rhetoric and reality.

The first problem facing the CIO was organization. Union organizations did not coincide geographically with political units. While the large urban centers were divided into five or six congressional districts, the CIO's organization in the same center was most likely divided into a multitude of local unions, several international unions, and a county-wide central union, none of which coincided with the all-important congressional districts. Effective political action dictated a change. To organize politically, the CIO needed one comprehensive membership list for each congressional district and one all-inclusive labor committee per political unit.

Only days after the creation of the two CIO political

16. A good, short account of the 1944 campaign can be found in James MacGregor Burns, *Roosevelt: The Soldier of Freedom* (New York: Harcourt Brace Jovanovich, 1970), 497–531.

17. Sidney Hillman to Franklin D. Roosevelt, July 27, 1943, White House File, 1942–1946, Sidney Hillman Papers, Amalgamated Clothing Workers Union, New York, N.Y.

committees, the Special Committee on Congressional Action, chaired by the United Automobile Workers' Secretary–Treasurer George Addes, prepared to remedy the CIO's organizational deficiencies.[18] On July 16, 1943, the Addes Committee sent out what was to be the first in a long series of memoranda carefully outlining the international unions' roles in the coming political struggle. The most important point was the call for organization at the congressional district level. The international unions were to instruct their local affiliates to join with other unions in their congressional districts to form integrated district committees. The new committees would then handle all the details of the local congressional campaign.[19] By August 14, Chairman Addes reported that several hundred integrated district committees were already in operation.[20] The first tactical problem had been solved.

Organization at the state level was a much easier task. There, the state CIO Industrial Union Council and the state as a political body were coterminous. The Political Action Committee made only one improvement on the existing system. Sidney Hillman set up fourteen regional PAC offices to better coordinate the CIO effort in key states. These offices ranged from multiple state operations, such as Region One, which covered all of New England, to single state offices, such as Region Six, which concentrated solely upon

18. The Special Committee (Addes Committee) was composed of the following: George Addes, secretary–treasurer of the United Automobile Workers; James Carey, CIO secretary–treasurer; Julius Emspak, secretary–treasurer of the Electrical Workers; David McDonald, secretary–treasurer of the United Steel Workers of America. *CIO News,* July 12, 1943, p. 3.

19. Special Committee on Congressional Action to all International Unions, July 16, 1943, CIO Political Programs Folder, Box 25, Wayne County AFL–CIO Papers, Archives of Labor History and Urban Affairs, Wayne State University, Detroit, Mich.

20. *CIO News,* August 16, 1943, p. 3. Even President Murray of the CIO was getting into the organization business. Through his subordinates David McDonald and Robert Lamb, he was organizing the Steel Workers into usable political action districts. Particular emphasis was placed on the USWA drive in Pennsylvania and New York. Robert Lamb to Philip Murray, n.d. (1944), CIO–PAC Folder, Box A4–9, Philip Murray Papers, Catholic University of America, Washington, D.C.

the problems of Michigan. All of the regional offices were financed by the national PAC and manned by national PAC appointees.[21]

The next problem was financing, and the solution involved more legal maneuver than financial manipulation. Under the provisions of the June, 1943, War Labor Disputes (Smith–Connally) Act, it was unlawful for any labor organization "to make a contribution in connection with any election" that chose presidential electors, senators, or representatives to Congress.[22] Yet, the PAC had to have funds to operate a patently political campaign. In fact, the CIO's international unions had already pledged over 700,000 dollars to the PAC in apparent violation of the Smith–Connally provisions forbidding union political contributions.[23] The PAC had to find legal means to finance its work.

According to the CIO–PAC's counsel, John Abt, the acceptance and use of union contributions was legally justified in two ways. First, Abt pointed out that the national unions' pledges to the PAC were not legally contributions but were rather to be considered expenditures. The legal definition of contribution stated that the money donated must go directly to the candidate. Because all of the money donated to the PAC had been spent on pamphlets, radio time, and various other publicity devices, and because no PAC funds had gone directly to candidates, the union contributions to the PAC were perfectly acceptable. Second, the Smith–Connally Act forbade union contributions to an election campaign. Yet, an election required a candidate, and any activity prior to the nomination of party candidates was not restricted. Moreover, the kind of activi-

21. Philip Murray and Sidney Hillman to West Virginia Industrial Union Council, September 11, 1943, Box 20, CIO Folder, West Virginia Industrial Union Council Papers, West Virginia University Library, Morgantown, W.Va. The West Virginia University Library will hereafter be cited as WVUL. U.S., Senate, Special Committee to Investigate Presidential, Vice-Presidential, and Senatorial Campaign Expenditures, *Hearings on S.R. 263,* 78th Cong., 2nd sess., 1944, p. 10.

22. U.S., *Statutes at Large,* 57, Part 1, p. 168.

23. U.S., Senate, Special Committee to Investigate Presidential, Vice-Presidential, and Senatorial Campaign Expenditures, *Hearings,* p. 15. Gaer, p. 177.

ties in which the PAC had been involved were better described as educational rather than political. Indeed, Sidney Hillman himself described PAC registration drives, primary campaigns, and other activities as only an encouragement of good citizenship.[24] There remained one small financial problem—how would the PAC finance its drive after the nominees had been chosen?

The PAC "dollar drive" was the device used to allow the PAC to circumvent the postnomination restrictions of the Smith–Connally Act. Although unions had been forbidden to contribute funds to an election campaign, Smith–Connally contained no specific prohibition of union member contributions. Thus, if the PAC could raise voluntary contributions from CIO members it could use such monies without legal restrictions. The "dollar drive" was simply a CIO-sponsored drive for members' CIO–PAC donations. The idea was that if every member gave but a dollar, the postnomination PAC financial picture would be rosy, indeed, and legally so.[25] Now that the PAC had an organizational structure and adequate financing, it could turn to the political problems of electing a pro-CIO Congress.

The PAC in 1944 relied upon a simple campaign strategy to elect a President and Congress that it believed would enact its program. Starting with the assumption that five million CIO members, if properly organized, would hold the balance of power in many congressional districts, CIO–PAC felt that membership registration and voting were the twin keys to success.[26] Indoctrination and education of union voters were also important, but not so vital as registration and a massive union vote.

The emphasis on registration was a direct result of CIO analysis of the 1942 elections, which brought one of the most antilabor Congresses in a decade into power. The

24. Ibid., pp. 23–26.
25. Ibid., p. 18. Sidney Hillman to all International Unions, December 9, 1943, CIO–PAC File, Sidney Hillman Papers, Amalgamated Clothing Workers Union of America, New York, N.Y.
26. *Report of President Philip Murray to the Sixth Constitutional Convention of the Congress of Industrial Organizations, Philadelphia, Pennsylvania, November 1–5, 1943*, pp. 52–55. Gaer, pp. 54–56.

official CIO view of the 1942 debacle was that it was caused by low voter turnout. Of a potential electorate of over 80 million, only 28 million bothered to vote. Since a small vote seemed to have been responsible for the most conservative Congress in years, a large vote in 1944 could be the path to a more liberal Congress.[27] Years later, James Carey, CIO secretary–treasurer, echoed that analysis. He blamed the low voter turnout in 1942 for the defeat of forty-two prolabor congressmen.[28] Two measures were required to increase voter participation. First, the CIO had to make sure that as many voters as possible were registered. Second, it had to find a way to get them to exercise their franchise.

The registration drive started at the 1943 CIO convention. Both CIO President Philip Murray and Political Action Committee Chairman Sidney Hillman emphasized the importance of the subject.[29] By early 1944, the drive was well underway at the state level. The registration campaign in Ohio was illustrative of the techniques used throughout the country. Because registration was the responsibility of county governments, the County Political Action Committee became the center of attention. The key to successful registration, Ohio PAC leaders wrote, was to convince county officials to set up voter registration booths at factories during the changing of the shift. Whatever stragglers this system might miss, CIO block workers, operating from master membership lists, would bring into the fold.[30] By late October, 1944, reports began to pour into national PAC headquarters telling of registration totals far in excess of even optimistic predictions. Detroit, Michigan, one of the centers of PAC activity, recorded an all time high in voter registration.[31]

27. Ibid.

28. James B. Carey to author, May 5, 1969.

29. *Proceedings of the Sixth Constitutional Convention of the Congress of Industrial Organizations, Philadelphia, Pa., November 1–5, 1943*, pp. 82–85, 239–42.

30. Ohio CIO Political Action Guide, pp. 19–21, PAC Folder, Box 27, West Virginia Industrial Union Council Papers, WVUL. "What Every Canvasser Should Know" in Gaer, pp. 135–48.

31. Release to all Local Unions, October 19, 1944, CIO–PAC Folder, Box 25, Wayne County AFL–CIO Papers,

Transforming record registration figures into a record Democratic vote was a much more complicated problem. The CIO did have certain advantages over such voting groups as political parties and other pressure groups. First, it had a membership of over five million members who shared some kind of loyalty to the national organization for substantial wage gains. Second, because the PAC worked through the existing union organization, it had access to the unionist voter for much of his forty-hour workweek. Few parties could claim to have had that much time to indoctrinate their voters. Finally, PAC had group pressure working for it. Since a substantial portion of the CIO's membership supported the same party and candidates as the PAC, the few dissidents could often be brought into line by informal shop ostracism. This pressure was the PAC's secret weapon.[32]

The best the Political Action Committee could hope to do outside the shop was to keep the union member interested in the issues, frequently by bombarding workers with the PAC message. Again, the PAC exploited certain CIO advantages. First, both the CIO and its many component unions had their own private newspapers. Utilizing this medium to the utmost, the unions showered their members with the 1944 message at least monthly, and often, in the *CIO News,* weekly. Second, the PAC's Publication Division, which published over 85 million pieces of campaign literature in 1943 and 1944, had the advantage of a direct line to the membership.[33] Working through local PACs, it easily could saturate CIO shops. However, keeping voter interest was only the first step in the PAC plan.

The second step toward PAC victory was active participation in the primary elections. Tactically, the PAC's

ALH. Records were also reported in Los Angeles, Atlanta, and Dayton, William H. Riker, "The CIO in Politics" (Ph.D. dissertation, Harvard University, 1948), pp. 307–10.

32. Riker, pp. 298–300. One worker to which the PAC paid attention in 1944 was the black. An entire campaign apparatus chaired by Henry Lee Moon was created solely to work on the black CIO voter. See C. B. Baldwin to Henry Lee Moon, April 6, 1944, CIO–PAC New York City, 1944–1947 Folder, Box 203, CIO Secretary–Treasurer's Papers, ALH.

33. Gaer, pp. 305–6.

chances would surely be enhanced in November if it could present attractive candidates to its voters. The Political Action Committee was thus forced to place its prestige on the line in the primaries.

Fortunately for the CIO–PAC, it never published a complete list of its primary endorsements. Thus, it was impossible for its detractors to gauge accurately the extent of PAC failure, or success, as the results came in. Even more fortunately, several influential conservatives, who were defeated in the primaries, blamed their defeats upon the PAC. As the summer came and went, the PAC could bolster its camp with tales of stunning victories instead of worrying its wavering supporters with early defeats.

Some of the PAC's victories were so spectacular that they provided ammunition for optimistic CIO writers up to election day. Perhaps the most famous of these was the political abdication of Martin Dies. Dies, as chairman of the House Un-American Activities Committee, had been an outspoken opponent of basic CIO issues, levelling blast after blast at labor unions in general and Sidney Hillman in particular. However, when his Texas constituency, which included the industrial towns of Beaumont and Port Arthur, began to feel the pressure of CIO political organization, Congressman Dies suddenly withdrew his bid for reelection. It was a gleeful *CIO News* that headed its May 22, 1944, issue with the story of Dies's withdrawal due to a "sore throat." It was even more satisfactory to report that Dies blamed the CIO for his premature retirement.[34]

Retreats similar to Dies's were repeated often enough in other districts to give the CIO–PAC an aura of invincibility. By early June, several of Dies's conservative colleagues joined him in flooding the press with tales of PAC perfidy. When Congressman John Costello, the California conservative, became the third Un-American Activities Committee member to experience defeat by the CIO,

34. *CIO News,* May 22, 1944, p. 1. *Washington Post,* May 19, 1944, p. 8. Dies's fears of the PAC were not justified by CIO strength in his home district, which probably did not exceed 8,000 workers. Jack Kroll to PAC Executive Board, n.d. (1948), PAC 1948 Folder, Box 85, CIO Secretary–Treasurer's Papers, ALH.

Congressman Howard Smith demanded that Congress investigate the PAC's political involvement. In August, senior Missouri Senator Champ Clark revived the tale of the unbeatable PAC. Senator Clark's vituperative postelection public statement paid an unwitting compliment to the effectiveness of the CIO campaign. It was the unusually high city vote and the "Communist-controlled CIO," said Clark, that ended his senatorial career. Apparently, the PAC emphasis on registration and the primaries had not been mistaken. Regardless of the total results of the polls, the benefits of the Dies, Costello, and Clark episodes made the whole primary push seem worthwhile.[35]

Sidney Hillman concentrated personally on politics in the state of New York. The New York voter had a choice between three parties, the Democratic, the Republican, or the small but influential American Labor party. Hillman's plan was to get both the Democrats and the American Labor party to endorse the Roosevelt ticket. Thus, if the race were close, the American Labor party ballots cast for Roosevelt might tip New York's important Electoral College vote into the Roosevelt column. As Hillman's biographer wrote, "Hillman had his eye on New York State's American Labor Party as a pivotal local organization that fitted well into the frame of his larger plan." [36]

Hillman's choice of the American Labor party was, historically, quite logical. Thrown together in 1936 by Hillman; David Dubinsky, president of the International Ladies Garment Workers' Union; and Alex Rose, president of United Hatters, Cap, and Millinery Workers International Union to support President Roosevelt's second term bid, the ALP served as a means of bringing the "regular" social-

35. *Washington Post,* May 18, 1944, p. 1; August 4, 1944, p. 5. *CIO News,* August 7, 1944, p. 3. On the question of Communists and the CIO see Max Kampelman, *The Communist Party Vs. the CIO* (New York: Praeger, 1957). The three defeated congressmen all came from districts with a number of CIO voters. They were Joseph Starnes (Alabama 5), Dies (Texas 2), and Costello (California 15). See Jack Kroll to PAC Executive Board, n.d. (1948), PAC 1948 Folder, CIO Secretary–Treasurer's Papers, ALH.

36. Matthew Josephson, *Sidney Hillman, Statesman of American Labor* (Garden City: Doubleday and Co., 1952), p. 600. A similar view is expressed in Gaer, pp. 223–24.

ists into the Roosevelt vanguard. The ALP, like the CIO
itself, attracted a mixture of New Deal liberals, socialists,
and Communists. By 1944, this mixed bag of leftists had
moved to the point of holding the balance of power in
New York state politics. In 1938, the Labor party's
420,000 votes were responsible for Democrat Herbert
Lehman's victory in the gubernatorial race. Although
Lehman's Democratic total was more than 300,000 votes
less than that of his Republican opponent, votes cast for
Lehman under the ALP banner decided the election.
President Roosevelt carried New York in a similar manner in 1940 with about 400,000 votes cast for him on the
Labor party ticket.[37] Thus, in an election that promised to
be very close, the 400,000 ballots cast for the ALP slate
could well decide who would receive New York's decisive
Electoral College vote.

Getting American Labor party support for Hillman's
master plan, however, proved to be no simple task. By
1944, the leadership of the ALP had passed into the hands
of David Dubinsky's anti-Communist forces, the right wing
of the party. Although the Dubinsky faction had control
of the state machinery, his opponents, those who were willing to work with the Communists, controlled the influential
CIO New York City Industrial Union Council. If Hillman
were to place his hopes on the Dubinsky faction, he was
sure to offend what was potentially the largest Labor party
voting bloc. Yet, if the PAC decided to go with the New
York city dissidents, it would surely lose the favor of the
ALP right, a group that included Dubinsky's ILGWU.[38]
Hillman chose neither route.

Early in 1944, New York Mayor and ALP leader

37. Josephson, pp. 400–401. David J. Saposs, *Communism
in American Politics* (Washington: Public Affairs Press, 1960),
pp. 70–71. For election statistics see U.S., Bureau of the
Census, *Vote Cast in Presidential and Congressional Elections*
(Washington: G.P.O., 1946), p. 161.

38. *Report of the General Executive Board to the Twenty-
Fifth Convention of the International Ladies Garment Workers'
Union, May 29–June 9, 1944, Boston, Mass.*, pp. 18–20. Alan
Schaffer, *Vito Marcantonio, Radical in Congress* (Syracuse:
Syracuse University Press, 1966), pp. 142–44. Saposs, pp.
74–79.

Fiorello LaGuardia appointed the Committee for a United Labor Party. The purpose of the committee was to reconcile all factions within the party by assuring each one representation on the ALP Executive Council. Thus, the ALP could boost Roosevelt's cause with a united front in 1944. The Dubinsky right wing immediately rejected the CULP proposal. Having worked for years to rid the Labor party's Executive Committee of its Communists, Dubinsky was not about to abandon his purification project for a one-shot election victory. Hillman, who saw his immediate plans for 1944 slowly evaporating because of Dubinsky's intransigence, immediately denounced the rejection as being tantamount to an endorsement of such FDR enemies as Dies. After all, the sole purpose of CULP had been to better Roosevelt's chances in New York.[39] The showdown was at hand.

The 1944 American Labor party convention proved to be the very antithesis of what Hillman had hoped. The entire CULP strategy, prayerfully formed to avoid conflict, resulted in one of the bitterest confrontations in the Labor party's history. As the delegates began to fall in line behind the LaGuardia compromise, the Dubinsky faction bitterly watched their years of party purification go up in smoke. When the final balloting proved Hillman and the compromise the winners, the right walked out.[40] Hillman had his party.

Although the CIO–PAC had won the allegiance of the ALP, Hillman's personal involvement in the Labor party struggle (he was elected the new party head) did have its negative effect on the PAC's campaign. The CULP stand had offended the ILGWU, a union that the PAC had hoped to enlist in the national fight, and at the 1944 ILGWU convention anti-PAC feeling was much in evidence. Not only did Dubinsky and the executive board of the ILGWU condemn Hillman and the CIO–PAC for

39. *Report of the General Executive Board . . . 1944,* pp. 20–21. *CIO News,* March 27, 1944, p. 10. Gaer, pp. 223–25.

40. *Report of the General Executive Board . . . 1944,* pp. 20–21. *CIO News,* April 17, 1944, p. 2. Josephson, pp. 600–606.

their New York maneuvering, but the delegates also made their displeasure with Hillman obvious and vocal.[41] Yet, ILGWU displeasure was the least of PAC's ALP worries.

While Hillman was making headlines with his ALP involvement, CIO members outside New York were not universally impressed. Noting the time, publicity, and money that the PAC was investing in a minor intraparty struggle, union leaders began to question PAC priorities. An example of the grumbling in the ranks was the letter of a PAC coordinator in the South. Writing to C. B. Baldwin, assistant director of the Political Action Committee, the coordinator complained about lack of CIO political activity in the South. The membership had worked hard to raise PAC dollars, he wrote, but for what purpose, except perhaps "to reorganize the A.L.P.?" [42] The American Labor party strategy may have won votes in New York, but elsewhere it was a potential liability.

Now that the CIO–PAC had a strategy for 1944 and the tactical planning to implement it, the PAC began to tune its electoral machine. At this point, Thomas R. Amlie entered the scene.

Thomas Amlie was the Political Action Committee's resident expert on congressional campaigns. Amlie had excellent credentials for the job, having distinguished himself as a political planner for over two decades. Starting as an organizer for the Non-Partisan League in Elkhorn, Wisconsin, during the 1920s, he had worked his way up to a congressional seat by 1931. His defeat for reelection in 1932 prompted him to turn to Philip LaFollette's cause, the Progressive party. With Amlie as campaign planner, LaFollette and the Progressives swept the Wisconsin gubernatorial race in 1934. After two more terms in Congress, Amlie was defeated in the Wisconsin senatorial primary in 1938. Four years later, he organized the na-

41. *Proceedings of the Twenty-Fifth Convention of the International Ladies Garment Workers' Union, May 29–June 9, 1944, Boston, Mass.,* pp. 20–23, 274–75, 511–13.

42. R. R. Lawrence to C. Benham Baldwin, February 10, 1944, CIO–PAC 1946 Folder, Box 3, Series 1A, Textile Workers Union of America Papers, Wisconsin State Historical Society, Madison, Wis. The Society will hereafter be cited as WSHS.

tional liberal group, the Union for Democratic Action, and, in 1944, joined Hillman's staff.[43] In late July, 1944, Thomas Amlie gave Hillman an overall plan for congressional campaign tactics.

Amlie began his memorandum with a review of what he believed were the chief aims of the CIO–PAC in 1944. These he listed as registration of the maximum number of voters and education of these voters to cast their ballots for liberal presidential and congressional candidates. He defined liberal candidates as those who would support the domestic programs of President Roosevelt and the CIO.[44]

The second section of Amlie's plan dealt with the course that the PAC should follow in the campaign. First, Amlie insisted that the PAC push only a few essential issues. Have no fear of repeating these ideas over and over again, he wrote; repetition is an important road to success. Second, plan speakers, subjects, and occasions so that the selected ideas can be driven home to the worker–voter from as many angles as possible. Third, always emphasize the historic failures of the Republican party. It is important, he advised Hillman, never to let the voter forget 1929. Finally, he listed a series of issues that would help emphasize the good points of the Roosevelt Administration and the CIO program. These enumerated issues included full employment and economic stability, reconversion, housing, social security, small business, agriculture (including Tennessee Valley Authority and Rural Electrification Administration), and the problems of minority workers. The PAC was supposed to pick its campaign issues from this list, which was accompanied by a more specific compilation of state by state goals.[45]

Limiting himself to the twenty states that he believed were capable of sustaining a labor drive, Amlie candidly assessed the CIO's chances in each. Five of the most important of these states were Wisconsin, Minnesota, Indiana, Massachusetts, and New York. Of particular interest to

43. Notes on Thomas R. Amlie, Historical Society Guide, Thomas R. Amlie Papers, WSHS.

44. Overall Plan for the Political Action Committee, July 26, 1944, CIO Campaign Plans and Memoranda to Sidney Hillman Folder, Box 58, Thomas R. Amlie Papers, WSHS.

45. Ibid.

Amlie was his home state, Wisconsin. Wisconsin could go in one of two directions in 1944, and either alternative would have profound impact on the future of politics in that state. Either Congressman Howard McMurray and Democratic gubernatorial candidate Daniel Hoan would make a good showing in 1944, a showing that would relegate the Progressives to a poor third place in the balloting, or the Progressives would continue to hold the Democrats enthralled in the third spot. If McMurray and Hoan could capture even forty per cent of the vote, then the Progressive party would wither away and the state's liberals could once again unite under one Democratic banner. Because the CIO controlled a number of votes in such key liberal counties as Dane, Milwaukee, and Kenosha, the CIO–PAC would be in a position to determine the political future of the state. As Amlie put it, a CIO–Democratic victory would help clear up "the whole three-way split . . . for the future." [46] The CIO role could be just as decisive in other states.

"From a labor standpoint," wrote Amlie, "it is extremely important that a good showing be made in Minnesota." The importance of the 1944 contest in that state was that Hubert Humphrey, an unsuccessful candidate in the Minneapolis mayoralty race of 1943, was trying to merge the radicals of the Farmer–Labor party with the Catholics and political professionals of the Democratic party. Apart, neither had the strength to carry the state. Together, they might win the state for Roosevelt. Thus, national leaders like Thomas Amlie were concerned with the fusion of the two groups and did everything possible to help Humphrey and the fusion convention. Again, the CIO would have a critical position in the proceedings, because the CIO radicals of the Farmer–Labor party were among the chief roadblocks to the onrushing merger movement. Moreover, with its strong position in the third and eighth congressional districts, the CIO could help the merged party to at least two congressional victories.[47]

46. *Wisconsin,* n.d. (1944), Records on Congressmen, CIO–PAC Folder, Box 58, Thomas R. Amlie Papers, WSHS.

47. *Minnesota,* n.d. (1944), Records on Congressmen, CIO–PAC Folder, Box 58, Thomas R. Amlie Papers, WSHS. G. Theodore Mitau, *Politics in Minnesota* (Minneapolis: University of Minnesota Press, 1970), pp. 13–26.

Indiana's political situation was not quite so complex, but, again, it was a state in which the CIO might hold the key to Democratic victory. Although Amlie saw no chance of winning the state for Roosevelt, he did see that increasing CIO concentrations in a number of key cities might help win three congressional seats for the Democrats. Wartime industry had attracted a number of workers to Fort Wayne, South Bend, Indianapolis, and LaFayette. Because the CIO had registered substantial gains in all of these communities, the new CIO members were to be utilized as the spearhead of a drive to capture the third, fourth, and fifth congressional districts. Victory was possible in all three areas.[48]

The race in Massachusetts promised to be very close and, of course, such a race gave the CIO added incentive. Even the shift of a few hundred votes might win the state for Roosevelt. Thus, Amlie counseled Hillman to run candidates in every possible congressional district. The object would not be to win congressional seats, but rather to increase interest in the election. If voters saw that the Democrats were really contesting a number of "safe" Republican seats, perhaps they would come out to cast a Democratic and Roosevelt ballot. It would probably be easier, wrote Amlie, to bring out another 10,000 votes in this manner, rather than spending more time and money in a close district, where both parties will mount their maximum money efforts. Looking at the 1940 returns, Amlie could see no reason why Republican Congresswoman Edith Rogers could have captured the industrial fifth district by winning almost eighty per cent of the vote. Obviously, a number of workers were staying home. Such districts should feel the impact of the CIO–PAC in 1944.[49]

While Sidney Hillman was working for the New York city vote through his American Labor party, Amlie felt that the ALP effort should be supplemented, especially in the upstate area. There, a number of vulnerable Republican congressmen could be defeated with the aid of the regular Democratic machine. These were Hamilton Fish, a chief critic of the President, Clarence Hancock, Walter

48. *Indiana*, n.d. (1944), Records on Congressmen, CIO–PAC Folder, Box 58, Thomas R. Amlie Papers, WSHS.
49. *Massachusetts*, n.d. (1944), Records on Congressmen, CIO–PAC Folder, Box 58, Thomas R. Amlie Papers, WSHS.

Andrews, and John Butler. The last two names on his list were included because of the industrial nature of their Buffalo districts. Fish's violent anti-Roosevelt position made him politically vulnerable; the others were much more secure. As in Massachusetts, the various contests in New York were as important for attracting marginal voters as they were for winning new Democratic congressional seats.[50] The statewide vote for Roosevelt was all-important.

The PAC, in running its campaign, followed Amlie's advice to the letter. Although the official PAC program (as expressed in "The People's Program for 1944") included no less than twenty-four demands, the CIO–PAC campaign revolved around only four basic Amlie themes: inflation, civil rights, reconversion, and the historic failure of the Republicans (and a conservative Congress).[51] These four themes were repeated over and over in PAC pamphlets, local union leaflets, and the editorial pages of a score of union newspapers.

The Political Action Committee speaker's manual set the tone for the campaign. Citing a California study that showed that workingmen were receiving less than living wages, the manual blamed inflation caused by excessive profits and Congress's refusal to tax the rich. To the CIO, industrialists, not workers, were responsible for inflation. As far as governmental responsibility was concerned, the blame for the rising cost of living should be placed squarely on the shoulders of Congress, not the prolabor President.[52] Although its arguments may have been questionable, the manual's pitch made good political sense. It was a bit hard to blame the worker for inflation and then expect him to vote for one's candidates.

Blaming Congress for inflation and the fifteen per cent wage ceiling of the War Labor Board may not have been

50. *New York,* n.d. (1944), Records on Congressmen, CIO–PAC Folder, Box 58, Thomas R. Amlie Papers, WSHS.
51. "People's Program for 1944" in Gaer, pp. 185–212. All four of the fields fitted well into the PAC scheme. For instance, inflation and reconversion would give the CIO member good economic reasons to vote with the CIO. Civil rights talk would hopefully attract the black CIO member. Republican failures would give anyone a reason to reconsider an anti-CIO vote.
52. "Speaker's Manual" in Gaer, pp. 379–85.

completely fair, but it made good propaganda. After all, Congress had ignored President Roosevelt's 1942 call for higher taxes and holding the line on prices. Moreover, Congress, not the War Labor Board, was coming up for election in 1944. Inflation was a real problem with plenty of political potential. If the CIO–PAC could pin the blame for inflation on Congress, it would certainly have an effective issue for November.[53]

As the *News* continued to publicize the CIO program, the campaign began to get underway at the state level. Although the national PAC was instrumental in formulating strategy and tactics, the state political action committees really determined the success of the campaign. They had to deliver the votes.

One state that was particularly active, considering its small CIO population, was West Virginia.[54] A review of the state PAC director's correspondence during the last months of the campaign is illustrative of the problems encountered by small PACs throughout the United States.[55]

During the month of September, West Virginia PAC Director John Easton flooded regional CIO–PAC headquarters with pleas for aid and guidance. Reporting on what he had hoped would be a major PAC rally in Huntington, Easton dejectedly called it a "complete failure." He noted that he had followed the political action script carefully, having sent out notices to all the locals, CIO

53. The Little Steel formula of 1942 set a theoretical fifteen per cent ceiling on any future wartime wage negotiations, except in cases where prevailing wages were unusually low. Roosevelt's seven-point antiinflation program included a call for an equitable hike in income and corporate taxes. Philip Taft, *Organized Labor in American History* (New York: Harper and Row, 1964), pp. 549–50. Congress had also passed the Price Control Act of 1944 in June. This act lent credence to the CIO charge since it virtually took the lid off of cotton textile prices. *Washington Post,* July 3, 1944. *CIO News,* June 19, 1944, p. 3.

54. Only one West Virginia congressional district had substantial numbers of CIO members. Yet, even there the CIO represented only five per cent of the population. Riker, pp. 203–12.

55. Similar problems were encountered in Wisconsin and Minnesota. *Minnesota, Wisconsin,* n.d. (1944), CIO–PAC Campaign Folder, Box 58, Thomas R. Amlie Papers, WSHS.

councils, and the Amalgamated Clothing Workers of America, but almost nobody bothered to come. He thought it an insult to the Tennessee PAC man who had been invited to speak. Not only was the attendance slight, but the big United Steel Workers of America local had also insisted upon holding its own rump session. In the meantime, those loyal PAC workers who were trying to run a campaign were severely handicapped by poor communication with the national office. Internal bickering and lack of national support compounded the local failures experienced by the West Virginia director.[56]

By early October, the situation looked no better. The national CIO–PAC had decided to back Congressman Jennings Randolph because, despite his generally conservative record, he had voted against the poll tax and against the easing of price controls. The West Virginia CIO, on the other hand, would have nothing to do with Randolph. His record, which included a vote for Smith–Connally, was simply too bad. Easton correspondence with the Fifth Region's PAC director, Jack Kroll, began to be dominated by the Randolph controversy. Yet, while the two bodies were feuding over supporting Randolph, Easton still had to admit that "none of our PAC local organizations are functioning to any extent."[57]

Fortunately for the PAC, the election was not held in early October. By November 7, the West Virginia CIO had managed to patch up its campaign organization. It had negotiated a simple agreement with the national PAC over Randolph (by agreeing to support neither Randolph nor his opponent) and proceeded with more substantive local electioneering. According to Easton's account, the state PAC had distributed millions of pieces of campaign literature in the last month before the election alone. This, with statewide radio broadcasts and a good deal of campaigning among non-CIO miners, helped to push CIO-endorsed can-

56. John B. Easton to Jack Kroll, September 13, 1944, PAC. Folder, Box 27, West Virginia Industrial Union Council Papers, WVUL.

57. Jack Kroll to John Easton, September 26, 1944; John Easton to Jack Kroll, October 6, 1944, PAC Folder, Box 27, West Virginia Industrial Union Council Papers, WVUL.

didates into office.[58] At least, that was the official story.

While the CIO–PAC was pursuing the labor vote, the Democrats were faced with Republican charges that Roosevelt had sold out to the Communists and Sidney Hillman.

On September 25, Republican presidential candidate Thomas E. Dewey had entered a new campaign phase with a major policy speech at Oklahoma City. Making reference to a September Roosevelt speech, the New York governor noted that the only people who found Roosevelt indispensable were that "motley crew" that included "Sidney Hillman and the Political Action Committee" and "Earl Browder, the ex-convict and pardoned Communist leader." [59] If Dewey had anything to say about the campaign, it would be fought on the issues of communism and the PAC, not the war.

Although the President could easily deny Dewey's charges that he was soft on communism, a denial that would probably have carried much weight, he could not deny his sympathy for the PAC so easily. Indeed, his outspoken defense of the PAC and Hillman was Dewey's best hope of pinning the Communist label on the President. Although Hillman was obviously not a Communist, Dewey hoped to parley his involvement with the American Labor party into something that would arouse the public's suspicions. Since Hillman was a friend and confidant of the President, a fact that had only recently been bolstered by columnist Arthur Krock's sensational (although questionable) revelation that FDR had cleared the Truman nomination with "Sidney," Hillman's suspicious actions concerning the ALP could then be used to discredit Roosevelt.[60]

As the campaign progressed, a number of the minor Republicans jumped on the anti-PAC bandwagon that Dewey had begun. A prime example was Congresswoman Clare Booth Luce. In a Pittsburgh speech on October 13,

58. John B. Easton to Jack Kroll, November 14, 1944, PAC Folder, Box 27, West Virginia Industrial Union Council, WVUL.

59. *New York Times,* September 26, 1944, p. 1.

60. For the Krock column see, *New York Times,* July 25, 1944, p. 18.

Luce claimed that FDR was trading Communist and PAC support for presidential acceptance of a Communist take-over of the CIO, and later, of the Democratic party. These extravagant charges were soon followed by such ploys as Republican billboards that, playing to the Hillman–Communist pitch, asked, "This is your country; why let Hillman run it?" [61]

As time would prove, the Republican anti-PAC strategy did not work. Wild charges of Communist influence and the Hillman conspiracy meant less to 1944 voters than did the eleven-year New Deal record.

The day after the election was one of elation in the PAC camp. PAC-endorsed Franklin D. Roosevelt and the Democrats had won a major victory. However, many of the victory claims were met with skepticism even from within the organization.

Perhaps the most searching examination of the PAC role in 1944 was the report of Charles Ervin, an official of Sidney Hillman's own Amalgamated Clothing Workers of America. Analyzing only the 1944 presidential election, Ervin came to the conclusion that 1944 was not a Democratic victory. Instead, it was a personal tribute to a President who had carried the United States through depression and global war. Although the victory was not as sweeping as PAC leaders had believed, Ervin found that PAC activities had been effective in some areas. Only by comparing these few successful efforts with the tactics used in losing districts, wrote Ervin, could the CIO realistically plan for the future. [62]

Ervin chose Michigan's as an example of a successful PAC campaign. In 1944, Michigan went from the Republican to the Democratic column because of an increased vote in the state's industrial counties where the PAC worked hardest. Wayne County (Detroit), where PAC workers had been active in block and precinct organizations since

61. *New York Times,* October 14, 1944, p. 9; October 17, 1944, p. 14. *New York Post,* October 12, 1944, p. 10; October 24, 1944, p. 18.
62. Charles W. Ervin, "What Really Happened in the National Campaign of 1944," June, 1945, CIO–PAC 1944 Election Folder, Box 202, CIO Secretary–Treasurer's Papers, ALH.

August, 1943, showed a Roosevelt plurality of over 234,000 votes.[63] Although the Republicans took sixty-six of Michigan's eighty-three counties, Roosevelt's strong showing in the PAC-organized industrial counties won him a 21,000 vote plurality in the state.[64]

While Michigan was an example of successful PAC campaigning, the Wisconsin campaign was Ervin's example of the failures of the PAC effort. Milwaukee County, where CIO votes should have raised Roosevelt's total, showed a 15,000 net gain by the Republicans over 1940. The other two industrial counties in the state raised their Roosevelt totals slightly, but not enough to save the state from going to Dewey. As did several other industrial states, Wisconsin revealed that Labor would not automatically follow the PAC line.[65]

Ervin concluded his study with a warning about future PAC campaigns. In the future, he wrote, there will be no great national leader, such as Roosevelt, with whom the PAC can appeal to workers. CIO leaders must find new ways to attract the labor vote.[66]

Thomas Amlie's analysis of the PAC's electoral success was even more pessimistic than Ervin's. Although some of his goals had been attained, notably the creation of the Minnesota Democratic–Farmer–Labor party and the defeat of the troublesome Wisconsin Progressives, his key congressional districts were still in Republican hands. With such exceptions as the defeat of Hamilton Fish in New York and the capture of St. Paul's Fourth Congressional District by DFL candidate Frank Starkey, Amlie's campaign to remake Congress had failed. His hope that such strong industrial locales as Michigan's Seventh Congressional District would be transformed into Democratic–PAC strongholds was not realized. Even his dream of building a nucleus of Democratic–PAC congressmen from CIO cities

63. Ibid., pp. 30–31. Minutes of the Progressive Labor League, August 2, 1943, CIO Political Programs Folder, Box 25, Wayne County AFL–CIO Papers, ALH.

64. Ervin, pp. 36–37.

65. Ibid., pp. 32–33, 36–37, 66–69.

66. Ibid., pp. 66–69.

did not materialize.[67] Remarking to Sidney Hillman, he wrote:

> The most striking thing about the campaign that has just been concluded is the fact that on the Presidential level it has been conducted with utmost competency; while on the Congressional level the various campaigns . . . have been conducted in a wholly ineffectual manner.[68]

Although both Amlie and Ervin had strong reservations concerning PAC victory claims, an assessment of the PAC's 1944 campaign requires more than the assertions of either.[69] Ideally, an assessment of the PAC would involve an exact polling of all CIO voters in 1944. However, since such an ideal is hardly realizable, the best indicators of PAC success can be found in the returns from CIO voting districts. On the simplest level, such a voting analysis should examine two facets of the PAC campaign.

The first goal would be to assess the relative impact of the CIO's campaign approach. After all, the first facet of the PAC campaign was the detailed choice of the CIO–PAC's campaign tactics. In other words, did all the registration campaigns, propaganda barrages, and armies of block workers succeed in achieving higher Democratic totals in the congressional districts in which the PAC operated? How did the voters, both labor and nonlabor, react in those few congressional districts where the PAC was the major campaign organization?

The second facet of the CIO–PAC electoral campaign was the development of the CIO voter. Union members were to become union voters whose liberal sympathies would lead them to support the PAC's endorsees on every political level. Here, the question was whether unionists

67. Records on Congressmen, n.d. (1944), CIO Campaign Folder, Box 58, Thomas R. Amlie Papers, WSHS.

68. Thomas Amlie to Sidney Hillman, Memorandum on Congressional Elections, November 8, 1944, CIO–PAC Campaign Folder, Box 58, Thomas R. Amlie Papers, WSHS.

69. Hillman had admitted privately that the PAC had "found the formula" to electoral success in 1944. James Loeb to Mrs. Franklin D. Roosevelt, November 15, 1944, James Loeb Correspondence Folder, Box 18, Series 1, Americans for Democratic Action Papers, WSHS.

in CIO wards followed PAC dictates in all the political races. Did the PAC translate labor sympathy for President Roosevelt into high vote totals for other PAC-endorsed candidates?

Considering these questions, what, then, did the 1944 election returns reveal? [70]

At the presidential level, Amlie had noted that the campaign seemed to have been run with utmost competence. A quick survey of the top twenty CIO counties in the nation (See Appendix) seems to reveal some PAC impact on the election. While the country as a whole supported Roosevelt slightly less enthusiastically than it did in 1940 (Roosevelt's total declined by two percentage points and almost two million votes), Roosevelt's totals rose slightly in those counties where the PAC conducted its most vigorous campaigns.[71] Whether because of the CIO's intensive registration drives, its propaganda campaigns, or a variety of other reasons, the Roosevelt vote did show an increase in CIO counties, an increase that may have been attributable to PAC activity.

In the congressional races, the Democratic vote did not show any significant increase that would bolster a CIO victory claim. Although CIO–PAC had campaigned almost exclusively in those districts where CIO members comprised a significant percentage of the electorate, the Democratic congressional vote in the twenty strongest CIO districts differed only slightly from the Democratic vote in a series of districts where the PAC had not even trod (See Appendix). If anything, the margin of support offered Democratic candidates in non-CIO districts was slightly higher

70. The procedure that I have chosen for analyzing the 1944 voting returns is a simple descriptive method comparing CIO and non-CIO voting areas over a period of several elections. The labor wards used all contained an overwhelming majority of citizens in the "operative," "skilled labor," and "laborer" categories of the U.S. Census (the median labor ward had almost all of its inhabitants, according to census tract statistics, in these unionized occupational divisions). The object of comparing wards with virtually their entire voting populations in unionized occupational categories was to test the labor vote without committing an ecological error.

71. 1944 Table in Appendix.

than in CIO districts.[72] Perhaps Amlie's statement had some basis in fact.

The mute indictment of the district comparison was even further buttressed by another Amlie comment. In his report to Hillman, Amlie directly attributed Democratic and Progressive losses in Wisconsin to the failure of the PAC to organize effectively in Milwaukee County. The PAC's failure in this respect had squandered one of the few reserves of liberal voters in the state.[73] It hurt the ex-congressman to note that one of the big PAC mistakes in 1944 had taken place in his home state.

The final gauge of PAC effectiveness in 1944 involved the union voter. A survey of labor wards in four major CIO cities does reveal that labor voters did support the President by a greater margin than did the nation as a whole (See Appendix). Yet, a closer look shows that voters in nonlabor wards actually increased their support of Roosevelt to a greater degree than did labor ward voters in 1944. With the single exception of Pittsburgh, the increase in the Roosevelt percentage was significantly greater in nonlabor areas than in labor wards.[74] This would hardly support the thesis that 1944 was primarily a labor victory. After all, labor voters in CIO cities were less committed to Roosevelt in 1944 than in 1940.

Pursuing the union vote further, a comparison of presidential and nonpresidential Democratic percentages in labor wards shows that labor support for lesser Democrats increased no more than nonlabor support for the same candidates.[75] Seemingly, whatever bait the PAC had set out to lure labor voters into the Democratic fold had worked no more effectively than traditional political methods. Indeed, considering Amlie's proximity to the situation, perhaps his analysis of the situation was correct. Amlie's access to exact CIO ward membership figures meant that he could rather easily convert voting returns into an accurate estimate of CIO voter preferences.

72. Ibid.
73. Memorandum on Congressional Elections, November 8, 1944, CIO–PAC Campaign Folder, Box 58, Thomas R. Amlie Papers, WSHS.
74. 1944 Table in Appendix.
75. Ibid.

The PAC record, as far as the election returns indicated, was not particularly glorious in 1944, but the campaign did have its positive side.

Perhaps as important as electoral success was the reputation the PAC won in its initial outing. Electing a few Democrats in labor districts was one thing, but being credited by the *New York Times* with the selection of the Vice President was quite another. Eventually, the *Times* credit would prove to be the cornerstone upon which the myth of PAC power was built.

The whole vice presidential story began July 25, 1944, when the *Times'* Arthur Krock had revealed the details behind the nomination of Senator Harry Truman of Missouri. According to Krock, Franklin Roosevelt had asked Democratic National Chairman Robert Hannegan "to clear" Truman with "Sidney." [76] The charge had been a blockbuster in two ways. First, the Republicans now had the proof they needed to show that FDR had capitulated to big labor in general and to "Red" Sidney Hillman in particular. As the campaign wore on, Dewey had used the Krock charge repeatedly in red-baiting Roosevelt.[77] Second, and more important to the PAC, the Krock article had intimated that the CIO's political action arm was so strong that even the President of the United States had feared to act without its approval. Suddenly, the PAC was transformed from a minor political machine to a power behind the throne. The myth that began with the Dies defeat took on a whole new dimension after July 25.

Strangely enough, most of the principals in the Krock story denied the truth of the *Times* allegation. Hannegan, Roosevelt, and Hillman all denied knowledge of a "clear it with Sidney" message. Krock himself refused to reveal his sources. By the end of 1944, the PAC's Joseph Gaer dismissed the July 25 article as nothing more than Republican anti-Semitism.[78] However, later accounts differed dramatically with Gaer.

76. *New York Times,* July 25, 1944, p. 18.
77. For example, an Oklahoma City speech, *New York Times,* September 26, 1944, p. 1.
78. Gaer, pp. 171–73. Also, see Samuel Rosenman, *Working with Roosevelt* (New York: Harper and Brothers, 1952), pp. 444–50.

When James Byrnes published his autobiography in 1958, he entitled his thirteenth chapter "Clear It with Sidney." Recalling the 1944 convention, Byrnes bitterly documented Hillman's part in the vice presidential sweepstakes. In conversations with both Hannegan and Brotherhood of Railroad Trainmen President Allen F. Whitney, Byrnes had seen his own vice-presidential hopes vanish as the Truman bandwagon began to roll. In Byrnes's eyes, the sudden Truman momentum was the work of none other than the PAC's Sidney Hillman. Pretending to support Vice President Henry Wallace, Hillman was really directing the Truman campaign. After all, had not Hannegan admitted that the nomination had to be "cleared" with Hillman? Had not Whitney revealed that Hillman had breakfasted with Truman just prior to the push? Finally, had not Federal Deposit Insurance Commissioner Leo Crowley reported that Roosevelt abandoned Byrnes's candidacy only after Hillman personally warned the President that labor would not stand by Byrnes? To the defeated Byrnes, everything seemed to point to Hillman as the man behind the nomination of Truman.[79] Others backed the story.

In 1968, Arthur Krock finally published his account of the 1944 convention. Revealing that his source for the 1944 story was Turner Catledge of the *New York Times,* Krock reconstructed the conversation between Byrnes and Hannegan in much the same way as Byrnes. Indeed, Krock cited the Byrnes autobiography as proof that his original story had been correct. Yet, all he really documented was that Hannegan had told Byrnes that the nomination had to be "cleared" with Hillman. He did not prove that the PAC boss had actually swayed Roosevelt.[80] In fact, the true situation may have been quite different.

Undoubtedly, Wallace was in trouble in 1944. FDR realized that his liberal and outspoken Vice President would be a liability in what promised to be a close election. For this reason, the President sought an alternate, and Byrnes may well have been his first choice. However, as Byrnes

79. James F. Byrnes, *All in One Lifetime* (New York: Harper and Brothers, 1958), pp. 220–31.
80. Arthur Krock, *Memoirs: Sixty Years on the Firing Line* (New York: Funk and Wagnalls, 1968), pp. 217–19.

and others revealed, neither Byrnes nor Wallace were acceptable to both the bosses and the liberals of the party. Just as the bosses had vetoed Wallace, so had the liberals vetoed Byrnes. Since Hillman was the leader of one of the largest liberal blocs, his advice was doubtlessly sought when the time came to choose a compromise candidate. Yet, his was not the only advice sought.[81] There was, for instance, the case of the UDA.

The Union for Democratic Action, a prowar and anti-Communist collection of liberals, controlled a small but influential bloc of votes in 1944. As soon as its leaders heard of the possibility of a Byrnes nomination, they began to bombard Hannegan, Roosevelt, and other party leaders with letters demanding either Wallace or a compromise candidate. Byrnes was simply unacceptable. UDA surveys had shown that a Byrnes nomination could result in serious Democratic losses in labor districts. In the words of UDA Executive–Secretary James Loeb, Jr., a boss–Byrnes victory at the convention might well lose "a campaign in November in order to remember having won a skirmish in July." [82] Hillman was not the only influential opponent of Byrnes. Yet, there remained the July 25 Krock column.

In retrospect, Krock's "clear it with Sidney" story was generally accurate. However, Hannegan's chance comment of July 16 was blown all out of proportion by late November. Although Hannegan may have checked with Hillman in regard to the Truman name, the actual selection of Truman had been made at a July 11 White House meeting, a meeting to which Hillman had not been invited.[83] Far from being a power behind the throne, Sidney Hillman was little more than an influential Wallace-backer whose support was important in the coming election. He and others

81. This seems to be the general conclusion reached by the latest researcher on the subject. See Leon Friedman, "Election of 1944," *History of American Presidential Elections,* ed. Arthur M. Schlesinger, Jr., Fred L. Isreal, and William P. Hansen (New York: Chelsea House Publishers in association with McGraw–Hill Book Co., 1971), Vol. 4, pp. 3022–28.
82. James Loeb, Jr. to Robert Hannegan, July 13, 1944, Folder 5, Box 18, Series 1, Americans for Democratic Action Papers, WSHS.
83. Friedman, "Election of 1944," p. 3025.

in the Wallace camp had forced the Truman nomination only in the sense that they had consistently refused to accept Byrnes. Even so, the legend of PAC power remained.

As the year 1944 came to an end, the PAC could look back upon a number of accomplishments. It had helped Roosevelt boost his vote total, quite probably, in a number of urban centers. It had created a campaign machine that had pushed the Democrats into a number of congressional seats. Just as importantly, it had earned a reputation as a power in American politics. From the Dies defeat to the Krock column, it had continued to polish its political image.

The PAC had posited its program upon a simple belief, the belief that workers should think and vote as liberals. Although the CIO hierarchy had handed down a program calling for everything from reconversion to minority rights, its efforts had no easily measured effect on Democratic fortunes. Roosevelt carried CIO districts with stunning ease, but CIO-endorsed liberals all-too-often found his coattails quite difficult to ride. The hoped-for liberal labor constituency seemed as elusive as ever.

When the CIO convention met in Chicago, Sidney Hillman knew that the PAC had not lived up to its expectations. He knew that he had faltered in his larger purpose. Then the crowd's roar began to build. He received a standing ovation. He knew what the convention wanted to hear. Hillman spoke of vainglory, not victory.

3

From a Dubious Victory to Taft–Hartley

In the two years following the 1944 elections, the CIO and its Political Action Committee endured a painful introduction to the realities of national politics. Almost before the 1944 postelection glow had worn off, Congress began an aggressive attack against organized labor. This two-year offensive culminated in the 1947 passage of the Taft–Hartley Act. Congressional antipathy, however, was but one facet of the CIO's political education. In 1946, the CIO–PAC's attempt to reuse the successful campaign formula of 1944 led to complete disaster; CIO candidates were crushed at the polls.

The postwar push against labor began at the state level. Only months after the elections of November, 1944, CIO Industrial Union Council head John Brophy warned the state councils (state branches of the CIO) that legislatures were seriously considering the passage of acts known as right-to-work laws. Such measures, which were pending in the legislatures of Arizona, Colorado, Maryland, New Hampshire, New Mexico, Tennessee, Texas, and Vermont, would have forbidden any form of union security agreement. In other words, closed and union shops, where employees were required to join a union, would be forbidden.[1] To CIO leaders, such laws may well have undone all the organizational work of the 1930s.

While the CIO was still worrying about state right-to-work laws, it suffered a much more serious blow: On April 12, 1945, President Franklin D. Roosevelt died. No longer would labor have so sympathetic a leader in the White House. No longer would the man who vetoed such antiunion measures as the Smith–Connally bill occupy the President's chair. Most importantly, no longer would the

1. *CIO News,* March 12, 1945, p. 1.

CIO have the dynamic figure of President Roosevelt with which to inspire labor voters. As the *CIO News* noted, April 12 marked the passing of the "Champion." [2]

The death of Roosevelt seemed to be the signal for the release of a series of antiunion bills in Congress. The first of this series was the Ball–Burton–Hatch bill (S.1171), which was introduced in the Senate in mid-June. The CIO immediately dubbed it the "Ball and Chain Bill," since among its provisions was a section calling for compulsory arbitration of national emergency strikes.[3] So strong was the CIO's opposition to this bill that the *CIO News* carried a weekly article on its progress for almost three months. The *News* decried the bill's repeal of the antilabor injunction ban set forth in the 1932 Norris–LaGuardia Act, its provision allowing an employer to petition for an NLRB election, and its changing of the wording of the Wagner Act so as to grant NLRB protection to "national" not "interstate" commerce.[4] Fortunately for the CIO, the Ball–Burton–Hatch bill never reached the floor of the Senate.

No sooner had one worry subsided than the CIO was faced with a first-rate economic crisis. As the war effort wound down in the summer of 1945, thousands of war industry employees and thousands of returning veterans were left without jobs. The CIO, as bargaining agent for millions of war workers, was closely involved in the crisis.

By August, 1945, the *CIO News* was warning of massive unemployment that would surely follow the war's victorious conclusion. Fearing that as many as ten million war workers would soon be among the unemployed, the *News* took the occasion to set forth the CIO's solutions for reconversion problems. The major assumption of the CIO plan was that only through increased domestic purchasing power could industry afford to hire the increasing number of unemployed. Thus, the CIO called for an upward revision of existing wages, a sixty-five cent minimum hourly wage, federal unemployment compensation for at least twenty-six weeks, a substantial mustering-out bonus for veterans, and firm government price controls to ensure that any new injection of money into the economy would not be wasted

2. *CIO News,* April 16, 1945, pp. 1–2.
3. *CIO News,* June 25, 1945, p. 4.
4. *CIO News,* July 23, 1945, p. 6; July 30, 1945, p. 10.

in inflation.[5] By September, it seemed that CIO fears were indeed justified.

The very first issue of the *News* in September featured the charge that over four million people were unemployed. In response to the unemployment crisis, the CIO and other labor organizations held mass demonstrations to initiate congressional action on unemployment.[6] Even the usually cautious Bureau of Labor Statistics recognized the seriousness of the situation and warned that industrial employment had declined by almost four million jobs since December, 1944.[7]

However, massive unemployment was no guarantee of congressional success for the CIO reconversion program. During the months of September and October, Congress demolished the CIO plan piece by piece. The first victim was the sixty-five cent minimum wage bill. Even before the bill reached the Senate floor, CIO leaders feared that Congress would settle for a fifty-five cent compromise. When such fears were realized, President Murray called the compromise a brazen "retreat" from responsible reconversion.[8] At almost the same time, the House scuttled another CIO pet project, supplementary unemployment insurance. The CIO-supported Kilgore–Murray–Wagner bill (S. 1274) would have provided twenty-five dollars a week for twenty-six weeks to unemployed persons as a supplement to state unemployment benefits. The Senate had approved the measure by voice vote on September 20, but the House Ways and Means Committee ended consideration of the measure by voting to indefinitely postpone it. Within days, the last hope of the CIO plan, the Murray–Wagner Full Employment bill (S.380) was amended beyond recognition by the Senate. Whereas the original bill had authorized the President to submit a budget that would initiate projects to maintain full employment, the Senate-passed bill specified that such a budget

5. *CIO News,* August 20, 1945, pp. 1–2. U.S., House, Labor Committee, *Hearings on Proposed Amendments to the Fair Labor Standards Act,* 79th Cong., 1st sess., 1945, pp. 121–29.

6. *CIO News,* September 3, 1945, p. 5.

7. U.S., Bureau of Labor Statistics, *Monthly Labor Review,* 62 (March 1946), 510.

8. *CIO News,* October 22, 1945, p. 5.

could not increase the national debt. Deficit spending was forbidden. The House finished off the Murray–Wagner measure by changing the bill's provision for a "right" to "full employment" to the desirability of a "high level of employment." [9]

As Congress was putting an end to CIO-backed reconversion programs, a new proposal threatened the CIO even more directly. Early in October, Congressman Howard Smith of Virginia (a chief critic of the CIO) convinced the House Military Affairs Committee to begin hearings on his H.R. 3937, a bill to repeal the War Labor Disputes Act (Smith–Connally Act). As Smith explained to the assembled committee, the War Labor Disputes Act had proven to be completely incapable of controlling the nefarious activities of organized labor. The coal shortage of 1945, which he blamed on the United Mine Workers of America and John L. Lewis, was proof of the inability of the act to provide adequate means to stop national emergency strikes. Moreover, the recent involvement of the CIO Political Action Committee in the 1944 elections had proven to Smith that the act's ban on union political involvement was totally unworkable. What was needed was new legislation.[10]

Congressman Smith's call for new labor legislation was soon answered. When his bill (H.R. 3937) came to the floor of the House, Representative Leslie Arends of Illinois amended it in order to tie the repeal of Smith–Connally to a series of labor "reforms." The reforms incorporated in the Arends Amendment covered three aspects of labor regulation. First, no labor organization could make contributions in connection with a federal election or primary. This closed the Smith–Connally loophole allowing primary contributions, a loophole that the CIO–PAC had taken

9. U.S., *Congressional Record,* 79th Cong., 1st sess., 1945, 91, Part 7, 8830–8831, 8948, 9153; Part 9, 12095. However, as Arthur McClure argues, even the watered-down bill was a labor victory. Truman himself felt that passage signified public acceptance of economic planning, a CIO objective. Arthur F. McClure, *The Truman Administration and the Problems of Postwar Labor* (Rutherford: Fairleigh Dickinson University Press, 1969), pp. 192–202.

10. U.S., House, Committee on Military Affairs, *Hearings on H.R. 3937 to Repeal the War Labor Disputes Act,* 79th Cong., 1st sess., 1945, pp. 1–7.

ample advantage of in the 1944 elections. Second, any union that violated the no-strike provisions of its contract would have its collective bargaining rights suspended for one year. Finally, unions could be sued in federal court for any damages an employer might suffer as a result of a strike in violation of contract.[11] To CIO President Philip Murray, such provisions hardly merited the title, "reform."[12]

In the closing months of 1945, the political hopes of the CIO fell even lower. Congress appeared to be about to enact an entire series of antiunion measures. In addition to the Smith bill, which was being spiritedly debated in the House, action was pending on the Hobbs bill to prevent union racketeering, the Gwynee bill to prevent workers' suits for back pay, and the Norton bill to stop national emergency strikes. In reporting the calamitous situation in Congress, the *CIO News* began to sound as if the end were at hand.[13] In fact, as the CIO was about to discover, its political fortunes were in immediate danger of slipping even further downward.

On November 21, 1945, after weeks of fruitless negotiation, the United Automobile Workers struck the General Motors Corporation. Over 325,000 auto workers were out of work and very much in the public eye. As if to point to the shortcomings of existing labor legislation, the strike had developed after the failure of a series of mediation attempts. The company had refused President Truman's offer of mediation on November 6, and on November 20, General Motors had refused even to reply to the union's last offer. Since the United Automobile Workers had complied with the provisions of the Smith–Connally Act and had held a strike vote on October 24, a vote that revealed overwhelming support for the work stoppage, there remained no legal barrier to the strike of November 21.[14] However, in a nation that had grown sick of strikes, the GM walkout soon

11. U.S., *Congressional Record,* 79th Cong., 1st sess., 1945, 91, Part 8, 10211.

12. *CIO News,* November 5, 1945, p. 1.

13. *CIO News,* November 12, 1945, p. 12; December 10, 1945, p. 1.

14. *New York Times,* November 22, 1945, p. 1. *CIO News,* November 26, 1945, p. 3.

generated the kind of political backlash that made the task of labor's congressional enemies considerably easier.

While the UAW had been near a General Motors strike, President Truman had convened a national labor–management conference to work out basic hostilities before they resulted in strikes. The conference lasted only until November 30, when it finally broke up without agreeing to anything of substance.[15] On December 3, President Truman cited what he termed the "failure" of the conference as his reason for demanding new labor legislation.[16]

Truman's message proved to be a watershed in the CIO's relationship with the new President. Whereas the CIO and the head of the Democratic party had previously been on friendly terms, after December 3 Truman was a traitor in the eyes of the CIO. As the *CIO News* remarked, the December 3 speech was a "shameful betrayal of the public trust by an administration that labor's votes did much to elect." [17]

The speech that had so angered the leaders of the CIO was simply a call by Truman for application of the Railway Labor Act to nonrailway labor disputes. He asked for legislation that would allow the Secretary of Labor to certify certain national strikes as being against the public interest. Under Truman's plan, when a dispute was so certified, the President would appoint an investigating panel with the power to subpoena individuals and records. For a thirty-day period, while the panel was investigating the dispute, all lockouts and strikes would be prohibited. Truman stated that only under legislation of this sort could such disastrous strikes as the GM affair and a threatened steel walkout be prevented from ruining the Administration's plans for orderly reconversion.[18]

On December 5, Democratic Congresswoman Mary Norton of New Jersey submitted Truman's plan to Congress as H.R. 4908.[19] While the House Labor Committee was con-

15. Harry A. Millis and Emily Clark Brown, *From the Wagner Act to Taft–Hartley* (Chicago: University of Chicago Press, 1950), pp. 306–11.

16. *New York Times,* December 3, 1945, p. 1.

17. *CIO News,* December 10, 1945, p. 4.

18. *New York Times,* December 3, 1945, p. 1.

19. U.S., *Congressional Record,* 79th Cong., 1st sess., 1945, 91, Part 9, 11523.

sidering the bill, Congress hurried to enact its own anti-union legislation.

When the second session of the Seventy-ninth Congress convened in January, 1946, the CIO found itself at a great disadvantage. On January 21, the anticipated nationwide steel strike had begun.[20] The GM strike still seemed to be as far from settlement as in November. Two concurrent national strikes hardly provided the kind of publicity upon which to build a prolabor congressional coalition.

During this period of strike-engendered bitterness, the Norton bill once again made its appearance on the House floor. Almost immediately, everything except the enacting clause of H.R. 4908 was amended so as to agree with the much more antiunion Case bill (H.R. 5262). On February 7, the amended H.R. 4908 passed the House by the substantial margin of 258 to 155.[21] A major antiunion measure was on the road to enactment.

The Case bill, which under the title of H.R. 4908 passed the House in February, differed from the Norton bill in several ways. First, it provided for the appointment of a permanent Labor–Management Mediation Board that must be notified by labor management in the case of a "public interest" strike or lockout. When notified, the board, while it appointed a mediation panel, could ban strikes or lockouts for thirty days. Second, the board was empowered to issue antilabor injunctions, a tool that had been banned by the 1932 Norris–LaGuardia Act. Third, the bill prohibited organized boycotts and foremen's unions as unfair labor practices. Fourth, it made unions liable for any damages an employer might suffer as a result of a strike in breach of contract. Finally, the bill stated that any organization that prevented anyone from working, or quitting, through intimidation or threats would lose all of its collective bargaining rights.[22]

The CIO soon made its stand on the bill quite evident. The February 11 issue of the *CIO News* devoted several

---

20. *CIO News,* January 21, 1946, p. 3. *New York Times,* January 21, 1946, p. 1.

21. U.S., *Congressional Record,* 79th Cong., 2nd sess., 1946, 92, Part 1, 490, 661, 1069–1070.

22. Ibid., 1027–1029.

pages to the Case bill, which it termed a "best smeller." The bill was attacked on two grounds. First, it legalized the antiunion injunction, a hated weapon that organized labor had been fighting for more than fifty years. Second, while it banned many union practices, it left untouched "notorious employer misconduct." [23] From the CIO's viewpoint, the bill was simply intolerable.

While the *CIO News* was condemning the shortcomings of the Case bill, the measure moved from the House to the Senate. On May 25, after extensive debate, the Senate passed the bill in an amended form. The final legislation, which was approved by both houses of Congress, changed the cooling-off period from thirty to sixty days, added a provision forbidding interference with the movement of goods in interstate commerce, and prohibited employer contributions to welfare funds administered solely by unions. President Truman, however, because he had just settled the national railroad strike, vetoed the measure on June 11. The House failed to override the veto by a vote of 255 to 135.[24] The CIO had been saved from the Case bill; the traitor was vindicated.

At the same time that Congress was considering the Case bill, the CIO Political Action Committee was preparing for the 1946 elections. The campaign officially began on April 16, 1946, when Sidney Hillman called his lieutenants together to plan the fall operations. Emphasizing the importance of better organization at the local level, the PAC dedicated itself to electing candidates who would support its six-point program, which included the following: continuation of the Big Three alliance, construction of at least three million homes through federal spending, improved veterans' aid, expanded medical care under the Wagner–Murray–Dingell health bill, a minimum wage of sixty-five to seventy-five cents, and a continuation of the Office of Price Administration.[25] As the CIO–PAC had discovered in 1944, however, it took more than political pronouncements to elect candidates.

23. *CIO News,* February 11, 1946, p. 4; February 4, 1946, p. 12.
24. U.S., *Congressional Record,* 79th Cong., 2nd sess., 1946, 92, Part 5, 5739, 6674, 6678.
25. *CIO News,* April 22, 1946, p. 3.

While the PAC was publishing its program for 1946, it was also deeply involved in an internal debate concerning the precise role that the CIO should take in American politics. Some of the questions left unanswered in July, 1943, had to be resolved at once.

The debate had started in late 1944, when Sidney Hillman and Philip Murray had been presented with a most interesting proposition by the leaders of the Union for Democratic Action. Citing the important role CIO–PAC had played in 1945, James Loeb, Jr., UDA executive secretary, had asked the CIO leaders to use the PAC as a nucleus around which could be assembled a "national progressive federation." [26] Such groups as the UDA, the PAC's own National Citizens Political Action Committee (a 1944 PAC subsidiary composed of nonlabor liberals), and the PAC itself would be united in a superfederation that could bring the progressive cause tremendous political clout. Ideally, such a federation could reassemble the various components of the successful FDR reelection campaign and use them to make Congress more responsive to liberal demands.[27] With such important national figures as Mrs. Eleanor Roosevelt and Henry Wallace behind the move, it could not fail.[28] However, would the CIO cooperate?

From the start, Hillman was opposed to such a move. In conversations with Loeb, he had indicated that the liberal community had its champions already in PAC and NCPAC. In Hillman's words, "We have found the formula. Let's keep it!" [29] If a national federation were to be formed, the CIO–PAC and NCPAC would take the lead, not the UDA.

Murray had been thinking along quite different lines. Although he left no direct record of his feelings on the UDA

26. James Loeb, Jr. to Philip Murray, November 14, 1944, Folder 1–18–5, Box 18, Series 1, Union for Democratic Action Papers, WSHS.
27. "Hasty Suggestions and Ideas Concerning the Formulation of the National Progressive Organization," n.d. (November 1944), Folder 1–21–2, Box 21, Series 1, Union for Democratic Action Papers, WSHS.
28. James Loeb, Jr. to Mrs. Franklin D. Roosevelt, November 15, 1944, Folder 1–18–5, Box 18, Series 1, Union for Democratic Action Papers, WSHS.
29. Ibid.

proposition, Murray's actions and the rumors that filtered down the PAC chain of command made it clear that he was convinced of the soundness of neither the Loeb nor the Hillman master plan. Just as he had opposed the third-party supporters in July, 1943, now he clamped down on those in the CIO who viewed the PAC as more than a CIO-dominated campaign device. By mid-1945, it was rumored that Hillman was in Murray's disfavor. As a leading Detroit PAC official wrote, Murray objected to Hillman setting himself up as head of something that was "too far apart from the CIO." At the London founding conference for the World Federation of Trade Unions, UAW President R. J. Thomas also reported friction between Hillman and Murray over the PAC. According to Thomas, Murray was disgusted with the way Hillman had turned the WFTU meeting into a publicity device for an expanded PAC.[30] By late 1945, President Murray's opposition had killed both the Loeb and the Hillman plan.

A proposal made by John Brophy was more to Murray's liking than either the Hillman or the Loeb plan. Calling for closer ties between the CIO and the CIO-PAC, Brophy's plan put more political power into the hands of the State Industrial Union councils and the affiliated international unions. Brophy, too, said that some overtures should be made toward nonlabor groups, but he emphasized that the future PAC should be financially and politically controlled entirely by the national CIO leadership, not by non-CIO politicos.[31] With Murray's approval, the Brophy plan went into effect in 1945. Its first test was in Detroit.

With political control shifting from Hillman's office to the IUC's and the internationals, Detroit proved a most interesting test of the Brophy scheme. Detroit had both a strong international union upon the scene, in the person of the United Automobile Workers, and a strong Wayne County Industrial Union Council. Moreover, Detroit was a labor city (almost 400,000 CIO members) with a key 1945

30. Paul Weber to Rev. Benjamin Masse, May 27, 1945, PAC for America Folder, Box 32, Association of Catholic Trade Unionists–Detroit Papers, ALH.

31. "Suggestions on PAC," n.d. (1944–1945), CIO–PAC Folder, Box A4–33, Philip Murray Papers, Catholic University of America, Washington, D.C. (hereafter cited as CUA).

mayoral contest. The CIO–PAC policymakers decided that a CIO city needed a CIO mayor.

What made the Detroit race particularly appealing to the CIO was mayoral candidate Richard T. Frankensteen, a thirty-eight-year-old vice president of the UAW. With a strong PAC aldermanic slate to back him and a great deal of UAW money, Frankensteen had breezed through the August primary with a 83,000 to 69,000 vote victory over his nearest rival, Mayor Edward Jeffries.[32] Victory seemingly assured, Frankensteen had trusted the last months of his final campaign to the Wayne County CIO–PAC, which went to unprecedented lengths to elect him mayor. From August to November, the PAC dumped over 100,000 dollars into the Frankensteen effort, 50,000 dollars of that being reserved for sophisticated radio ads. With 550 Detroit precincts organized and almost 400,000 CIO voters registered, the PAC candidate was a certain victor.[33]

On election day, Frankensteen lost by a vote of 274,000 to 217,000. Later analysis showed that Jeffries had won the election in the very labor precincts where Frankensteen should have piled up huge majorities. While black unionists had gone for Frankensteen, their Polish and southern counterparts had turned to Jeffries overwhelmingly.[34]

As the PAC would later determine, one of the greatest weaknesses of the Frankensteen campaign had been the naivete of the Wayne County PAC in choosing its campaign issues. Sticking close to the 1944 PAC platform's emphasis on Negro rights, the Frankensteen campaign managers assumed that such a liberal platform would appeal to all CIO workers. Edward Jeffries did not make that mistake. Calling Frankensteen a Jew when addressing anti-Semites, a Coughlinite when speaking to Jews, and a "Nigger-lover" when campaigning among southerners, Jeffries expertly manipulated racial tensions to overcome whatever liberal

32. "Political Action—City Level," n.d. (1948), CIO–PAC 1948 Election Folder, Box 202, CIO Secretary–Treasurer's Papers, ALH. Hereafter, this report will be cited as "Political Action—City Level."

33. Report of Secretary–Treasurer (PAC), December 3, 1945, PAC Wayne County Folder, Box 31, Association of Catholic Trade Unionists, Detroit Papers, ALH.

34. "Political Action—City Level."

tendencies Detroit auto workers may have had originally. While Frankensteen steadfastly kept to the high road of racial peace and civil rights, Mayor Jeffries used every racial slur imaginable to defeat the PAC-endorsed candidate.[35] The PAC learned a lesson.

What was surprising was that the CIO–PAC would forget that Detroit was still recovering from the emotional fever of the 1943 race riot. The CIO leadership was so impressed with the supposed success of the 1944 new CIO voter campaign that it forsook logic in a mad scramble to duplicate the 1944 effort, liberal rhetoric and all. According to the 1944 PAC formula, such things as Negro rights, public housing, expanded social security, and even limited nationalization of industry (a concept found in "Toward a New Day") were all programs that would appeal to CIO member–voters. The Frankensteen defeat proved that liberal programs were not always the best way to win labor votes. The drive to turn CIO members into CIO voters would continue, but, after 1945, the PAC was warned that it must substitute real political issues for its liberal rhetoric.[36]

With the lessons of the Frankensteen defeat in mind, Hillman began the 1946 attack with the southern primaries. By early May, 1946, the *CIO News* began to print stories of the PAC's great Alabama triumphs. The *News* claimed that CIO–PAC had played a major part in the primary victories of gubernatorial candidate James Folsom and fifth district Congressman Albert Rains.[37] Closer examination of the two Alabama races, however, tended to discount PAC victory claims.

Although Folsom and Rains were PAC endorsees and victors, the CIO–PAC effort did not deserve Hillman's accolades. Folsom won his primary without capturing Jefferson County, the Birmingham stronghold of the Alabama CIO. Certainly an active CIO–PAC campaign should have been reflected in a Jefferson County triumph for a PAC endorsee. The situation was repeated in the case of Albert Rains. His congressional district, the fifth, had only one

35. Ibid.
36. Ibid.
37. *CIO News,* May 13, 1946, p. 12.

major labor area, Gadsden. In fact, in a district that cast over 50,000 votes, the CIO never claimed to have influenced more than 10,000 voters. How could one-fifth of the electorate have been responsible for a victory margin that was materially greater than the votes it represented? [38] It would seem that the PAC was building member confidence rather than accurately reporting the state of its southern campaign.

While the PAC was still involved in the primaries, it suffered a major loss. On July 10, 1946, Sidney Hillman, the CIO's political expert both as PAC chairman and leader of the old LNPL, suffered his third heart attack in four months. Three hours later he was dead.[39] The Political Action Committee became leaderless in the thick of the 1946 campaign.

The death of Hillman marked the beginning of a new era for the PAC. No longer would the PAC be led by the man who had been instrumental in founding the CIO; no longer could it depend upon the guidance of the man who had directed the CIO's political efforts since the days of Lewis. There was a new man waiting in the wings, however; a man who would lead the PAC for the rest of its existence. The era of Jack Kroll was at hand.

The CIO Executive Board met almost immediately after Hillman's death to decide upon the future course of the CIO's political effort. There was obviously no man of Hillman's stature who could fill immediately the void left by the PAC chairman's death. There were no other CIO international union presidents who were either as well respected or as politically able as Hillman. Yet, the PAC must have a leader; 1946 was a campaign year. With these considerations in mind, the board decided to reorganize the PAC completely. Henceforth, there would be no PAC chairman,

38. Primary returns were from Alexander Heard and Douglas S. Strong, *Southern Primaries and Elections, 1920–1949* (University: University of Alabama Press, 1955), p. 13. The CIO membership figures were from Jack Kroll to PAC Executive Board, Memorandum on Southern Primaries, n.d. (1948), PAC 1948 Folder, Box 85, CIO Secretary–Treasurer's Papers, ALH.

39. *CIO News,* July 15, 1946, pp. 1, 3. Josephson, pp. 669–70.

which was Hillman's title; but Hillman's assistant, Jack Kroll of the Amalgamated Clothing Workers of America, would be moved up to the new position of PAC director. In addition, the Committee itself would now be run by a five-man executive board. Kroll would take care of the day-to-day staff activities of the PAC, but the new executive board would determine long-range PAC policy.[40] The PAC was once more prepared for action.

Almost as soon as he assumed the directorship, Jack Kroll began to reorganize and strengthen the PAC. The first change came at the state level. There, Kroll finished implementing the Brophy plan by turning all remaining regional PAC functions over to the state Industrial Union councils. The second change was Kroll's emphasis on waging the electoral battle more fiercely in what he saw as the eighteen most crucial cities. These cities (essentially the eighteen largest cities in the United States), noted Kroll, would be the deciding factor in the 1946 elections.[41] With this strategy in mind, Kroll immediately announced that the PAC would hold a series of special city-level CIO political meetings.[42] The transition from Hillman to Kroll had been made.

As the campaign progressed, the *CIO News* noted more and more PAC primary victories. One of the most notable of these was the CIO–PAC triumph in Jack Kroll's old PAC region, West Virginia.

The West Virginia CIO had begun working for a slate of liberal Democrats early in 1946. The chief tasks confronting the PAC were the renomination of Senator Harley Kilgore, a strong prolabor Democrat, and the job of swinging the Fourth Congressional District nomination to Marshall College Professor M. G. Burnside. To ensure the

40. *CIO News,* July 22, 1946, p. 2. The five-man board included: Kroll, David McDonald (secretary–treasurer of the United Steel Workers of America), Julius Emspak (secretary–treasurer of the United Electrical Workers), George Addes (secretary–treasurer of the United Automobile Workers), and William Pollock (secretary–treasurer of the Textile Workers Union of America).

41. Outline of Remarks, October 7, 1946, Box 1, Group 2, Jack Kroll Papers, Library of Congress Manuscripts Division, Washington, D.C. Hereafter cited as "Outline of Remarks."

42. *CIO News,* August 5, 1946, p. 6.

nomination of these two, as well as the renomination of prolabor congressmen Matthew Neely, Cleveland Bailey, and John Kee, CIO West Virginia Chairman John Easton immediately began to open up lines of communication with other labor groups. The first group whose cooperation he sought was the West Virginia branch of the Brotherhood of Railroad Trainmen. Writing to a representative of the trainmen, J. M. Houchins, Easton soon reached agreement on the common candidates of the labor movement. The next step was to inform the national PAC so that CIO publications could be put to full use in the candidates' cause. In the meantime, Easton had been advising Professor Burnside on proper techniques for gaining the favorable publicity that was needed to keep himself in the public eye. With cooperation, candidates, and publicity, West Virginia seemed to be ready for the primary.[43]

On August 12, 1946, the *CIO News* took special note of the sweeping victory of the PAC in West Virginia. Not only had the incumbent Senator Kilgore been renominated, but the entire PAC congressional slate had also won spots on the Democratic ticket.[44] It began to seem as if 1946 was going to be the year of a massive PAC victory. That was, however, merely the impression that the *CIO News* tried to give its readers.

The very day that the *New York Times* announced the primary triumph of the PAC and Senator Kilgore, it also announced the primary defeat of PAC's greatest hope, senatorial aspirant Martin Hutchinson. Hutchinson had been the beneficiary of an enormous amount of PAC aid in his attempt to unseat Senator Harry F. Byrd in the Democratic primary election. Yet, in spite of the CIO–PAC's funds and campaign workers, Senator Byrd, who had campaigned on a platform condemning the CIO outsiders, managed to defeat Hutchinson by almost 60,000 votes.[45]

43. John B. Easton to J. M. Houchins, May 17, 1946; John B. Easton to Tilford E. Dudley, May 20, 1946; M. G. Burnside to John B. Easton, March 13, 1946, Political Action Committee Folder, Box 7, West Virginia Labor Federation AFL–CIO Papers, WVUL.
44. *CIO News,* August 12, 1946, p. 3. *New York Times,* August 7, 1946, p. 2; August 8, 1946, pp. 1, 15.
45. *New York Times,* August 8, 1946, p. 1.

As the primary fights of August were replaced by the congressional campaigns of September, the PAC turned again to the National Citizens Political Action Committee. Created during the 1944 battle to reelect President Roosevelt, the NCPAC had provided a means for the PAC to carry on a campaign outside of the immediate labor community without being burdened by the restrictions that the Smith–Connally Act placed upon the CIO. During the 1944 campaign, the NCPAC served mainly as a source of funds for the Roosevelt rallies. A sampling of the names of the NCPAC's Executive Committee revealed both the committee's close relationship to the PAC and the distinguished nature of its membership. For example, the PAC origins of the NCPAC were hardly hidden by an Executive Committee that included Sidney Hillman (chairman), R. J. Thomas (treasurer), and Van Bittner, all of the CIO–PAC. Moreover, the non-PAC members of the NCPAC Executive Committee made up a most distinguished list of American liberals. From James Loeb, Jr.; Freda Kirchway, the publisher of *Nation;* and Gifford Pinchot, former governor of Pennsylvania; to such prominent politicians as George Norris and Elmer Benson, the ex-governor of Minnesota, the NCPAC had almost a monopoly of nonlabor, New Deal liberals. At the end of the 1944 campaign, the NCPAC, which numbered almost 4,200 members, voted to become a permanent political organization.[46] This was the organization that Hillman had seen as a nucleus for a broad liberal federation, and this was the organization that would back the PAC in 1946.

By September, 1946, the NCPAC was fighting its own campaign to "elect a liberal Congress." However, there was one important difference between the NCPAC and the CIO–PAC. Whereas the CIO–PAC could always fall back upon union financing, the NCPAC had to depend upon voluntary contributions. With this in mind, NCPAC Chairman Frank Kingdon turned to several CIO union organizations for financing. Although the CIO–PAC agreed basically with the objectives of the NCPAC, it was not

---

46. Gaer, pp. 213–21. Gaer devotes several pages to defending the NCPAC from the "Communist" charges of the 1944 campaign.

willing to finance an organization that, by 1946, had ceased to be even an unofficial CIO organ. Even so, there were political bonds that still tied the CIO–PAC and the NCPAC.[47]

Late in September, the paths of the PAC and the NCPAC crossed once again. The two groups were co-sponsors, along with the Independent Citizens Committee of the Arts, Sciences, and Professions, of the Chicago Conference of Progressives. About 300 delegates of the three organizations met in Chicago to discuss ways of bringing the spirit of the New Deal back into the national government. Condemning the aggressive foreign policy of the United States, the reactionary elements in the Seventy-ninth Congress, and the illiberal path of the Truman Administration, the conference managed to throw the PAC into the national spotlight only weeks before the election. Although the conferees had promised to aid the PAC in its drive to liberalize Congress, the association of the PAC with the NCPAC and the ICC, two groups of the left, may have had more effect on an election held in a time of strong anti-Russian feeling than a million Progressive promises.[48]

As the last weeks of the campaign came and went, the CIO–PAC continued to voice the party line of the Progressive conference. In the public mind, the conference was most closely associated with its condemnation of Truman's bellicose attitude toward the Russians. Thus, when Kroll told a national radio audience that the Chicago conference "must keep on working," many Americans associated the PAC not with the electoral pledges of the conference (to which Kroll was referring), but with a pro-Russian stance that offended too many potential voters. As the November elections would prove, participation in the Chicago conference, where the PAC was identified with the NCPAC and the ICC, may have been a major tactical blunder. The blunder was hardly helped by the October 18 announce-

47. Frank Kingdon to Michigan CIO, September 4, 1946; Barney Hopkins to Frank Kingdon, October 1, 1946, PAC 1946 Folder, Box 104, Michigan AFL–CIO Papers, ALH.
48. *New York Times,* September 28, 1946, p. 7. *CIO News,* October 7, 1946, p. 3. Saposs, pp. 126–28. Apparently Murray was willing to try something in 1946 he had opposed in 1945.

ment, which made the front page of the *New York Times,* that the Soviet government had officially endorsed all CIO–PAC candidates as true "progressives."[49]

To add even more to CIO–PAC problems, bickering within the United Automobile Workers had brought Michigan PAC activity to a halt in the last months of the campaign. With one of the strongest blocs of CIO voters in the country, Michigan was an important key to national CIO–PAC victory.

The situation came about because of the 1946 UAW presidential sweepstakes. President R. J. Thomas, a key figure in the national PAC, was finding his position challenged by Walter Reuther. Seeing Reuther rapidly overtaking him, Thomas found it necessary to use every means at his disposal to hang on to the UAW presidency. The means that hurt the Michigan PAC effort was Thomas's demotion of two key PAC coordinators, Newman Jeffrey and Frank Hook. Since the two were Reuther supporters, the move was an obvious one, but what was not so obvious was the importance of the coordinators to the campaign. As chief planners for the Michigan PAC since 1945 and the sole link between the national PAC and the Michigan affiliate, Jeffrey and Hook were vitally important to the 1946 effort. President Milton Murray of the American Newspaper Guild summed up the ensuing mess best. Calling the fiasco the work of a "thickheaded stupid Dutchman," he concluded that the action would wipe out all Michigan PAC groundwork simply for spite.[50]

49. "Outline of Remarks," October 7, 1946. All the national newspapers had emphasized the pro-Russian stance of the conference. See, *New York Times,* September 28, 1946, p. 7. As Eric Goldman noted, the Russians' control of Poland, Yugoslavia, and East Germany was becoming an increasingly offensive issue to most U.S. citizens. Furthermore, most Americans were spurred by these international actions into an aggressively anti-Communist attitude at home. The NCPAC and the ICC were already under suspicion as Communist fronts. See, Eric Goldman, *The Crucial Decade and After* (New York: Random House, 1960), pp. 25–45. Also, *New York Times,* October 20, 1946, p. 1.

50. Milton Murray to Paul Weber, n.d. (1946), Milton Murray Folder, Box 28, Association of Catholic Trade Unionists—Detroit Papers, ALH.

As the end of the campaign brought the magnitude of the Michigan disaster to light, Thomas defended his actions to President Murray in a blistering letter. Blaming the Michigan PAC for the defeat, Thomas blasted state PAC boss Gus Scholle for red-baiting to the detriment of campaigning. Moreover, Thomas claimed, Scholle and Reuther were in league with Republican gubernatorial candidate Kim Sigler to defeat CIO–Democratic nominee Van Wagoner.[51] It was all a plot.

On the national level, the results of the 1946 elections were nothing short of a disaster. Whereas the PAC had cherished hopes of winning twenty-three new House seats for the liberal bloc, the returns revealed a fifty-four seat loss by the Democrats in that body. In the Senate, the Democrats lost eleven seats—but the importance of the defeat to the CIO was not measured in numbers alone.[52]

The deposed Democrats included in their ranks a number of outstanding liberals whose prolabor votes would be sorely missed in the coming session of Congress. In the House, such liberals as California's Jerry Voorhis, whom Thomas Amlie (in 1944) had called idealistic, high-minded, and eminently worthy of PAC support, were defeated.[53] In the Senate, the 1946 elections took such casualties as the prolabor Senator Joseph Guffey of Pennsylvania and Progressive Robert LaFollette, Jr., of Wisconsin. Such men had been behind labor in the critical Case bill fight, but when antilabor legislation came up in the next Congress their places would be filled with such antilabor members as Wisconsin's new senator, Joseph McCarthy.[54] Such was the story of the 1946 elections on the national level.

In the CIO's own constituency, Democratic congressional aspirants fared no better. Only eight of twenty congressional

51. R. J. Thomas to Philip Murray, November 4, 1946, CIO–PAC Folder, Box A4–33, Philip Murray Papers, CUA.

52. The Senate and House breakdown were from Malcom Moos, *Politics, Presidents, and Coattails* (Baltimore: Johns Hopkins Press, 1952), p. 224.

53. Ibid., pp. 179–212. Thomas Amlie to Sidney Hillman, January 8, 1944, CIO–PAC Campaign Folder, Box 58, Thomas R. Amlie Papers, WSHS.

54. Moos, pp. 215–24.

districts in which CIO members composed a substantial percentage of the electorate sent Democrats to Congress in 1946. Compared to 1944, this represented a loss of two Democratic congressmen.[55] However, these losses did expose a number of the PAC's 1946 mistakes.

The first and most obvious mistake was the CIO–PAC identification with NCPAC and Communists. As Congressman Jerry Voorhis revealed in his autobiography, the single most effective weapon that the Republicans used against him was the NCPAC issue. Time and time again, his opponent tried to equate Voorhis's PAC endorsement with Kremlin approval. Voorhis was on the defensive for the entire campaign, trying to separate the PAC from the leftist NCPAC and himself from them both. By election day, the voters of California's Twelfth Congressional District were convinced that the PAC, the NCPAC, and Jerry Voorhis were all part of a Communist conspiracy. It mattered little that Voorhis never actually received PAC endorsement (since the Communist-influenced California CIO–PAC found him too much of a rightist); the voters put his opponent in Congress. His opponent, Richard M. Nixon, would have a prominent part in writing the Taft–Hartley Act.[56]

In Indiana's Third Congressional District, the PAC's situation was much the same. Although the third district was one of the twenty districts in which CIO members composed a significant percentage of the electorate, it had been represented since 1938 by Republican Congressman Robert A. Grant. In 1946, when the Communist issue was injected into the campaign, the CIO–PAC backing of Democrat John Gonas provided Grant with plenty of ammunition. Ever since the Chicago conference, the PAC and everyone it endorsed had been suspected of Communist

55. Moos, pp. 179–212. The twenty CIO districts were: Michigan 1, 2, 6, 13–17, Indiana 1, 3, Pennsylvania 20, 25, 27, 28, New York 31, Ohio 9, 14, 19, New Jersey 1, Wisconsin 1. See Chapter 3, Appendix. The two 1946 losses were in Wayne County, Mich., where the Democratic incumbents were defeated in districts 13 and 14.

56. Jerry Voorhis, *Confessions of a Congressman* (Garden City: Doubleday and Co., 1947), pp. 335–42.

sympathies. Congressman Grant was easily returned to Congress.[57]

The PAC had not taken into account the deep-seated, anti-Communist sympathies of the 1946 electorate. In a year when America had almost come to an armed show-down with Russia in Iran, American voters did not take kindly to the CIO hobnobbing with Russian leaders at the London Conference of the World Federation of Trade Unions, or to the PAC aligning itself with the red-lined members of the Chicago conference. Already the whispered rumor that Roosevelt had sold out the free Poles at Yalta was beginning to hurt even regular Democrats in Polish–American areas. With this kind of feeling sweeping the land, it was amazing that PAC candidates were not more soundly defeated, especially after the Soviet endorsement.[58]

The second major PAC mistake was the assumption that CIO voters would flock to the polls as in 1944. According to Clark Clifford, a key reason for the liberal defeat in 1946 was the failure of the CIO to convince its membership to register and vote as it had in 1944. Without the inspiration of Roosevelt, noted Clifford, the task of getting out the labor vote became extremely difficult.[59] The kind of minor adjustments that Kroll had made in 1946 were simply not enough to do the job.

As the year 1947 began, the immediate results of the PAC's 1946 failure became evident. President Truman, worried about a pending coal strike, made a call for new labor legislation in his State of the Union message. What

57. CIO members composed about twenty-six per cent of the third district's electorate. See Chapter 3, Appendix. For information on the third district, see Paul C. Bartholomew, *Indiana's Third Congressional District* (South Bend: University of Notre Dame Press, 1970), pp. 153–69, 170–71.

58. A number of CIO members wrote to President Murray after the election blaming PAC defeats upon the Communist issue and the NCPAC label that was being pinned upon the CIO–PAC. See for example, Philip J. Smith to Philip Murray, November 10, 1946, and Charles Weinstein to Philip Murray, November 14, 1946, CIO–PAC Folder, Box A4–33, Philip Murray Papers, CUA.

59. Memorandum for the President, November 19, 1947, p. 8., Clark M. Clifford Papers, Harry S. Truman Library, Independence, Mo.

was needed, he said, was legislation that would make contracts truly binding and render jurisdictional strikes illegal. Truman cautioned, however, that Congress must not go too far and enact punitive measures.[60] The Eightieth Congress ignored these cautionary remarks.

With the reorganization of Congress that followed the Republican victory of 1946, two names would become increasingly prominent in labor legislation. In the House, where six Democratic members of the crucial Labor Committee had been lost by the 1946 elections, the chairmanship of the newly-formed Committee on Education and Labor fell to the senior Republican congressman from New Jersey, Fred Hartley, Jr. In the Senate, a long-time critic of the CIO, Senator Robert Taft of Ohio, inherited the Labor Committee chairmanship. Below these two individuals, both House and Senate labor committees were packed with Republicans eager to return unions to their pre-Wagner Act status. Such men as Taft, Hartley, Congressman Clare Hoffman of Michigan (third ranking Republican on the Labor Committee), and Congressman Max Schwabe of Missouri (fifth ranking Labor Committee Republican and violently antiunion) would be the legislators whose tasks it became to revise the labor laws.[61]

By mid-January, the *CIO News* was deeply worried by the new antilabor Congress. The occasion for the *News'* concern was the introduction of the Taft bill (S.55) in the Senate. As the *News* noted, the Taft bill was but a reworked version of the narrowly defeated Case bill. The Congress that would pass on the Taft bill, however, was not as inclined to favor labor as its predecessor.[62] The fight was on.

Only weeks after its introduction, the Taft bill had already passed its first test. In January, the bill went through a series of favorable hearings held by the Labor and Public Welfare Committee. Senator Joseph Ball, a cosponsor of the bill, used one of the sessions to explain the provisions of the pending legislation. First, he explained, the bill set up an agency called the Federal Mediation Board. This

60. *New York Times,* January 7, 1947, p. 1.
61. Fred Hartley, Jr., *Our New National Labor Policy* (New York: Funk and Wagnalls Co., 1948), pp. 22–32.
62. *CIO News,* January 13, 1947, p. 3.

board would have the power to declare a sixty-day cooling-off period in any labor dispute in which it judged that a strike would be contrary to the public interest. The second major provision was a prohibition of collective bargaining for foremen, for the reason that foremen were essential agents of management and, therefore, should not be thought of as employees. The third provision would have allowed management to sue unions for breach of contract. No longer could unions violate no-strike contract with impunity. Other parts of the bill outlawed secondary boycotts, forbade jurisdictional strikes (strikes against other unions), and made unions publish financial statements that would be open to public scrutiny.[63] This was the bill jointly sponsored by senators Robert Taft, Joseph Ball, and Howard Smith.

During the second month of hearings on the Taft bill, President Philip Murray gave the CIO's view of the bill. Murray began his presentation with a long defense of industrial relations status quo. He called the 1940s the most peaceful era in American industrial relations. With the American worker at the peak of his efficiency and the labor relations system in its most peaceful era, why tamper with the status quo? The few major strikes of 1946, such as the steel strike, were, in Murray's view, caused by management's refusal to bargain in accordance with the wishes of President Truman. After all, when the steel strike finally ended, had not the steel companies granted the same wage increases recommended by Truman and the unions in the beginning? The terms of the Taft bill, which Murray referred to as compulsory arbitration, would do nothing but provoke loyal workers. There was clearly no need for new labor legislation.[64] When it came to labor legislation, however, Congress had other ideas.

As the Taft bill began to move toward passage, it differed only slightly from legislation recommended by President Truman in his State of the Union message. This de-

63. After the CIO split from the AFL, many of its unions tried to organize workers in shops already organized by the AFL. Such jurisdictional disputes would not be allowed to lead to strikes under the Taft bill. U.S., Senate, Committee on Labor and Public Welfare, *Hearings on S. J. Res. 22, A Labor Relations Program,* 80th Cong., 1st sess., 1947, Part 1, pp. 9–16.

64. Ibid., Part 2, pp. 1089–1145.

ficiency was soon remedied by congressional conservatives.

When the Taft bill was reported to the Senate in April, it had been transformed into an entirely different measure. Under its new designation, S.1126, the bill had added several new provisions. First, it banned industry-wide bargaining with competing employers. Second, it banned employer contributions to welfare funds administered in any way by a union (a Case bill provision). Third, the new bill forbade the closed shop, where only union members could be hired. Fourth, the Norris–LaGuardia ban on antilabor injunctions was amended so as to allow injunctions against public interest strikes. Finally, it changed the composition of the National Labor Relations Board by adding four new members.[65]

While Taft and his fellow Senators had been working on S.1126, the House had also been concerned with a labor relations bill. This was Congressman Fred Hartley's H.R. 3020, which had been reported on April 11. The Hartley bill contained five new clauses, in addition to the Taft bill provisions. First, the National Labor Relations Board would be transformed into the Labor–Management Relations Board. Second, unions would be forbidden to charge more than twenty-five dollars for an initiation fee. Third, no union could be certified as a bargaining agent that had an officer who was a Communist. Fourth, unions would be forbidden to make political campaign contributions (a provision that closed the loophole in the old Smith–Connally Act). Finally, in its amended form, the bill forbade government employees to strike. To the alarm of CIO officials, the two bills began to move quickly toward enactment. On April 17, only six days after it had been reported to the House, the Hartley bill was passed by that body.[66]

The Senate deliberated at a slower pace. As the upper house continued to debate the Taft bill throughout the month of April, the CIO mustered its forces to defeat the pending legislation. Jack Kroll declared the month of April to be "Defend Your Union Month." To raise a cry of public protest, the CIO instructed all its branches to distribute literature warning the membership and the public about

65. U.S., *Congressional Record,* 80th Cong., 1st sess., 1947, 93, Part 5, 6441–6445.
66. Ibid., Part 3, 3318, 3547–3553, 3670–3671.

the dangers of the Taft and Hartley bills. A massive letter-writing campaign was initiated that would be accompanied by public protest rallies and indignant citizens' delegations' visits to wavering senators. If things went as planned, the CIO hoped to see millions of citizens outside of the labor movement caught up in the spirit of the campaign. Leaving no stone unturned, all local PACs were instructed to start a new registration drive, a move that might scare a few wandering senators back into line. However, all the CIO's efforts seemed to be futile. The bills continued to move speedily toward passage.[67]

As increasing congressional pressure made it clear that some new labor legislation would be passed, labor's friends in the Senate made one last attempt to head off the Taft and Hartley bills. With the backing of the CIO, Senator James Murray of Montana submitted a substitute bill to the Senate on May 12. The Murray bill made only four slight changes in existing labor law. First, the bill called for the strengthening of government mediation and conciliation services. Second, the Murray substitute allowed foremen's unions only if they contained no rank-and-file workers. Third, the bill would have allowed the President to seize industries threatened by public safety strikes (a provision of Smith–Connally). Finally, secondary boycotts to further a jurisdictional strike were outlawed. Despite the strong support of the Senate's liberal bloc, the substitute measure was voted down by the substantial margin of seventy-three to nineteen. The Taft bill was assured of passage.[68]

The Taft bill finally gained passage by the margin of sixty-eight to twenty-four on May 13. In its final form, the bill was passed under the title of H.R. 3020 (Hartley bill), but its provisions were those of S.1126.[69] A Senate–House Conference Committee next awaited the measure.

The legislation that emerged from the Conference Committee differed from both bills considerably. First, it in-

67. Jack Kroll to John B. Easton, March 26, 1947, Political Action Committee Folder, Box 11, West Virginia Labor Federation AFL–CIO Papers, WVUL.

68. U.S., *Congressional Record,* 80th Cong., 1st sess., 1947, 93, Part 4, 4985–4986, 5117.

69. Ibid.

corporated most of the Hartley bill provisions with a few modifications. Foremen's unions were banned, but plant guard unions were allowed. The welfare fund proposal was amended to require participation of both employers and employees. Second, the committee report listed four basic unfair labor practices. These were: coercion of employees or employers, the jurisdictional strike and boycott, denial of union membership to anyone except for failure to pay dues, and refusal to bargain collectively. Third, the report allowed the Attorney General to obtain an eighty-day injunction against any public interest strike if the employees rejected the last offer of the employer (an NLRB secret ballot election would determine the latter point). Finally, the report closed the loophole left open by Smith–Connally; union campaign contributions and expenditures would be forbidden. The use of the word expenditures was interpreted to mean any support whatsoever. Even endorsement of a candidate by a union newspaper would be considered illegal.[70] If the report passed both houses, the CIO–PAC would be severely hindered in the future.

In the meantime, the CIO was continuing its anti-Taft–Hartley campaign. President Murray sent telegrams to every state industrial union council calling for letters to the President to veto the hostile measure.[71] However, the last appeal was a case of too little, too late: The bill could not be stopped even by the President.

On June 4, the House passed the conference report. The Senate followed suit two days later by a vote of fifty-four to seventeen. On June 20, citing the ban on union political expenditures as a "dangerous intrusion of free speech," President Truman vetoed the Taft–Hartley bill. The House waited only hours before it overrode the veto. The Senate took three days to make up its mind, but followed the House's example. The era of the Taft–Hartley Act began.[72]

The final passage of the Taft–Hartley Act in 1947 emphasized the failures of the PAC from 1944 to 1947. Claiming victory in 1944, the CIO–PAC watched in dismay

70. Ibid., Part 5, 6361–6381.

71. Philip Murray to August Scholle, May 15, 1947, PAC 1947 Folder, Box 104, Michigan AFL–CIO Papers, ALH.

72. U.S., *Congressional Record,* 80th Cong., 1st sess., 1947, 93, Part 5, 6392–6393, 6536; Part 6, 7488, 7489, 7538.

as the Seventy-ninth Congress almost enacted the Case bill. Hoping to start a new era of CIO victories, PAC saw its liberal pronouncements turned against it in the Detroit mayoral race. Next, ignoring the stormclouds over Europe, the PAC naively cooperated with the discredited NCPAC in the Chicago Conference of Progressives. As the 1946 election proved, associating with Communist fellow travelers was not the correct path to victory. Finally, as the passage of Taft–Hartley proved, the consequences of electoral defeat were much too serious to treat lightly. The CIO Political Action Committee had to do better—much better —in the coming elections.

4

Mr. Murray and the Great Red Menace

The passage of the Taft–Hartley Act deeply discouraged CIO members and their leaders. The November defeat at the polls, and then Taft–Hartley itself, had impressed everyone active in union politics with the seriousness of the situation. Not since the 1920s had union rights hung by so thin a thread. To make matters worse, national elections were only a year away, and the electoral machine that misfired in 1946 had yet to be fixed. Key policy decisions had to be made at once, and the only man with the power to make such decisions was the boss himself. For Philip Murray, it was one more instance when he was keenly aware of the message displayed on another President's desk: The buck stops here.

As Murray looked deeper into the problems of the coming campaign, he found one issue that arose time and time again. The issue, the times, and the election all seemed bound together. It was an issue that CIO officials had ducked for years and, for some time, the seeming secret of CIO electoral success had been such studied silence. However, the 1946 elections had shown that silence was no longer satisfactory. Silence could not compete with the strident tones of a Richard Nixon, a Parnell Thomas, or even a Harry Truman. The issue was communism.

To understand Philip Murray's approach to the red scare and the CIO, it is first necessary to understand that amazingly complex individual who took John L. Lewis's place as president of the Congress of Industrial Organizations. Philip Murray was his own man.

Irving Bernstein, in trying to sum up the life of Phil Murray, called him "the Good Man of the labor movement." [1] Although nobody could argue with the merit of

1. Irving Bernstein, *Turbulent Years* (Boston: Houghton Mifflin Co., 1971), p. 443.

that description, an even better key to the Murray character was given by Monsignor Charles Owen Rice, who
described his long-time confidant as labor's "tough unionist." [2] While all would concede such a title to beetle-
browed and bullying John L. Lewis, few realized how tough
quiet, charming Phil Murray was in the depths of his union
soul.

There was good reason for Murray to be tough and
union to the core. Born the son of a union miner in a
Scottish colliery town, he was steeped in the trade union
ethic from the first union meeting he attended at age six
(chaired by his father, Will Murray) through a twenty-year
subterranean career in the pits on both sides of the Atlantic.
The story goes that on his first day at the pit head the
superintendent greeted his father with, "Well, Will, I see
you've brought another man for the union." [3] And right
he was.

Coming to America with union transfer cards and hope,
Will and Phil Murray headed for Madison, Pennsylvania,
the home of an uncle, where they found mine work. Although he roomed with the family of Pat Fagan (later
president of United Mine Workers District Five and the
man who introduced Father Rice to Murray), Phil Murray
did not get into the thick of mine union activity until age
eighteen. Then, disgusted with a cheating check weighman,
Phil took a little "direct action" (as it would later be
termed by Bill Haywood), was fired, and found himself the
leader of a spontaneous strike of 600 fellow workers. He
lost the strike, but he had found a home in the United
Mine Workers of America. In 1912, he was elected to the
UMWA international executive board and moved from
there to the presidency of UMWA District Five in 1916.
Hitching his wagon to the rising star of John L. Lewis, the
District Five presidency was replaced by the UMWA vice
presidency in 1920. For the next twenty years, he would
be Lewis's second-in-command. When Lewis broke with
the AFL, Murray came with him. When Lewis created the

2. Monsignor Charles O. Rice Interview, October 18, 1967,
pp. 6–8, Pennsylvania State University Oral History Collection, Pennsylvania State University Library, University Park,
Pa. (hereafter cited as PSUL).

3. Bernstein, p. 442.

United Steel Workers of America, Murray took charge of its day-to-day operation. When Lewis negotiated a contract with big steel, Murray signed the papers.[4] And then came October, 1940.

On October 25, 1940, CIO members throughout the country tuned their radio sets to hear John L. Lewis announce his support for Wendell Willkie, the Republican presidential nominee. Such an announcement had been expected, but what really shocked the audience was Lewis's promise that if Willkie were not elected, he would "retire as President of the CIO at its convention in November." [5] It was a tough choice. CIO members must either reject the founder of the CIO or the founder of the New Deal and the most popular President in history. Telegrams flooded CIO headquarters that night and were joined by scores of letters the next day. The message was always the same: "With all due respect and loyalty to John L. Lewis, I cannot accept his alternative Willkie." [6]

Again, Murray was left in the background as CIO directors Allan Haywood and John Brophy were assigned the task of answering the critics. Most of such answers followed the pattern set by a letter to Detroit CIO boss Gus Scholle. "My choice is with Lewis," wrote Haywood. Roosevelt gladly accepted the title "friend of labor," but his real friends were such antilabor figures as Boss Edward Kelley of Chicago and Boss Frank Hague of "Jersey." Lewis, on the other hand, went against the Administration in supporting the workers in the Little Steel and Ford strikes. "Politicians will come and go," concluded the CIO director, "but the labor movement must go on forever." [7] That was precisely the attitude of the next head of the CIO.

When Lewis resigned as promised, the CIO convention turned not to Haywood or Brophy, but rather to the mild-mannered vice president of the organization, Philip Mur-

4. Ibid., pp. 442–43, 447.

5. *United Mine Workers Journal,* November 1, 1940, pp. 4–6. This was the complete and official version of the speech.

6. August Scholle to Allan Haywood, October 27, 1940, Lewis and 1940 Election Folder, Box A5–8, John Brophy Papers, CUA.

7. Allan Haywood to Gus Scholle, October 31, 1940, Lewis and 1940 Election Folder, John Brophy Papers, CUA.

ray.[8] His was not exactly a case of overnight success; it had taken Phil Murray forty-four years to rise from the pit head to the CIO penthouse. Yet, after 1940, it would be the gentle Murray, not the blustery Lewis, who would guide CIO fortunes.

Many a national politician and many a labor leader has fancied himself a man of the people. Phil Murray was one of the few who truly deserved such a *sobriquet*. As Father Rice related, Murray had real empathy with working people. One of Rice's favorite stories revolved around this point.

A visitor to Pittsburgh hailed a cab and was somewhat annoyed to find the cabby in a terrible hurry to get rid of him. "What's the rush?" he asked.

"I want to go back and pick up Philip Murray. I'll have a chance if I hurry now," came the reply.

"Why?" asked the passenger. "Is he a big tipper?"

"No bigger tip than most. But," said the driver, "it's just a wonderful thing to have him in the cab." [9] Few self-styled men of the people ever rated such a compliment.

Murray was also tough. A trade unionist through and through, he never let his associates forget for exactly whom they worked. Another Rice story showed that side of the Murray character.

During the middle of World War Two, Father Rice was having lunch with Murray and Clinton Golden, the northeastern regional director for the United Steel Workers of America. Golden, college-educated and urbane, was waxing poetic about how he was "representing the country" in a negotiating session before a wartime agency. Murray did not accept that argument for a minute.

"You're not!" he cried. "You're representing the labor organizations, that's who you're representing, and don't think for a minute that the people on the other side are representing the country as a whole. If you don't represent our organization, we are underrepresented!" [10] Yet how

8. Bernstein, pp. 721–26.

9. Monsignor Charles O. Rice Interview, October 18, 1967, p. 10, Pennsylvania State University Oral History Collection, PSUL.

10. Ibid., p. 11.

did the trade union ethic guide him in his treatment of communism?

The CIO had been dealing with critics of its stance on communism ever since its birth. As an organization director of the United Electrical, Machine, and Radio Workers of America noted, young Communists were active in the organizing drives of "all" CIO unions.[11] They were the only experienced labor organizers John L. Lewis could rely on during the first years of the CIO. However, with the Communist organizers came a public relations problem. As seen in the 1944 and 1946 elections, one of the Republicans' favorite ploys was to cite the Communist character of the CIO. How could CIO leaders answer such a charge?

John Brophy, as director of the CIO, had been the first to stand on the firing line, as the newly-formed Association of Catholic Trade Unionists began to take potshots at communism in the CIO in 1939. Answering a letter from Father Thomas Darby, who had wondered how a good Catholic like Brophy could accept the presence of Communists in the CIO, Brophy set forth a position that would have major influence on Philip Murray's anticommunism in later years.[12] The CIO, wrote Brophy, had consistently denied any political party the right to "control its life." When CIO members tried to bend the organization to the ends of any outside party, they were severely disciplined. "To meet your point about the Communists," he wrote, "if the CP members in our union conduct themselves in such a manner as to constitute themselves a challenge to the existence of the CIO, it is only then they become a 'menace' and we deal with them accordingly. . . ." This was the official position of the CIO until World War Two.

With the beginning of the war and, more importantly, the end of James Carey's control of the United Electrical Workers Union, the CIO's Communist debate suddenly became more heated. Carey was not only the *Wunderkind* of 1930s unionism (he was a president of the United Elec-

11. James Matles Interview, May 6, 1968, p. 56, Pennsylvania State University Oral History Collection, PSUL.

12. Reverend Thomas Darby to John Brophy, November 24, 1939; John Brophy to Reverend Thomas Darby, November 29, 1939, Folder D, Box A5–7, John Brophy Papers, CUA.

trical Workers Union at twenty-five), but was also a close and intimate friend of Philip Murray. When CIO Secretary–Treasurer Carey became concerned about an issue, Murray had at least to give it thought. Thus, when Carey took up the anti-Communist cudgel in 1941, Murray was forced to face the issue that the CIO had been ducking through the agile pen of John Brophy.[13] Before a decision could be reached, war intervened.

In the tangle that was the United Electrical Workers–CIO Communist controversy, only a few basic facts were accepted by both sides. First, and most importantly, both agreed that the Communists were excellent organizers. It was in great part their work that made such new unions as the UE successful. Second, as successful organizers, both sides agreed they deserved some representation on the UE executive board. Indeed, that right was rarely challenged until 1940, when the UE anti-Communists (James Carey, Matthew Campbell, and Harry Block) felt that the union's Communists (James Matles and Julius Emspak) were following the Soviet line too slavishly on the Lend-Lease issue. Finally, both agreed that the critical shift in UE power occurred at the September, 1941 UE convention, when Matthew Campbell's executive board replacement (Campbell had died in 1941), sided with the Communists in ousting Carey as UE president. Because the critical party in that coup was the replacement, Albert Fitzgerald, his views of the Carey overthrow and succeeding CIO red scare cast an interesting light on the whole situation.[14]

Fitzgerald fit into a rather novel slot in the UE controversy. A non-Communist (a member of the UE's "pure Catholic" Local 201), he was courted by both sides before the 1941 convention. Although the Matles–Emspak offer of the presidency obviously swayed him, his views of Carey may also have affected his course. In his view, Carey was but an imitation John L. Lewis. The majestic phrases that cascaded from Lewis always sounded "corny" to Fitzgerald

13. Monsignor Charles O. Rice Interview, October 18, 1967, pp. 17–18, Pennsylvania State University Oral History Collection, PSUL.
14. Harry Block Interview, September 25, 1967, pp. 7, 10–17, Pennsylvania State University Oral History Collection, PSUL.

when echoed by the diminutive Carey; they never for a moment distracted him from the realization that effective control of the UE was held by Matles and Emspak, not by CIO officer and liberal politician Carey. As far as Fitzgerald was concerned, there was no Communist controversy in the UE in 1941. The factionalism was merely the division of the UE into pro- and anti-Carey camps. Only later did Carey try to convert anti-Careyism into procommunism.[15]

Because the war pushed the entire CIO into Murray's "production for victory" drive, the UE split was forced underground for the next few years. Although the fight was underground, it still had direct effect on Murray. Because he had supported Carey for the position of CIO secretary–treasurer in 1942 (and had supported him as CIO secretary before that), Emspak, Matles, and Fitzgerald held him responsible for Carey's sniping at the new UE leadership. Things got so far out of hand in 1943 that Murray called a special meeting of all UE factions on February 4 to settle their differences. The outcome of the meeting was Murray's censure of Carey and an indirect endorsement of the existing UE administration.[16] As Father Rice admitted, Murray was not anti-Communist during the war.[17]

The renewal of CIO anticommunism and the UE battle occurred just as President Murray saw the 1946 PAC election effort fall apart. Indeed, the Cold War began in the CIO almost before it did in the larger political world.

Again, according to Rice, Murray was not particularly impressed when Carey renewed hostilities by forming the UE Members for Democratic Action in 1946. While Carey, by then, saw the UE affair as part of a world-wide conspiracy, the CIO boss still looked upon the UE leaders

15. Ibid. Also, Albert J. Fitzgerald Interview, May 7, 1968, pp. 7–14, Pennsylvania State University Oral History Collection, PSUL.

16. Julius Emspak to Philip Murray, January 28, 1943 and Julius Emspak to Central Executive Board–UE, February 8, 1943, both in UEW, 1943 Folder, Box 62, CIO Secretary–Treasurer's Papers, ALH.

17. Monsignor Charles O. Rice Interview, October 18, 1967, pp. 12–13, Pennsylvania State University Oral History Collection, PSUL.

as acceptable and successful trade unionists. After all, they had recently won very impressive contracts from both the General Electric Company and the Westinghouse Electric Corporation.[18] Despite Murray's lack of concern, other CIO leaders were doing their best to get the CIO involved in the growing Communist controversy.

Probably the first organization that tried to influence Murray and his fellows was the Association of Catholic Trade Unionists. Ever since the 1939 letter by Father Darby, the ACTU had done its utmost to turn the key Catholic CIO leaders (Philip Murray, John Brophy, James Carey, and David McDonald) into anti-Communists. By 1946, its efforts had borne some fruit.

As Carey threw himself into the UE fight, he was not opposed to ACTU help. Although his critics were quick to accuse him of ACTU membership, Carey never actually joined the association; he merely used it. In the years 1945 to 1949, Carey even brought ACTU activists onto his staff; of these, the most important was Harry Read.[19]

Harry Read was a newspaperman by trade, Catholic by upbringing, and union by choice. Born in Chicago in 1892, Read was reared in a staunchly Catholic household. After graduating from Northwestern University, he sought work in the world of Chicago journalism. By the 1930s, when he became active in American Newspaper Guild organizing (the ANG was a CIO affiliate), he had moved up to the position of city editor of the *Chicago American*. A CIO man of such stature could not be overlooked by CIO national headquarters. So, in 1941, Read was hired as editor of the Michigan *CIO News*. In the meantime, as Read had been moving up in CIO circles, he had also been moving up in the ACTU. A founder of the Chicago chapter of the association, he easily moved into a position of leadership in the Detroit branch after his arrival in that city in

18. Ibid., pp. 17–18.
19. The three most prominent ACTU members on the CIO payroll were Harry Read, Carey's administrative assistant, Paul Weber of the Wayne County PAC, and Richard Deverall of the CIO's Education Department. Francis W. Sullivan to Harry Read, January 25, 1941; Harry Read to Paul Weber, September 11, 1946, ACTU Folder, Box A8–3, Harry Read Papers, CUA.

1941.[20] He and ACTU associate Paul Weber were even successful in moving the ACTU into labor politics. First with the Wayne County LNPL and then with the CIO–PAC, Read and his friends helped shift control of the Detroit organizations to ACTU cells that were pledged to keep Communists out. The association did its work so well that in 1945 most key Wayne County CIO–PAC positions were held by ACTU sympathizers.[21] Then, Carey called Read to Washington to be his administrative assistant.

Even before he took the new job in April, 1945, Read was besieged by ACTU requests to use secret CIO data to further association ends. Father John Cronin, Detroit's Paul Weber, and the New York ACTU's John Cort were Read's chief contacts in this endeavor. Father Cronin of Baltimore felt that CIO insiders such as Read would surely have access to material that Catholic action groups could use to discredit CIO Communists. In collecting such material, Cronin found Read a ready coconspirator, or "Sherlock Holmes" as Cronin liked to put it. From April to October, 1945, Harry Read worked for two bosses, Carey and Cronin. At the end of that period, Read's research on "our matter"—as he termed the project—yielded Father Cronin a local-by-local breakdown of Communist strength within the CIO. Not only were the locals revealed, but the investigation also found the names of key local Communists, the types of appeals they used most successfully, and the ethnic groups with whom they were most successful. Although much of the work was based upon Read's experiences in Chicago and Detroit, some must certainly have come from those secret CIO files that Cronin had sought. By December, Father Cronin was able to piece Read's reports into a guide for the parish priest in his fight against Communist unions.[22]

20. Harry Read Biography, January 1, 1954, Harry Read Biography Folder, Box A8–5, Harry Read Papers, CUA.
21. To All CIO Activists, June 30, 1944, PAC, 1944 Folder, Box 31 and ACTU to All CIO Activists, n.d. (April 1945) both in Association of Catholic Trade Unionists—Detroit Papers, ALH. The latter broadside also lists the leaders of the ACTU cell within the PAC. Of those listed, Paul Weber, Tracy Doll, and Ernest Bennett were all key Wayne County CIO–PAC leaders.
22. Father John Cronin to Harry Read, April 2, 1945;

Through the entire CIO Communist crisis, Read stayed in Carey's office and relayed key material to his ACTU correspondents. Harry Read carried out two quite similar errands for Paul Weber. In 1946, Read used his position to discover and report on two suspected Communists in Detroit.[23] A year later, Read obtained secret CIO correspondence on the UE that he supplied Weber.[24] In neither case were the favors supplied of critical importance, but Read and—*de facto*—Carey were certainly bending the national office to some unusual ends.

The Harry Read–John Cort correspondence revealed even more bending. In a series of letters that began in 1948 and lasted until 1952, John Cort, a leader of the New York ACTU, revealed that some association members hoped to gain more than information from Read's office. In 1948, Cort acted as a communications link between Catholic trade unions in Europe and the CIO. When the Catholic unions discovered that they could not control the World Federations of Trade Unions, they began to cast about for allies. One of the most likely allies seemed to be the CIO, but the Catholic unionists could find no direct link with that federation. That is, they could find no link until the ACTU appeared. Using Cort and Read as a pipeline, Erwin Altenburger, a German Catholic trade union official, tried to convince James Carey and the CIO leadership that their proper allies in the WFTU should be Altenburger's Catholic unions, not the CIO's socialist

---

Harry Read to Father John Cronin, March 20, 1945; Father John Cronin to Harry Read, October 18, 1945; Material Sought for C.P.A. Report, n.d. (1945), Father Cronin Folder, Box A8–3, Harry Read Papers, CUA.

23. Marguerite Gahagan to Harry Read, October 20, 1946, ACTU Folder, Box A8–3, Harry Read Papers, CUA.

24. Harry Read to Paul Weber, February 21, 1947, James Carey, 1943–1947 Folder, Box 11, Association of Catholic Trade Unionists—Detroit Papers, ALH.

A more spectacular, but less successful, quest by Paul Weber's office was for Read to put an ACTU man named Henry McCusker into a high position in the CIO's Michigan region, where he would torpedo efforts of Gus Scholle's socialists to control the Michigan state CIO–PAC. Marguerite Gahagan to Harry Read, March 14, 1950, ACTU Folder, Box A8–3, Harry Read Papers, CUA.

friends. By the time that the message reached Carey, it was too late. Most of the Catholic unions had withdrawn from the WFTU and the CIO was on the verge of similar action. Cort's second demand of Read was that he help make President Murray into a public ACTU supporter. Harry Read replied that such a course was foolish; Murray did not support outside organizations.[25]

In the whole Communist crisis, Murray maintained the independence and basic voluntarism of the CIO. While Read and Carey could not swing Murray to the right, others were equally unsuccessful in moving him to the left. The case that best revealed this was Murray's involvement with the Progressive Citizens of America.

President Murray was one of the first CIO leaders to realize the folly of that 1946 Progressive conference in Chicago. When January, 1947, brought a letter from C. B. Baldwin, head of the newly-formed Progressive Citizens of America (the national liberal alliance that came out of the Chicago Conference), Murray was decidedly cool toward the new organization. While he was well aware of the importance of the 1948 campaign, he could see no advantage to be gained by allying the CIO with the PCA. PCA identification could only aggravate the CIO–PAC weaknesses exposed by the 1946 elections. Murray replied to Baldwin's plea for CIO help with a demand that the CIO name not be used in conjunction with the PCA until all CIO vice presidents could discuss the matter. In the meantime, he sent instructions to CIO officials to stay clear of the PCA.[26]

At the state level, Murray's caution found itself reflected

25. John Cort to Harry Read, October 1, 1947; John Cort to Harry Read, October 12, 1948; Harry Read to John Cort, October 15, 1948, ACTU Folder, Box A8–3, Harry Read Papers, CUA. Although the reply to the 1947 inquiry of Cort does not exist in the Harry Read Papers, his response would probably have been the same in 1947 as it was in 1952 to a similar request involving Murray. Harry Read to John Cort, August 14, 1952, ACTU Folder, Box A8–3, Harry Read Papers, CUA.

26. C. B. Baldwin to Philip Murray, January 31, 1947; C. B. Baldwin to Philip Murray, February 3, 1947; Philip Murray to C. B. Baldwin, February 5, 1947, CIO–PAC Folder, Box A4–33, Philip Murray Papers, CUA.

in the stance of CIO–Industrial Council Department director, John Brophy. When California CIO leaders asked to join a liberal coalition whose aim was progressive state legislation, Brophy's instructions were explicit. Stay away from such PCA coalitions, he wrote. Make absolutely certain that the CIO is "not a party to" anything resembling the PCA. The PCA, with its membership composed of the party-lining NCPAC, the questionable Independent Citizens Committee for the Arts, Sciences, and Professions, and an assortment of liberals who stayed close to the Communist party position, could do nothing but give the CIO a red reputation.[27]

Not until later in 1947 did Murray finally deviate from his path of CIO neutrality in the Communist controversy. Even then, the reason for deviation was not his ideological concern with the issue, but rather a practical, trade union bent that forced him to keep the CIO clear of communism.

The first overt action came in forcing the resignation of *CIO News* Editor Leonard DeCaux. DeCaux had been brought into the organization to serve as *News* editor and CIO publicity director by John L. Lewis. An admitted Communist, DeCaux had come under more and more criticism for his use of the *News* as a sounding board for the views of the Communist unions of the CIO. By mid-1946, DeCaux had managed to offend almost everybody from Barney Taylor of the National Farm Labor Union–AFL to Van Bittner, head of the CIO's southern organizing campaign.[28] The CIO headquarters staff, headed by the anti-Communists James Carey, John Brophy, and Nathan Cowan, had never been fond of DeCaux and they were quick to back Bittner's and Taylor's charges that DeCaux's

27. John Brophy to Irwin DeShetler, December 30, 1946; John Brophy to Mervyn Rathbone, n.d. (December 1946), California CIO Folder, Box A5–11, John Brophy Papers, CUA.

28. Barney Taylor to John Brophy, July 9, 1946, "M–T" Folder, Box A5–11, John Brophy Papers, CUA.

Also see Kampelman, pp. 106–8. Kampelman is a reliable source since much of his book is based upon secret CIO sources (see Maron Lindbergh to Charlotte Orton, September 20, 1950, Hubert Humphrey 1948–1950 Folder, Box 174, CIO Secretary–Treasurer's Papers, ALH).

stand hurt further organizing efforts.[29] To Murray, the important point was not DeCaux's communism, which he could tolerate, but rather the editor's inability to keep his politics out of CIO business.[30]

DeCaux resigned on June 26 to do some "writing." Replaced by anti-Communist Allen Swim, public relations director of the CIO Organizing Committee, the purged editor left muttering about an ACTU plot.[31] In part, he was right.

Looking back with the hindsight gained by the passage of twenty years, Charles O. Rice did admit that he and the anti-Communists of the CIO had put pressure on Murray. Indeed, in the 1960s, Rice felt that the pressure he, Carey, and the others exerted may have been unwarranted. After all, the Communist party was on its last legs. The Communist leaders of the United Electrical Workers and other unions never did succeed in winning the membership to their political views. Maybe, in a few years, the UE members would have come around to the Rice–Carey point of view without the CIO purge. Yet, even in the 1960s, Rice was adamant about one point. Pressure or not, Philip Murray did not move—even in 1947—unless he was certain that his course was necessary only for the well-being of the trade union movement and the CIO. He was a union man first, last, and always.[32]

It is hard to reconstruct exactly what passed through Murray's mind in that critical year 1947. One thing is certain: Time and time again, he mentioned to his associates the critical nature of the coming presidential campaign. With Taft–Hartley on the books, Murray saw the coming fight as a time to close ranks and win.[33] To keep

29. Kampelman, pp. 106–8.
30. This was Father Rice's view of the action. Monsignor Charles O. Rice Interview, October 18, 1967, pp. 15–18, Pennsylvania State University Oral History Collection, PSUL.
31. In DeCaux's autobiography, he makes the charge that Murray was acting under ACTU influence when he fired him. See Len DeCaux, *Labor Radical* (Boston: Beacon Press, 1970), pp. 470–74.
32. Monsignor Charles O. Rice Interview, April 5, 1968 (the second Rice interview), pp. 12–16, Pennsylvania State University Oral History Collection, PSUL.
33. Harry Block Interview, September 25, 1967, pp. 40–41,

labor unity, Murray had again to abandon his traditional neutrality in the Communist controversy.

One participant had yet to be heard from in the CIO's Communist tangle. In 1947, this new combatant would have a central role in President Murray's plans for the solution of the mess started by UE's rejection of Carey in 1941. Fittingly enough, Jim Carey, too, would have a part in the Murray design.

Critical as the coming election was, it demanded that Murray seek some *rapprochement* with the CIO left. Even then, *rapprochement* could not go too far. A leftward drift that exposed the CIO to the ire of the anti-Communists would be as bad as disunity. Because the PCA was too far left and the ACTU too far right, Murray had very little room in which to appease the CIO liberals. Fortunately, a third body existed with its political feet planted firmly on that middle ground.

While Phil Murray had been fighting with C. B. Baldwin over the PCA problem in January, other CIO executives had been active in the formation of an anti-Communist liberal coalition based upon James Loeb's 1944 proposition. With key leadership supplied by the Union for Democratic Action, the new Americans for Democratic Action (founded in January, 1947) had much more labor participation than the older body. The AFL had supplied David Dubinsky and the healthy treasuries of the International Ladies Garment Workers' Union and the International Association of Machinists. From the CIO had come James Carey, Emil Rieve (Textile Workers Union of America president), Walter Reuther (Thomas's successor as United Automobile Workers chief), and Samuel Wolchok (Wholesale and Retail Workers boss). Although neither delegation

Pennsylvania State University Oral History Collection, PSUL.

Block's views were shared both by Rice and by UE leaders Fitzgerald and Matles. The only difference in interpretation is Fitzgerald's insistence that Murray acted only after direct pressure from President Truman through Secretary Forrestal (Rice denied that such pressure existed).

Monsignor Charles O. Rice Interview, October 18, 1967, pp. 17–18; James Matles Interview, May 6, 1968, pp. 65–68; and Albert J. Fitzgerald Interview, May 7, 1968, pp. 20–21. All in the Pennsylvania State University Oral History Collection, PSUL.

had the backing of its parent federation, all of the ADA labor leaders were of national stature and executive board rank. At first, Murray had shunned this coalition as much as PCA.[34] What changed his mind was the Henry Wallace threat.

In 1944, Vice President Henry Wallace had been the darling of both the PAC and the UDA. He was a genuine liberal of the Sidney Hillman school—but perhaps that should have been a warning. Like Hillman, Wallace dreamed of a national liberal coalition that could force Congress and the presidency into what he viewed as the New Deal mold. He participated in the 1946 Chicago conference and he was one of the first backers of the new PCA. In the meantime, he had been demoted from Vice President to Commerce Secretary in 1944 and had left the Truman Administration altogether two years later. Cut off from Capitol Hill, Wallace had become more and more critical of Truman's anti-Soviet foreign policy. Hoping to unite anti-Truman liberals with this stand, Wallace had instead won the devotion of the PCA. By 1947, Henry Wallace had found PCA cheers so convincing that he was clearly running for the presidency. Little did he realize that PCA support cut him off not only from the President, but also from the increasingly strong ADA left. He unwittingly was selling what little chance he had for the Democratic nomination in return for PCA pampering. Yet, this very PCA support was sufficient to make him a potent possibility for a third-ticket try. This was what worried Murray.[35]

As the Cowan–Brophy–Walsh report had stated, the CIO's only political hope rested with the Democrats.

34. Statement on Americans for Democratic Action and the Progressive Citizens of America, n.d. (March 1947), Americans for Democratic Action Folder, Box 6, CIO Secretary–Treasurer's Papers, ALH.

35. For a detailed picture of the Wallace candidacy, see Edward L. Schapsmeier and Frederick H. Schapsmeier, *Prophet in Politics: Henry A. Wallace and the War Years* (Ames: Iowa State University Press, 1970).

Murray's concern with the Wallace candidacy was echoed time and time again by Father Rice. Monsignor Charles O. Rice Interview, October 18, 1967, pp. 17–18, Pennsylvania State University Oral History Collection, PSUL.

Unless a Democrat won in 1948, Taft–Hartley could have been the start of a major antiunion push. A Republican in the White House would not have vetoed Taft–Hartley as Truman had done. In such a situation, Henry Wallace posed a real threat to the CIO as a third-party candidate. If he ran in 1948, he could easily drain off enough liberal votes to give the presidential prize to the party of Taft and Hartley. Faced with this possibility, Murray could see but one course—he must isolate Wallace.[36]

In the final analysis, it was this Wallace threat that forced Phil Murray to take sides in the CIO Communist controversy. A strong anti-Communist himself, Murray had kept his personal feelings out of the fight until mid-1947. Admittedly, he had never hidden his views. A 1946 blast at Communists in the United Steel Workers of America had shown this. Yet, the CIO president had scrupulously avoided interfering in the internal affairs of the Communist unions before 1947. The federation president had to be above such squabbles.[37] After 1947, he was not.

The first proof of Murray's change of heart came in his dealings with the non-Communist liberals of the ADA. In the spring of 1947, he had condemned both the ADA and the PCA in the same breath. By October, Walter Reuther noted that Murray was on the verge of publicly committing himself to the ADA cause. Only months later, Allan Haywood wrote that Murray had not only allowed him to attend the ADA national convention as a CIO delegate, but might also allow the appointment of a second CIO representative.[38] From that point on, President Murray became more and more deeply involved in ADA affairs.

As the _1947_ Democratic National Convention approached that summer, Phil Murray found himself increasingly drawn into the ADA's inner councils. As James Loeb, ADA director, revealed to Carey, ADA leaders

36. Ibid.
37. The Murray blast occurred at the 1946 United Steel Workers of America convention. *New York Times,* May 15, 1946, p. 1.
38. James Loeb, Jr. to Andrew Biemiller, October 16, 1947, Folder 2–26–5, Box 26; Allan Haywood to Leon Henderson, February 16, 1948, Folder 2–30–4, Box 30, Series 2, Americans for Democratic Action Papers, WSHS.

viewed the CIO and Murray as vitally necessary to the liberal body's operation. "It is absolutely imperative," Loeb wrote, "that somebody from the CIO be present at all (executive committee) meetings." The somebody most desired was, of course, Murray. In June, ADA Executive Committee Chairman Leon Henderson refused to adopt any Democratic convention strategy without prior consultations with the CIO president. A meeting was arranged, and the ADA executive travelled to Pittsburgh to work out an ADA–CIO strategy for the convention.[39] The meeting must have been fruitful. According to Jack Kroll's convention log, CIO–PAC strategy was formulated from the beginning upon the premise of ADA–CIO cooperation.[40] Yet, even at this point, Murray had not publicly committed himself to the ADA. Not until September would the CIO boss reveal himself with a public statement and a CIO check for 5,000 dollars in support of the liberal organization.[41] Only then would the CIO be committed.

Although the ADA was not Philip Murray's only anti-Communist commitment in 1947 and 1948, the ADA–Murray operation did seem to confirm Father Rice's judgment that it was politics, not ideology, which drove the CIO president to action. A liberal, Democratic President was the CIO's foremost objective for 1948. Rejection of the Communists and acceptance of the ADA was but a means to achieve that end. Events following the 1948 election seemed to support such a thesis.

Only months after the 1948 contest, the CIO began a rather rapid disengagement from the ADA. In December, Al Barkan of the Textile Workers Union wrote that the CIO unions were no longer funding the ADA as they had

39. James Loeb, Jr. to James Carey, April 20, 1948; Leon Henderson to Philip Murray, June 18, 1948; Philip Murray to Leon Henderson, June 21, 1948, Folder 2–30–4, Box 30, Series 2, Americans for Democratic Action Papers, WSHS.

40. "A Day to Day Account of the Activities of CIO–PAC at the Democratic National Convention," n.d. (July 1948), Box 1, Group 2, Jack Kroll Papers, Library of Congress Manuscripts Division (hereafter cited as LCMD).

41. James Loeb, Jr. to Philip Murray, September 3, 1948, Folder 2–30–4, Box 30, Series 2, Americans for Democratic Action Papers, WSHS.

in the election year. Moreover, CIO Secretary–Treasurer Carey, Vice President Walter Reuther, and Vice President Emil Rieve were all on the verge of pulling out of the Americans for Democratic Action body.[42] The crisis past, the CIO no longer needed the ADA.[43]

Meanwhile, the CIO had begun deliberations concerning the fate of its Communist unions. Murray had entertained the thought of expulsion only after the UE and others had defied CIO policy in the matter of Henry Wallace. Even though Murray had emphasized the utter necessity of keeping the CIO vote in the Democratic column, the Communist unions had backed Henry Wallace on the third-party ticket. This seemed to have been the final straw. Murray agreed that the Communists should be purged.[44]

Although the year of the great expulsions was 1949, the CIO anti-Communists had been working toward such an end since 1941. Carey had been carefully compiling dossiers on his UE opponents; Brophy had been faced with the problem of Reid Robinson's International Union of Mine, Mill, and Smelter Workers; and even the state Industrial Union councils were conducting anti-Communist

42. Al Barkan to Emil Rieve, December 19, 1949, Political Action Department, 1949 Folder, Box 12, Series 1A, Textile Workers Union of America Papers, WSHS.

43. The CIO was won back into the ADA fold only after some adroit maneuvering on the part of the new ADA Director Charles LaFollette. By using the ADA as a public relations bureau for the Steel Workers' case in the 1949 big steel negotiations, LaFollette apparently convinced Murray that the ADA could help the CIO. His thanks for the public relations effort was accompanied by a 7,000 dollar steel workers' check. See Charles LaFollette to Philip Murray, August 31, 1949; and Philip Murray to Charles LaFollette, November 15, 1949, Folder 2–30–4, Box 30, Series 2, Americans for Democratic Action Papers, WSHS.

44. Again, these were the conclusions of Father Rice and Harry Block. Monsignor Charles O. Rice Interview, October 18, 1967, pp. 17–18; Harry Block Interview, September 25, 1967, pp. 40–41, Pennsylvania State University Oral History Collection, PSUL.

Harry Block also mentioned that Murray had a second reason for expelling the Communists. Their refusal to sign the Talt–Hartley non-Communist pledge cut off all of their NLRB rights. For this reason they ceased organizing, which was a cardinal sin the CIO president's eyes.

purges.[45] Indeed, some CIO officials had started anti-Communist drives long before Murray had approved of such actions.[46] In many ways, the Murray decision reached during 1947 and 1948 was merely the final stamp of approval placed upon actions initiated by Carey and others in the early 1940s. Yet, that final stamp was most definitely needed. Murray was the president.

Thus, Philip Murray finally violated his self-imposed pledge not to tamper in the internal workings of CIO unions. The decision was momentous and, just as importantly, political. To win the day in 1948, the CIO had to reject the red tag. Now that the task had been accomplished, it was time for the PAC to prepare for battle.

45. Carey's interest was obvious. Brophy, as head of the Industrial Council Department, had been worrying about the possibility of CIO losses in the West that might be attributed to the IUMMSW. J. Frank Marble to Philip Murray, November 12, 1946, "M–T" Folder, Box A5–11, John Brophy Papers, CUA.

46. A case in point was the Indiana Industrial Union Council, where President Neal Edwards and United Chemical Workers President Martin Wagner attempted to oust a union official for criticizing "America, right or wrong" thinking. It was obvious to the two that such criticism was close to communism. Neal Edwards to Martin Wagner, December 16, 1947, Correspondence, October–December, 1947 Folder, Box 1, Neal Edwards Papers, ALH.

5

1947: "Mistaken Political Tactics"

Andrew Biemiller was a pro. A veteran of a decade of political wars, champion of a host of liberal causes, he was to the ADA of 1947 what Tom Amlie was to the PAC of 1944. When he looked back on the campaigns of 1947, he had but one comment: "The entire liberal cause has been done irreparable harm," he wrote, "because of the mistaken political tactics of labor."[1] He referred directly to the CIO–PAC.

While Philip Murray was wrestling with the Communist problem, Jack Kroll and his PAC staff were preparing for the 1947 elections. Fortunately for the PAC, the 1947 campaign was but a dress rehearsal. With only a few municipal elections up for grabs, it offered all the ingredients of a major effort save one. While the issues, the voters, and even the tactics would be much the same as in 1948, the stakes were not so high. If its plans went awry, the CIO would lose only a few isolated contests, not Congress.

As the disastrous 1946 elections had proven, the PAC was badly in need of a complete overhaul. The plans hatched by Amlie and Hillman in the optimistic 1944 campaign had to be reconsidered in light of the Cold War and the 1946 defeat. Taft–Hartley had proven to the CIO that a prolabor Congress was now an absolute necessity, and that a review of the three-part Hillman strategy was in order.

From the appointment of Hillman in July, 1943, and until the 1947 campaign, three ideas had dominated CIO–PAC strategy. First, the union voter concept of Hillman and "Toward a New Day" had been all-important.[2] Second,

1. Andrew J. Biemiller, "Observations and Conclusions on Special Elections in Wisconsin and Pennsylvania," October 6, 1947, Folder 2–26–5, Box 26, Series 2, Americans for Democratic Action Papers, WSHS.
2. For a more complete explanation see Chapter 2.

PAC leaders believed that a large vote was a good vote. Since the disaster of 1942, which CIO believed had fallen to the Republicans because of the small (less than thirty-five per cent of the electorate) voter turnout, CIO politicians had equated a large vote with electoral success. Because a light turnout had to be avoided at all costs, much of the CIO–PAC's campaign was necessarily devoted to increasing registration and voter interest. As Joseph Gaer, PAC's 1944 publication director wrote, "Registration and voting became the test and proof of PAC's worth from the start." [3] The two would continue to be the proof of PAC's worth in 1948.

Finally, the PAC prior to 1948 usually had bowed to the popular front syndrome. The PAC believed that all liberals, regardless of ideology, were acceptable allies. Earl Browder was as valued an ally as William Green. In 1944, this syndrome had been made manifest both in the CIO's capture of New York's leftist American Labor party and in the creation of the National Citizens Political Action Committee, a collection of prominent liberals that carried the PAC message to the nonlabor community.[4] In 1946, the PAC had again cooperated with the NCPAC and, in addition, had cosponsored the Chicago Conference of Progressives, a meeting that was not devoid of Communists.[5] However, in a country that had grown increasingly suspicious of Russian moves in Iran, Greece, and Czechoslovakia, cooperation with such pro-Russian organizations as the NCPAC was not greeted enthusiastically by the public. Moreover, the CIO itself, both leadership and rank and file, found cooperation with the far left increasingly distasteful.

By the start of the 1948 campaign, the Political Action Committee had been forced to reassess all of its previous plans. The union voter concept was tried and found lacking. In perhaps its greatest test, the 1945 Detroit mayoral race, the union voter approach proved to be less reliable than appeals to racial prejudice. The CIO voters of Detroit overwhelmingly rejected the overtures of a PAC-backed

3. Gaer, pp. 49–60, 104.
4. Ibid., pp. 213–25.
5. *CIO News*, October 7, 1946, p. 3. *New York Times*, September 18, 1946, p. 7.

liberal and solidly supported a candidate who based his campaign on racial slurs.[6] The union voter ideal was not held so highly after 1945.

The PAC also reviewed its policy concerning voter turnout. In the case of this strategic concept, however, the 1944 and 1946 elections tended to affirm the validity of the PAC's original stand. In 1944, a high voter turnout (about fifty-three per cent of the eligible electorate) had accompanied a PAC victory. Two years later, a small turnout (only thirty-seven per cent of the electorate voted) went hand in hand with a disastrous PAC defeat.[7] In only one respect was the concept questioned; the PAC doubted the usefulness of the registration drive as a successful tactic. The PAC had sponsored a large registration drive in 1946, but the voter turnout had been disappointingly small. Registration and voting were still the twin keys to success, but the CIO needed to learn more about how to achieve the desirable large vote.

The PAC hardly needed to review its popular front policy. The United States was in the midst of the Cold War; any policy that associated the CIO–PAC with the Communist party would certainly have a negative effect upon PAC political fortunes. That had been the PAC's greatest lesson in 1946.

After reviewing its blunders of 1946, the CIO–PAC was left with but one major strategic objective; it had to turn out a large labor vote in 1948. The tactics that Jack Kroll and his Political Action Committee staff adopted to achieve this objective did much to determine the outcome of the 1948 elections.

The first PAC innovation for 1948 took the form of a special program among minorities, a suggestion made by Henry Lee Moon, the PAC's expert on minority problems. Because almost 45,000,000 Americans belonged to some

6. "Political Action—City Level," Minutes of the National Citizens Political Action Committee Steering Committee, November 29, 1945, 1945 Correspondence Folder, Box 19, Elmer Benson Papers, Minnesota Historical Society, St. Paul, Minn.

7. Potential Vote and Vote Cast in Presidential and Recent Off-Year Elections, February, 1956, Box 4, Group 2, Jack Kroll Papers, LCMD.

minority group, it made good political sense to concentrate on these groups. Furthermore, because the CIO leadership had been drawn from minorities, the CIO–PAC should have a decided advantage when dealing with these groups. Moon warned, however, that the PAC should pay special attention to its foreign policy pronouncements. It must be remembered, he said, that United States attitudes toward Poland, Turkey, and the nations of central Europe did much to influence the voting patterns of their nationals in the United States. Quite specifically, this meant that the PAC would have to abandon many of its pro-Russian stands on foreign policy if it ever hoped to capture the crucial Polish vote in such cities as Buffalo, Detroit, and Chicago.[8] Yet, this was only one aspect of the minority question.

Just as important as the Polish, Irish, and Italian vote was the critical Negro and Mexican–American vote. Those two large minority groups had settled in the large industrial cities as had many immigrant minorities. In such cities as Detroit and Chicago, cities with large concentrations of CIO members, the Negro vote was an important building block in the assembling of an electoral majority. The PAC had attempted to win the Negro vote in the past and had met with some success. The problem for the PAC was not to win just black, or Polish, or Jewish voters, but to win both black and immigrant minority voters. The Detroit mayoral contest of 1945 had proven that the CIO could win black voters if it was willing to lose the Poles in the process. What was needed for 1948 was a problack civil rights program that would not awaken racial animosities in other groups. Jack Kroll began to work on just such a program.

The PAC's eventual solution to the problem involved three major points. First, the PAC would try to appeal to all groups with clear-cut economic programs that would avoid the racial issue. Second, before starting the campaign, the PAC would try to get all sides to agree to refrain from racial slurs. The local PAC leader was also urged to get church groups, etc., to witness the agreement for the PAC's protection. Finally, PAC workers were urged to unite all

8. Henry Lee Moon to Jack Kroll, March 27, 1947, CIO–PAC New York Folder, Box 203, CIO Secretary–Treasurer's Papers, ALH.

local CIO factions around the PAC-endorsed candidate so that no faction would be tempted to turn to racial slurs to show their disapproval of the candidate.[9]

As the year 1947 drew to a close, several important events outside CIO circles occurred that would have effects on the PAC campaign.

The first of these events was the creation of an AFL political auxiliary, cast in the mold of the PAC. Keeping close to the spirit of Gompers, the AFL had been less active politically than the CIO. However, the passage of the Taft–Hartley Act in June, 1947, had forced a change. To defeat Taft–Hartley and other antilabor legislation, the sixty-sixth convention of the AFL, held in December, 1947, voted to join the fight by creating Labor's League for Political Education. Under the leadership of Joseph Keenan, secretary of the Chicago Federation of Labor, the LLPE opened its office in March, 1948, and began to concentrate exclusively on the coming congressional elections.[10]

Although the AFL–LLPE had the potential for becoming an even greater political force than the CIO–PAC (because of the AFL's superior membership), its potential was not realized in 1948. First, it had neither the money nor the organization of the CIO–PAC; the LLPE, in 1948, was in the same position as the PAC in 1943. Second, because of its marginal resources, the LLPE limited itself to the congressional races. The glamour and excitement of the White House sweepstakes was left to the PAC and the political parties, organizations that had the money and manpower to play the game. Indeed, considering the divergent political views within the AFL, there was some question whether the federation could unite its membership behind a presidential endorsee. Finally, about midway in the campaign, the AFL–LLPE opted to involve itself only in the key senatorial races. Even the modest hopes of a full congressional campaign were sacrificed to political reality. The LLPE was not to be a major force in 1948.[11]

9. Ibid.
10. Report of Secretary George Meany, Minutes of Labor's League for Political Education meeting, November 17, 1948, pp. 1–2, Political Education Folder, Box 6, West Virginia State Federation of Labor Papers, WVUL.
11. Ibid.

While the AFL was laying the groundwork for the league, other parties were also casting eyes upon the labor vote. Prime among these interested groups was the Truman faction of the Democratic party.

Ever since the 1936 election, the labor vote had been taken for granted by the Democrats. Franklin Roosevelt was a President who could depend upon his personal friends in the labor movement. Sidney Hillman, David Dubinsky, Philip Murray, and numerous other labor leaders were as committed to the New Deal as Roosevelt himself.[12] However, President Truman did not have such support.

On November 19, 1947, Clark Clifford, Truman's campaign strategist, sent a memorandum to the President that outlined a plan for winning the following of labor. Clifford's basic premise was that victory in 1948 lay in attracting enough southern conservatives, western progressives, and big city laborers (the "three misfits" in Clifford's terminology) to the polls. These three were the basis of the Democratic party; no Democrat could win the presidency without them.[13]

More specifically, Clifford noted that the election would hinge on Truman's success in attracting the "progressives" of the country. This group included labor, farmers, liberals of the ADA school, and the ethnic minorities.[14] To attract labor, Clifford had an intriguing plan.

The first thing to learn about the labor vote, wrote Clifford, was not to take it for granted. As the 1946 elections had proven, labor could become a powerful enemy just by staying home. "The rank and file . . . are not yet politically minded; they will not . . . vote or work actively unless they are inspired to do so," he declared.[15] Therefore, the President had to do something that would inspire them in the coming election.

Of the three major leaders of labor—Murray of the CIO, William Green of the AFL, and George Meany of the New York State Federation of Labor—Clifford was most

12. Burns, pp. 524–25.
13. Memorandum for the President, November 19, 1947, p. 1. Clark M. Clifford Papers, Harry S. Truman Library, Independence, Mo.
14. Ibid., pp. 6–14.
15. Ibid., p. 8.

suspicious of Meany. Meany had actively supported Dewey, the probable Republican candidate, in his bid for the New York governor's chair. Indeed, Meany would demand a number of presidential favors over and above the recent Taft–Hartley veto; he was a question mark for 1948. The other two labor leaders, the presidents of the AFL and CIO, could probably be placated by calling them in as consultants on the Marshall Plan. Such a move would boost both their egos and their standing within their unions.[16]

Clifford had other suggestions that he felt would give labor leaders the impression that they were once more welcome in Democratic councils. For instance, such leaders as Daniel Tobin, David Dubinsky, Philip Murray, and William Green should be invited to "come by" and offer their advice on general matters. Clifford emphasized "general" matters because then the "advising" leader would not be able to ascertain if the President really followed his advice.[17] As the Marshall Plan proposal had been, this was but another way to win friends by boosting egos.

Clifford's final suggestion was that Truman appoint some member of his Administration as a special liaison man to work with labor in the campaign. After all, the objects of organized labor and the President were the same. Both wanted a Democratic President and Congress; a liaison man would, it was hoped, prevent labor from making the kind of campaign mistakes in 1948 that it had made in the past.[18]

While the Democrats were plotting to capture the labor vote, Americans for Democratic Action, the anti-Communist liberal group, was also deeply concerned about labor's role in the coming campaign. The ADA's equivalent of the Clifford memorandum was Andrew Biemiller's memorandum to the ADA political committee. On August 14, 1947, Biemiller, the liberal Democrat who had formerly represented Wisconsin's fifth district in Congress, told the ADA how it could win a liberal Congress in 1948.[19] Like Clif-

16. Ibid., pp. 8–9.
17. Ibid., p. 21.
18. Ibid., pp. 21–22.
19. Memorandum of Andrew J. Biemiller to the Americans for Democratic Action Political Committee, August 14, 1947, p. 1, Folder 2–34–9, Box 34, Series 2, Americans for Democratic Action Papers, WSHS.

ford's plan, the Biemiller proposal was essentially a blue-print for Democratic success.

The first thing we must realize, Biemiller wrote, is that Truman will be renominated. This, in itself, will not be an obstacle to the ADA. Truman has always been a liberal President, although his leadership has often left much to be desired. What must be done, as far as the nominating convention is concerned, is to make absolutely certain that President Truman will run with a liberal vice-presidential candidate on a liberal platform. If such objectives can be accomplished, the ADA will have a reason to turn out the vote.[20] Of course, organized labor was the key to the liberal vote.

Perhaps the most reassuring thing to Biemiller was the Republican contempt for labor. When even such liberal Republicans as Harold Stassen were campaigning for the Taft–Hartley Act, no working man would waste his vote on the Grand Old Party. Indeed, William Hutcheson himself, the most Republican of the AFL's old guard, would find it embarrassing to attend the Republican National Convention in 1948. However, labor's loyalty would be severely tested on the left. The PCA and the Communists would do everything in their power to defeat Truman.[21]

What did all this mean to the ADA and the labor vote? First, ADA leaders had an abiding faith in the liberal nature of the labor vote. If the PCA tried to paint Truman a reactionary and a cynical politician (especially concerning his Taft–Hartley veto), it would be the ADA's job to counter such an attack. Second, to counter the anti-Truman attack, the ADA must "out-huckster" the opposition. Point to congressional failures, such as the Taft–Hartley Act, refusal to act on an old-age pension bill, refusal to consider the Missouri Valley Authority bill (the TVA of the Missouri River basin), and outright attacks on soil conservation and farm loan programs. At the same time, point with pride at the Truman program (never enacted) that offered positive contributions in all of these fields. Finally, send a select committee of ADA leaders to the Democratic National Committee. Both the ADA and the Democrats

20. Ibid., p. 3.
21. Ibid., pp. 2–3.

would be concerned about an attack upon the left flank. Why not join forces? As far as labor was concerned, with the new Taft–Hartley restrictions on labor politics, the AFL and CIO would probably be happy to channel funds into the ADA to do the kind of campaigning that was no longer legally permissible for them. The two keys to 1948 would still be a liberal Democratic platform and effective sabotage of the far left.[22]

Biemiller appended a state-by-state survey of ADA strength to the political committee memorandum, a survey that emphasized the paramount importance of six states. In the West, California would prove especially crucial to ADA hopes. There, ex-Attorney General Robert Kenny had assembled an impressive group of California Democrats pledged to a Wallace candidacy. If the ADA were ever to stamp out the Wallace virus, then California would be the place to start. Unfortunately, the liberal CIO was not as strong in the Golden State as in other industrial centers. The ADA's chief ally would have to be the California AFL. The CIO and ADA could do the organizing, but the AFL would do the actual legwork.[23]

The Midwest was represented in the Biemiller report by three industrial states, Minnesota, Wisconsin, and Indiana. Minnesota seemed to offer the greatest hope of success, because the Hubert Humphrey faction of the Democratic–Farmer–Labor party was already in league with the ADA. As far as that state was concerned, the entire battle would occur at the DFL convention. Biemiller was confident that the ADA would emerge a winner.[24]

In his home state of Wisconsin, Biemiller viewed the Democratic party as a potential ally. Already, the ADA had a number of members in the Wisconsin organization. The Wisconsin Democratic delegation should prove to be the backbone of the ADA assault on the Democratic convention. Moreover, once the convention was over, the Wisconsin Democrats, with ADA help, should be able to pick off a number of congressional seats. Districts one, two, four,

22. Ibid., p. 5.
23. Andrew J. Biemiller, Notes on Political Situations in Various States, August 14, 1947, p. 1, Folder 2–34–9, Box 34, Series 2, Americans for Democratic Action Papers, WSHS.
24. Ibid., p. 3.

five, and ten should all produce liberal congressmen in the coming election.[25]

Indiana's Democratic prospects were especially intriguing to Biemiller. Small, disciplined blocks of voters could easily swing such key districts as the second, third, and eighth into the Democratic column. Especially in Indiana, the well-disciplined United Automobile Workers and other CIO voters should help push ADA candidates to victory. However, because of machine control, the state's Democratic convention offered the ADA little hope. Victory at the Democratic National Convention would have to come through the cooperation of other state parties.[26]

The state that was particularly promising in the East was West Virginia. There, the prominence of the United Mine Workers, coupled with John L. Lewis's oath to unseat every congressman who voted for Taft–Hartley, should result in a number of Democratic victories. Already, the city of Charleston had shown a marked Democratic preference in 1947 municipal elections, a preference that had not been displayed for over twenty-eight years. With such strong liberal Democrats as ex-congressmen Cleveland Bailey and Matthew Neely waiting in the wings, West Virginia was certain to register liberal gains in 1948.[27]

Biemiller's final state, Tennessee, was very much in question. Tennessee, Biemiller wrote, "is the only Southern state in which we should do any concentrated work in terms of '48." Although Boss "Ed" Crump's Memphis machine controlled the state Democratic party, there were good liberals who were willing to run if Crump could be temporarily stymied. Prime among the Tennessee liberals was Estes Kefauver, an excellent campaigner who had promised Biemiller to make a run for the Senate if the ADA and labor could pull for him in the primary. Fortunately for the liberals, Crump had deeply offended both the AFL and the CIO in Tennessee. George Googe, the southern AFL director, had even been forbidden to speak in Memphis by a Crump edict. With active labor support, the liberals and ADA might elect Kefauver to the Senate.

25. Ibid., p. 4.
26. Ibid., p. 7.
27. Ibid., p. 9.

Biemiller, like Clifford, was deeply concerned about the labor vote.[28]

While the ADA and the Democrats were quietly apportioning labor's 1948 votes, the CIO–PAC was preparing for the 1947 off-year elections. Its efforts along those lines would fizzle.

The 1947 campaign offered the PAC three real opportunities. Important House races were anticipated in Wisconsin and Pennsylvania, and CIO unions were strong in each contested district. Joint PAC–Democratic efforts could have succeeded in both.[29] At the same time, Democratic professionals had decided upon 1947 as the ideal time to cast the Republicans out of Philadelphia's city hall. Again, strong labor support from the CIO should have materially enhanced such a venture's chance of success.[30] In all three, the Democrats had a fighting chance. A fighting chance, that is, until CIO–PAC entered the ring.

In the first of the House contests, the Wisconsin CIO handled things almost respectably. As the ADA's Biemiller reported, the CIO's fault in Wisconsin's Second Congressional District was a sin of omission, not commission. Since the district was traditionally a Republican stronghold, the CIO and the Democrats had their work cut out for them. Both did well in agreeing to the candidacy of Carl Thompson, a liberal, a veteran, and a fresh young political face. Both seemed to work well in publicizing their man; Democrat and PAC workers were at their doorbell-ringing best. The CIO even printed a special newspaper that was distributed to all unionists in Madison, the district's key city. Even so, Thompson lost. In the heat of the campaign, both the Democrats and the PAC lost sight of that traditional tool, registration; the Republicans did not.[31] It was a minor fault. Such was not the case in Pennsylvania.

Pennsylvania's Eighth Congressional District seemed

28. Ibid., pp. 7–8.
29. Andrew Biemiller, "Observations and Conclusions on Special Elections in Wisconsin and Pennsylvania," October 6, 1947, Folder 2–26–5, Box 26, Series 2, Americans for Democratic Action Papers, WSHS.
30. John Edelman to Jack Kroll, November 7, 1947, CIO–PAC Folder, Box A4–45, Philip Murray Papers, CUA.
31. Biemiller, "Observations."

made to order for the CIO–PAC. Comprising most of the counties of Bucks and Lehigh, it featured both CIO-unionized cities (Allentown and Bethlehem) and Democratic-dominated villages. Over the years, only luck and a determined Republican machine had kept the Democrats out of power there. In 1947, the CIO set out to break that machine.[32] It did not succeed.

From the very beginning, the CIO's role in the campaign was obvious to all. Indeed, it was too obvious. Only two days after CIO member Philip Storch won the Democratic nomination, hundreds of strangers descended upon the district. Obviously city-bred and obviously CIO, the new political "experts" (some even from red unions) pushed their way into positions of leadership. Once there, they engineered a campaign that featured blaring loudspeaker trucks, hard-hitting, four-letter-worded union orators, and soaring denunciations of Taft–Hartley. The climax of the campaign came when the same outsiders actually locked Storch out of his campaign office. Impressed with their own wisdom, the CIO experts were not about to trust the canvass to a bunch of Bucks County "jerks." [33]

By the end of the campaign, the big city CIO–PAC had managed to offend almost everyone in the district. Unionists were offended by the UE organizers sent into UAW–Reuther strongholds, rural Democrats were shocked by union rhetoric, and almost everyone was unhappy with the emphasis on Taft–Hartley. As Biemiller noted, Bucks County Democrats actually favored Taft–Hartley. No wonder they joined the Republicans to give the Democratic–PAC ticket one of the worst defeats in the country.[34] Even the Philadelphia fiasco seemed mild in comparison.

At the same time, Democratic politicians in Philadelphia were trying to mount a major offensive. In the long run, it would be no more successful than the Bucks County caper.

Philadelphia was a city blessed with thousands of unionists. It would have seemed that with such assets, the

32. Ibid.
33. Ibid.
34. The Republicans' most optimistic forecast had shown their man winning by only 5,000 votes. When the results were finally in, their candidate had a lead of over 17,000.

Democrats should have ridden to power easily. Such was not the case. Since 1941, Philadelphia had been controlled by the machine of Republican Mayor Bernard Samuel. Yet, in 1947, Samuel seemed quite vulnerable due to the Republican tag on Taft–Hartley. If all those unionists could be coaxed to vote Democratic, Republican hegemony might end. The CIO–PAC was needed.[35]

All stood in readiness during the summer of 1947. Democratic leaders, mayoral candidates, and aldermanic candidates were ready and waiting for PAC help. That help never arrived; the Philadelphia CIO was split down the middle. Some leaders felt that the CIO should back only a few aldermanic candidates. All PAC-endorsees then proceeded to lose in the primary. Other leaders asked for endorsement of prominent mayoral candidates. These too lost in the primary. When the final campaign turned into a fight between liberal, prolabor Richardson Dilworth and Mayor Samuel, the twice-burned CIO stayed out. In so doing, the Philadelphia CIO virtually guaranteed the reelection of Samuel. An important opportunity was lost and Samuel won by a surprisingly narrow 90,000 vote margin.[36] The CIO–PAC had lost again.

Looking back on the three races, it was easy to understand why Biemiller was so critical of the PAC. Three golden opportunities had presented themselves and CIO–PAC had not taken advantage of a single one. The closest thing to success was a Wisconsin defeat. With that kind of track record, what could be expected of the PAC in 1948?

35. John Edelman to Jack Kroll, November 7, 1947, CIO–PAC Folder, Box A4–45, Philip Murray Papers, CUA.
36. Ibid. So split was the CIO that some locals actually ended up endorsing Samuel.

6

PAC Victorious: The 1948 Elections

The year 1948 was a memorable one in the annals of the Congress of Industrial Organizations and its Political Action Committee. Within that twelve-month span, the CIO won two major political battles but found that the price of victory was ideological schism. Although the organization won a court test of the Taft–Hartley Act and rode to November victory with Truman and the Democrats, a minority of its members decided that Henry Wallace and the Progressives were preferable to the PAC-backed President. Moreover, because Philip Murray had made the support of PAC-endorsed Truman a test of loyalty, several CIO unions found that their political preferences jeopardized their CIO standing.

For the CIO, the 1948 elections began with a subpoena. On February 4, a United States attorney entered the CIO national headquarters and served *CIO News* Editor Allen Swim a subpoena requiring him to appear in court to explain his violation of Section 304 of the Taft–Hartley Act.[1] Section 304 was that part of Taft–Hartley that forbade any political contributions or expenditures by a labor organization in a national election.[2] The February subpoena was the result of a violation of this provision in July, 1947.

When the Taft–Hartley Act passed over Truman's veto in June, 1947, the CIO was particularly disturbed about the expenditures prohibition of Section 304. Although a contributions ban had proven ineffective in the 1943 Smith–Connally Act, such antiunion congressmen as Howard Smith had discovered that a prohibition of union political expenditures quite effectively banned the CIO–PAC's cam-

1. *CIO News,* February 9, 1948, pp. 3–4.
2. U.S., *Statutes at Large,* 61, Part 1, 159.

paign activities.[3] Legally, an expenditures ban even forbade the use of a union newspaper to endorse a political candidate. With this in mind, Philip Murray ordered the *CIO News* to endorse Judge Edward Garmatz in a special congressional election in Maryland's Third Congressional District. Murray was fully aware that the endorsement, carried on the front page of the July 14 *News,* would provoke legal action under the controversial section of Taft–Hartley, but he felt that Section 304 could be invalidated in a court challenge.[4] The February subpoena came as no surprise.

The CIO case went to a federal grand jury on February 11. Because CIO officials did not claim to be innocent of the Taft–Hartley violation, the grand jury indicted Philip Murray and the CIO for ignoring the statute. The indictment was front-page news throughout the country. The publicity was such that it even moved Senator Robert Taft, one of the sponsors of the questioned legislation, to comment on the case. When confronted with the CIO's indictment, Senator Taft was quoted as saying that the Attorney General had made a "mistake" in prosecuting the CIO. According to Taft, the original intent of Section 304 was to ban union political broadsides, not newspaper endorsements.[5] The indictment, however, had started the wheels of justice rolling. The CIO's day in court had begun.

The next legal step in the CIO challenge of Section 304 was Murray's move to quash the indictment. Contending that the controversial section violated constitutional guarantees of free speech, CIO lawyers took their case to the United States District Court of Washington, D.C. On March 15, District Judge Benjamin Wheeler Moore dismissed the CIO indictment and ruled that Section 304 was an illegal violation of the right of free speech.[6] The district

3. U.S., House, Committee on Military Affairs, *Hearings on H. R. 3937, Repeal of the War Labor Disputes Act,* 79th Cong., 1st sess., 1945, pp. 1–7.
4. *CIO News,* July 14, 1947, p. 1. On Murray's feelings concerning the susceptibility of Taft–Hartley see *CIO News,* March 8, 1948, p. 3.
5. *New York Times,* February 12, 1948, p. 1. *CIO News,* February 16, 1948, p. 1.
6. *United States* v. *Congress of Industrial Organizations,* 77 F. Supp. 355 (1948). *New York Times,* March 16, 1948, pp. 1, 24.

court, however, did not end the case. The next stop was the United States Supreme Court.

The case of the *United States* versus the *Congress of Industrial Organizations* came before the Supreme Court on April 28. CIO counsel Lee Pressman led off the argument by contending that Taft–Hartley prohibitions of political expenditures violated the First Amendment of the Constitution, which forbade Congress to enact a law abridging the freedoms of speech and the press. Moreover, the Washington, D.C., district court had concurred in that contention. To Pressman's argument, Assistant Attorney General Jesse Climenko replied by citing the defendants' guilt under Section 304. There was no question, he noted, that the CIO had spent one hundred dollars to print and distribute the offending issue of the *News* in Maryland's Third Congressional District. There was also no question that Philip Murray had approved of the expenditure; he had admitted it. As far as the constitutionality of the statute was concerned, the First Amendment was obviously not intended to foster the kind of abuses that Section 304 was trying to outlaw. As the 1944 election had shown, a mere contribution ban was ineffective and had to be augmented by the expenditures provision of Section 304. By April 29, both sides had presented their cases; the CIO's fate was in the Court's hands.[7]

After a seemingly interminable wait, the Supreme Court rendered a verdict. The CIO proved to be the victor, but not in the sense that it had hoped. In its final decision, the Court had unanimously dismissed all charges against the CIO, but it had not ruled Section 304 unconstitutional. The majority opinion, written by Justice Stanley Reed, simply stated that the *CIO News* incident was not illegal under Section 304. The opinion rendered no judgment concerning the section's constitutionality. In Justice Felix Frankfurter's opinion, the charges against the CIO were dismissed also, but the constitutional question was termed far beyond the "necessities" of the case. In the third and final opinion, Justice Wiley Rutledge flatly declared the

7. *United States* v. *Congress of Industrial Organizations,* 92 U.S. (Law. Ed.) 1853–1855 (1948). Pressman was Murray's private lawyer even though he had resigned as CIO counsel in February. See, *CIO News,* March 15, 1948, p. 6.

section unconstitutional. His opinion, however, was backed by only a minority of the Court. Thus, the CIO had won its case, but Taft–Hartley emerged unscathed. In the words of the vindicated *CIO News,* "This case represents the beginning of our legal campaign against the Taft–Hartley Law." [8] The most important part of that campaign involved the election of a new Congress.

As Jack Kroll and Philip Murray laid preliminary plans for the 1948 congressional campaign, one matter seemed of utmost importance. Both agreed that if the CIO were to avoid the blunders of the past, it must devise some new way of matching its campaign objectives to the public temper. All previous mistakes—the 1945 Detroit Negro rights campaign, the 1946 refusal to take a stand on communism, or the Pennsylvania carpetbag and Taft–Hartley fiasco of 1947—were due to the CIO's misreading of public opinion.[9] To avoid this error, Kroll decided to investigate the new science of public opinion testing for 1948.

In the first week of March, 1948, the Green–Brodie public relations firm of New York that was testing public opinion for Kroll issued its report. The Green–Brodie report, which was based upon surveys of twenty-five major cities, made three major points. First, because neither President Truman nor any of his opponents aroused the kind of personal following that marked Franklin D. Roosevelt, the 1948 campaign would be fought on the basis of issues, not personalities. The CIO–PAC simply could not hope to arouse the kind of support for Truman, the man, that they had rallied for Roosevelt in 1944.[10] However, there were advantages to an issues campaign; the CIO

8. Ibid., 1861–1863; 1864–1866; 1867–1868. *CIO News,* June 28, 1948, p. 1.

9. In two letters addressed to Murray after the 1947 Bucks County disaster, prominent Pennsylvania Democrats urged President Murray to quit being so "idealistic" and become more practical in his approach to politics and political issues. This was precisely what the Kroll opinion polling experiment was trying to do. See, John Welsh to Philip Murray, September 12, 1947, and Elmer J. Holland to Philip Murray, n.d. (September 1947), CIO–PAC Folder, Box A4–45, Philip Murray Papers, CUA.

10. Palmer Weber to Jack Kroll, March 11, 1948, Box 1, Group 2, Jack Kroll Papers, LCMD.

could start to campaign before the candidates were even nominated, secure in the knowledge that its early campaign would benefit any man who chose to run on the PAC platform.[11]

The report's second conclusion backed the CIO's large vote policy with but few modifications. There is abundant proof, the report noted, that a "large vote is usually a progressive one." Yet, all too often, registration and voting drives had been aimed only at the CIO's male voters. The result had been that working-class women had voted only half as frequently as working-class men, even though affluent women voted almost as often as their mates. The PAC program for 1948 would have to concentrate on the distaff side.[12]

The final conclusion of the Green–Brodie report concerned a tactical problem. Where should the PAC concentrate its efforts? According to the report, there were twenty-two states that had both a high concentration of CIO members and a large number of marginal electoral districts (districts that had been decided by less than five per cent of the vote). In these areas, the CIO–PAC could operate most effectively.[13] Green–Brodie's three simple suggestions combined with the PAC program for 1948 to create the basis for the coming CIO campaign.

No sooner had PAC headquarters accepted the Green–Brodie report than it found itself in the midst of the primaries. The PAC, following the report's suggestions, emphasized three aspects of the 1948 primary campaign. First, having lost their great drawing-card, Roosevelt, PAC workers placed special emphasis on the issues themselves.

11. Jack Kroll to James Carey, March 8, 1948, 1948 Political Action Committee Folder, Box 85, CIO Secretary–Treasurer's Papers, ALH.

12. Ibid.

13. Ibid. The CIO–PAC would exclude all the South and the Trans-Mississippi West (except California, Oregon, Minnesota, Missouri, and Washington) from its intensive effort.

A month later, an even more interesting Green–Brodie report, this time a study of CIO voters only, surfaced. It noted that from sixty-five to ninety-three per cent of CIO members intended to vote for the PAC's 1948 choice. See Jack Kroll to James Carey, April 16, 1948 Political Action Committee Folder, Box 85, CIO Secretary–Treasurer's Papers, ALH.

In CIO terms, this meant the PAC program, a national declaration of campaign policy, called for the reinstitution of price controls (not wage controls), rent controls (coupled with federal housing), and President Roosevelt's Four Freedoms. In addition, the PAC Program favored the Marshall Plan, a national health plan (similar to England's program), a nationwide unemployment compensation plan (coupled with a substantial rise in Social Security benefits), and the enactment of a four-point civil rights plan (including abolition of the poll tax, an antilynching law, abolition of discrimination in the armed forces, and endorsement of the President's Committee on Civil Rights). Finally, the PAC Program demanded an immediate end to Taft–Hartley.[14] These were the issues that PAC felt were important in 1948.

Second, PAC headquarters underlined the political necessity of successfully nominating the kind of candidates who would not offend potential CIO voters. Without the right kind of candidates, the PAC's November job was doubly difficult.[15]

Last, but not least, the PAC stressed the need for a national system of block and ward organizations that could be depended upon to turn out the faithful on election day. The primaries would be the first test of a system that included over a million blockworkers.[16]

14. *CIO News,* February 2, 1948, pp. 1, 3; July 12, 1948, pp. 6–7. The PAC's February program was almost identical to the one it submitted to the Democratic and Republican conventions in the summer.

15. For the emphasis on the primaries, see Jack Kroll's speech, *Proceedings of the Sixteenth Biennial Convention of the Amalgamated Clothing Workers of America, Atlantic City, N.J., May 10–14, 1948,* pp. 277–82, 286–87. Also Gaer, p. 56.

16. Ibid. The 1948 campaign for blockworkers was highlighted by a publication, "How We Win Blockworkers," which the PAC sent out to PAC local organizations to instruct them in the art of recruiting the million campaign workers needed for 1948 (Kroll claimed to have had 2 million in May, 1948. See, Amalgamated *Proceedings . . . 1948,* p. 280). The key points were the need for women workers (they must act as neighbors), and the techniques of recruiting them (union meetings are the best place), see "How We Win Blockworkers," n.d. (1948), 1948 Folder, John Melseth Jacobsen Papers, Minnesota Historical Society, St. Paul, Minn.

The PAC's success in the primaries was, as in previous campaigns, encouraging, but not complete. In May, CIO–PAC workers combined with Dallas County liberals and helped elect a prolabor slate of candidates to the Texas Democratic Convention.[17] In the same month, CIO members won both the senatorial nomination and the Democratic National Committeeman's post in Oregon.[18] In July, CIO, AFL, and independent union leaders formed a United Labor Political Committee that helped defeat an incumbent senator and nominate a prolabor governor in North Carolina.[19] Yet, even with these successes, CIO–PAC did not succeed in defeating as many of its prominent foes in the primaries as it had in 1944.[20]

As the primaries reached the halfway mark, Jack Kroll and his PAC staff prepared to attend the Democratic National Convention in Philadelphia. To a great extent, the success of their 1948 venture would depend upon the candidate that the convention chose.

Even before Kroll and his staff arrived in Philadelphia on July 10, the PAC had been working quietly with other groups to promote the candidacy of a liberal alternative to Truman. The first choice had been Dwight D. Eisenhower, a war hero and a liberal who had the backing of such prominent democrats as James Roosevelt and New York Mayor William O'Dwyer. Eisenhower had publicly disavowed any intention of accepting the Democratic nomination on July 5, however, leaving the CIO without a candidate. After months of planning, distributing literature, and committing delega-

17. *CIO News,* May 24, 1948, p. 7. All the CIO–PAC workers had really succeeded in doing was carrying the Dallas County Democratic Convention into their camp on the Taft–Hartley issue.

18. *New York Times,* May 23, 1948, p. 40. *CIO News,* May 30, 1948, p. 7.

19. *Washington Post,* May 31, 1948, pp. 1–2. *CIO News,* July 5, 1948, p. 8. The *News* cited a letter from Democratic gubernatorial aspirant Kerr Scott's manager claiming that the AFL and CIO campaign committee was the decisive factor in the election of Scott.

20. In 1944, CIO–PAC helped eliminate some of the best known conservatives in Congress. Martin Dies, Joseph Starnes, and Senator Champ Clark were all defeated with CIO aid. On the Dies defeat see *CIO News,* May 22, 1944, p. 1. *Washington Post,* May 19, 1944, p. 8.

tions, all for the Eisenhower cause, the CIO decided on July 9 to follow the ADA and back Justice William O. Douglas.[21] That was the official CIO position on the eve of the convention. Apparently, Clifford's clever advice to Truman had not worked; the CIO was not going into the convention as a Truman-backer.

Kroll arrived in Philadelphia on July 10 and immediately caucused with the PAC men who had preceded him. As a recently-burned suitor, the PAC delegation was afraid that Douglas might "pull an Eisenhower" and refuse to run. Kroll, his assistant Tilford Dudley, and United Steel Workers Secretary–Treasurer David McDonald decided that the best tactical move for the CIO–PAC was to find an alternative to Douglas, "just in case. . . ." At this point, the CIO leaders called in their good friend, Senator Claude Pepper of Florida, whom they persuaded to be the CIO's "favorite son" in case of a Douglas withdrawal. The CIO strategy was to choose some figurehead liberal, such as Pepper, who could be depended upon to hold the anti-Truman forces together long enough to break down Truman's early strength. A quick Kroll poll revealed that Pepper was acceptable to most of the anti-Truman delegates; Kroll ended his first day at the convention as a Douglas delegate leaning toward Pepper.[22]

The highlight of the second day of the convention was the CIO caucus. Over one hundred CIO members who were delegates (fifty-five in number) and alternates (over fifty) listened to McDonald push for an anti-Taft–Hartley platform; James Carey caution them about the disruptive activities of Communists such as Pressman; and Emil Rieve, an ADA member and Textile Workers president, plead Truman's cause. The consensus of the meeting was that many supported the Eisenhower drive, but few were willing to commit themselves either to Douglas or Pepper. Shortly after the CIO caucus broke up, word arrived from Douglas that he would not run. Pepper announced his candidacy an hour later.[23]

21. "A Day to Day Account of the Activities of CIO–PAC at the Democratic National Convention," p. 1, n.d. (1948), Box 1, Group 2, Jack Kroll Papers, LCMD.

22. Ibid., pp. 1–2.

23. Ibid., pp. 3–4.

The convention officially opened on Monday, July 12; Jack Kroll spent most of that day closeted with Hubert Humphrey of the ADA urging Humphrey to push for a stronger civil rights plank in the Democratic platform. If Humphrey were willing to make the attempt, Kroll promised complete CIO support.[24] The following day promised plenty of fireworks, as the Platform Committee was scheduled to debate the various civil rights proposals.

July 13 was a busy day for Kroll and his staff. The first item of business was the Platform Committee meeting, where Humphrey disappointed his CIO backers by agreeing to a watered-down civil rights statement. The civil rights issue, however, was far from dead. Kroll's assistant Tilford Dudley succeeded in getting his friends in the District of Columbia delegation to protest the seating of the segregated Mississippi contingent, a move that restarted the civil rights battle. No sooner had Dudley succeeded in bringing the rights issue back to the floor than the ADA held a special caucus at Kroll's suggestion. The caucus voted overwhelmingly to push for a stronger civil rights plank and elected Humphrey to be their leader in the coming fight.[25] Before the issue could come to the floor, the convention adjourned for the day.

By Wednesday, the CIO was ready to give up hope on nominating Pepper, or any alternate candidate. However, it felt that it could save the day by strengthening the Democratic platform. The labor sections of the platform were perfectly acceptable, the Platform Committee having followed the CIO's anti-Taft–Hartley line perfectly. On the other hand, the civil rights plank came nowhere near equalling CIO demands on the subject. Thus, the Wednesday session, in CIO circles, was devoted to lining up support for the minority report on civil rights, a measure Humphrey was scheduled to defend in a speech. When the roll call came, following Humphrey's harangue, the minority report passed by a scant seventy votes. The important margin came from several midwestern state delegations (Michigan, Wisconsin, and Illinois), in which CIO delegates had a crucial voice.[26]

24. Ibid., p. 4.
25. Ibid., pp. 5–6.
26. Ibid., pp. 7–8. The author of a "Day to Day Account"

After the excitement of the civil rights fight, the nominations were an anticlimax. Truman won on the first ballot; his running mate Barkley was nominated by acclamation.[27] The CIO now had its candidate and a platform. The campaign began.

Surprisingly enough, the CIO waited almost two months before officially jumping on the Truman bandwagon. Although Kroll, Dudley, Rieve, and McDonald, the union's politicians, supported the President, Murray waited until the last minute to endorse Truman because of strong Wallace pressure within the CIO. When the CIO Executive Board finally voted on the Truman candidacy, the vote followed strict Communist–anti-Communist lines. By a vote of thirty-five to twelve (the twelve votes coming from the representatives of the eleven Communist-influenced unions in the CIO), the board decided to stay with the Democrats in November.[28]

After the board came out with an official endorsement of President Truman, the PAC began to campaign. In early October, PAC Director Kroll announced that registration had reached record levels in four labor states. Pennsylvania, West Virginia, Maryland, and Washington had all surpassed the record registration totals of 1944 and 1940. Kroll's clear implication was that his PAC workers, the one group that was publicly committed to registration, were responsible for the new record.[29] As the PAC had learned in 1944, however, record registration did not automatically assure

---

(probably Kroll's secretary) gives the distinct impression that Kroll and the CIO were the prime movers behind the famous Humphrey speech of 1948.

27. Ibid.

28. *CIO News,* September 6, 1948, p. 1. The twelve opponents and their unions were: Ben Gold (Fur and Leather Workers Union), Julius Emspak and Albert Fitzgerald (UE), Grant Oakes (Farm Equipment Workers Union), Donald Henderson (Food, Tobacco, Agricultural, and Allied Workers Union), Reid Robinson (IUMMSW), James Durkin (United Office and Professional Workers), Abram Flaxer (United Public Workers Union), Joseph Selly (American Communications Association), Morris Pizer (United Furniture Workers), Irving Dvornin (National Union of Marine Cooks and Stewards), and J. F. Jurich (Fishermen and Allied Workers Union).

29. *CIO News,* October 4, 1948, p. 8.

record voting. The PAC needed one last big issue to stimulate voter interest.

Almost as if to oblige the PAC, Congressman Fred Hartley, one of the cosponsors of the Taft–Hartley Act, published a book called *Our New National Labor Policy* in early October. The theme of Hartley's book was that the Taft–Hartley Act simply had not gone far enough in restoring the balance between unions (which he thought too powerful) and management (which he sought to protect). Calling for a national right-to-work law, stronger bans against union's political activities, and a return to prosecution of unions under the antitrust laws, he made it clear that only such measures would "complete the job the Republican Party set out to do in November, 1946." [30] Such statements provided all the ammunition the CIO needed to pull its wavering troops into line.

The October 11 issue of the *CIO News* carried banner headlines proclaiming, "Hartley Squeals on GOP." [31] The CIO message was clear, if not altogether fair. Hartley, a retiring congressman, was made to seem the spokesman of the entire Republican party. His promises of new and more restrictive labor legislation were twisted to appear to be the promises of candidate Dewey and the Republicans.[32] If anything could have stirred unionists out of their apathy in November, the Hartley threat could.

While the national CIO–PAC had been involved in the glamour and excitement of the convention and the national campaign, the state and local PACs were involved in the equally important job of getting out the labor vote. An examination of four state and one local campaign reveals the difficulties that these committees faced.

One of the most interesting state PAC campaigns was waged in California. In that state, the CIO–PAC found itself fighting its own CIO dissidents almost as strenuously as it was battling the Republicans.

Publicly, the PAC presented two faces in southern Cali-

30. Hartley, pp. 171, 173–74. The section that the CIO publicized most was Chapter 15, which called for an immediate change in the national labor policy.

31. *CIO News,* October 11, 1948, pp. 11.

32. Ibid., pp. 6–7. Thousands of copies of this article were distributed by PAC as campaign propaganda.

fornia. The legitimate arm of the national PAC called itself the California National CIO–PAC and had the strong anti-Communist backing of John Brophy and his Industrial Union Department staff. The problem was that the Independent Progressive party, a Wallace group, had the backing of another organization using the CIO–PAC title. The second, or fraudulent, CIO–PAC spent most of its energies denouncing the national CIO–PAC for its "purge" of Wallacites and third-party supporters from the CIO.[33] Considering this handicap, the national PAC faction ran a very respectable campaign in California.

Because the dissidents had managed to win control of the California PAC office and records, the national faction began the campaign laboriously trying to reassemble the CIO ward and precinct lists. By late August, Kroll's staff had helped the national group reassemble its files and renew shipment of the *CIO News* (complete with its anti-Wallace editorials) directly to California members of the CIO. In the same month, the national faction, headed by Morris Zusman and Jerome Posner, even went so far as to endorse fourteen congressional candidates. Of particular interest was the organization's backing of Democrat Cecil White, a congressional candidate in antilabor Fresno County (district nine). In complete contrast to the naive efforts of the previous election, the CIO–PAC agreed to back White secretly. White had made it quite clear that he wanted CIO support, but that open CIO endorsement would amount to a political kiss of death. Therefore, PAC funneled funds into the ninth district, but kept its campaign workers out. Among the other thirteen PAC endorsees, Helen Gahagan Douglas, Clyde Doyle, and Chet

33. The best way to understand the split would be to read both sides' propaganda pieces. For the Wallace side see "An Analysis of the Primary Election Endorsements of the California Committee for the National CIO–PAC," n.d. (1948), CIO Western Region, 1948–1950 Folder, Box 19, Adolph Germer Papers, WSHS. Germer was Murray's trouble-shooter sent into southern California to purge the Communists in the local CIO. For the loyalist side see, John Brophy to Morris Zusman and Jerome Posner, April 7, 1948, 1948 Political Action Committee Folder, CIO Secretary–Treasurer's Papers, ALH. The latter document is Brophy's defense of the actions of the California National CIO–PAC.

Holifield were all faced with opponents not only from the Republican party, but also from the Independent Progressives.[34] In a three-way race the California National PAC would have quite a task.

From August through the November election, the Zusman–Posner PAC managed to mount a determined offensive against both the Republicans and the Progressives. In the important Los Angeles area, PAC had over 450 door-to-door campaigners and hundreds of unpaid volunteers. Thousands of pieces of CIO–PAC literature were distributed among union groups including PAC's condemnation of Wallace and over 50,000 copies of the *CIO News* exposé of Fred Hartley's book. When election day was over, the California PAC found that ten of its fourteen endorsees had won House seats. White, Douglas, Holifield, and Doyle had all won; White and Doyle had managed to unseat Republican incumbents.[35] All in all, CIO–PAC candidates had done quite well in California.

The PAC's success in the Golden State was matched by victories in a number of other industrial areas. Perhaps the most notable of these victories were won in Michigan and Indiana.

In Michigan, the CIO–PAC had formally agreed to ally itself with the Democratic party. The PAC and the ADA were the two most important parties in a liberal alliance that had taken the Michigan party by storm. The details of the party takeover were almost as fascinating as the campaign.[36]

Because the Michigan Democratic party was dominated by the state convention, the ADA–CIO alliance had sought some means of gaining influence at the biennial meeting.

34. Minutes of the California CIO–PAC Executive Board, August 28–29, 1948, California National CIO–PAC Folder, Box 23, Irwin L. DeShetler Papers, ALH. DeShetler was the man who would lead CIO Region 13 in the 1952 and 1954 elections.

35. Report on Campaign Activity of the California National CIO–PAC, n.d. (December 1948), California National CIO–PAC Folder, Box 23, Irwin L. DeShetler Papers, ALH.

36. The most complete and accurate analysis of the PAC–Democrat alliance in Michigan is Fay Calkins, *The CIO and the Democratic Party* (Chicago: University of Chicago Press, 1952), pp. 112–46.

The surest but most difficult means of achieving such influence was through the election of precinct delegates; these were elected every two years. As spring, 1948, rolled around, the alliance was ready and made its move in populous Wayne County. There, the preponderant number of CIO Democrats ensured the alliance victory in every precinct. CIO and ADA members were elected chairmen, or executive board members, in every Wayne County congressional district.[37] When the September convention finally arrived, the alliance had an absolute majority of the delegates.

The convention proved to be an AFL versus CIO battle. The ADA–CIO faction controlled the votes and the obvious gubernatorial candidate, ADA member G. Mennen Williams. The conservative AFL faction, however, led by teamster Jimmy Hoffa, controlled the Democrats' treasury and the old-line party machinery. Hoffa's ally, state party chairman John Franco, brought the full weight of the conservative faction to bear on the choice for state attorney general. The Hoffa–Franco faction tried to push for Edward Kane, a prominent but conservative Algonac attorney. However, Williams and the CIO–ADA faction succeeded not only in vetoing the Kane nomination, but also in getting its own man, CIO attorney Stephan Roth, the nod. Hoffa walked out of the convention, leaving the CIO–ADA liberals in complete control (except for the treasury, which was kept sealed by Franco). As state CIO Director August Scholle left the convention in triumph, he was heard to say, "Now we've got a labor party in Michigan, what the hell are we going to do with it?"[38]

Even before the convention, the Michigan CIO had begun to experience some of the perquisites of power. As the candidates began to line up in the primaries, clearing their candidacies with the state CIO became almost a universal practice.[39] Indeed, the practice became so open that Scholle

37. Edith Fountain to Violet Megrath, September 30, 1948, Folder 6–2–9, Box 2, Series 6, Americans for Democratic Action Papers, WSHS.
38. Ibid.
39. The files of the Michigan CIO are filled with notes of candidates begging CIO help in getting them the nomination, or aiding their election campaign. For example, see G. Mennen

had to caution national labor columnist Victor Reisel to quit emphasizing the success of the politicized Michigan CIO. "I am afraid," he wrote, "it is arousing the antagonism of the oldtime 'hack' politicians, whom [sic] I am sure are resentful about us coming into the Democratic Party." [40]

Although the perquisites of a labor party may have been enjoyable, they did not distract the Michigan CIO from the business at hand. Liberal Michigan Democracy was faced with two problems: money and Wallace. To ease the situation, CIO–PAC combined its dollar drive with mass distribution of anti-Wallace broadsides. Of course, the dollar drive had always been one of PAC's best means of circumventing union political restrictions, but in Michigan, where the anti-CIO Democratic faction held the purse strings of the party, it was doubly important. The Wallace problem was less easy to solve, but, again, the PAC fell back on an old political trick. By convincing the voter that a Progressive vote was a wasted vote, CIO broadsides seemed to offer some hope of diminishing Wallace's following in CIO circles. The most popular of the CIO–PAC broadsides even equated a Wallace vote with a Republican vote; only the GOP would benefit from a Truman defeat.[41]

With an army of campaign workers (especially in Wayne County), adequate financing, and attractive liberal candidates, the CIO–Democrats managed to win a modest victory in Michigan. Liberal Democrats were elected to the governor's chair (G. Mennen Williams) and two new congressional seats (George O'Brien in the thirteenth district and Louis Rabaut in the fourteenth district). Although the Wallace vote was negligible, it was strong

---

Williams to August Scholle, May 29, 1948, Box 7, Michigan AFL–CIO Papers, ALH. E. J. Daugherty to August Scholle, July 31, 1948, Folder 7, Box 21, Michigan AFL–CIO Papers, ALH.

40. August Scholle to Victor Reisel, April 2, 1948, Folder 6, Box 21, Michigan AFL–CIO Papers, ALH.

41. August Scholle to Walter Reuther, August 17, 1948, Folder 8, Box 21; Robert T. McCreedy to August Scholle, n.d. (1948), 1948 PAC Folder, Box 105, Michigan AFL–CIO Papers, ALH.

enough in liberal Detroit to keep the state out of the Truman column.[42]

In Indiana, different problems led to the same statewide result. As the ADA had noted in 1947, there were only a few congressional seats that the Democrats might win. The two strongest Democratic districts were the labor-dominated first (Gary) and the eleventh (Indianapolis). However, a strong concentration of CIO members enhanced Democratic chances in the third (South Bend), and a liberal tradition might pull the eighth (Evansville) into the Democratic camp.[43] After an extensive CIO–PAC campaign in the first and third, as well as a strong labor–ADA effort in the fourth, eighth, and eleventh, the Democrats surprised even themselves by capturing all but the second (Charles Halleck), sixth, ninth, and tenth. Among the newly-elected Democrats was Winfield Denton, a congressman who would win PAC support for every electoral campaign through 1954. Yet, even with a virtual sweep of the congressional districts, the Democratic–ADA–CIO alliance was not able to bring Indiana into the Truman column.[44]

One of the states that had always had a strong PAC organization made an excellent showing in 1948. This state was West Virginia. With John L. Lewis and the United Mine Workers of America having declared war on the Republican miscreants who had passed Taft–Hartley, the work of the anti-Republican PAC was made substantially easier. Instead of having to fight both Lewis and the GOP, PAC leader John Easton and his staff could concentrate on more prosaic and more rewarding political tasks. Having started its campaign in March, the West Virginia CIO–PAC had time to saturate the public with its views on issues and

42. This (and other analyses) of the success or failure of PAC on the state level was taken from the AFL–LLPE post-election assessment of the 1948 election. See, Minutes of Labor's League for Political Education meeting, November 17, 1948, Political Education Folder, Box 6, West Virginia State Federation of Labor Papers, WVUL.

43. Andrew J. Biemiller, Notes on Political Situations in Various States, August 14, 1947, Folder 2–34–9, Box 34, Series 2, Americans for Democratic Action Papers, WSHS.

44. Minutes of Labor's League for Political Education Meeting, November 17, 1948, Political Education Folder, Box 6, West Virginia State Federation of Labor Papers, WVUL.

candidates well before the usual beginning of the campaign in September. PAC alliance with such prominent candidates as ex-congressmen Cleveland Bailey and Robert Ramsay did not hurt its chances. Added to its stable of two incumbent congressmen (John Kee and Earl Hedrick) and two ex-congressmen, the PAC had two attractive and liberal candidates in college professor M. G. Burnside and novice politician Harley Staggers. Money was still a problem, because of the restrictions of Taft–Hartley, but Easton's staff hit upon an ideal method of dodging the law. Unions would donate gifts to a raffle, the proceeds of which would go to PAC. Because the raffles always brought in a substantial profit, the PAC could afford to reimburse the unions for their original donations plus keep a tidy profit for strings-free political spending. After all, not one cent of PAC's funds came from union dues.[45]

The final push in West Virginia came in late October, when Jack Kroll dispatched his special assistant, Anne Mason, to give the effort the benefit of national CIO expertise. In her report to Kroll, Mason noted that the West Virginia PAC had done an excellent job, having organized the four districts in which the CIO played even a slight role. In fact, Mason, who repesented the CIO–PAC in such strong labor areas as Philadelphia, wrote that she thought her twelve days in West Virginia were the most profitably spent in the whole campaign.[46] Anne Mason's estimate was borne out by the results on election day.

The Democrats picked up all four seats that the PAC had contested; Ramsay, Staggers, Bailey, and Burnside all defeated incumbent Republicans. Besides carrying the state for Truman, the local Democrats had even elected a governor from their own ranks.[47] Such success was also found in at least one city PAC campaign, that in Philadelphia.

45. John Easton to Earl Crowder, May 25, 1948, Political Action Committee Folder, Box 11, West Virginia Labor Federation Papers, WVUL.

46. Anne Mason to Jack Kroll, October 21, 1948, CIO–PAC Miscellaneous Folder, Box 203, CIO Secretary–Treasurer's Papers, ALH.

47. Minutes of Labor's League for Political Education Meeting, November 17, 1948, Political Education Folder, Box 6, West Virginia State Federation of Labor Papers, WVUL.

As early as 1947, Biemiller and the ADA had marveled at the PAC's Philadelphia organization. In a city where the regular Democrats were barely able to staff half of the precincts, the CIO had made up the slack by employing enough of its members (at fifteen dollars a day) to man every polling district.[48] Although the Democratic machine supposedly had a secure hold on Philadelphia, it remained to the PAC to organize the important Negro districts as well as to gather up the scattered ADA liberals. The key union in the Philadelphia drive was the United Steel Workers of America, whose George Pennington was in charge of the PAC's eastern seaboard operation. In a mid-October report to Kroll, Anne Mason noted that the Democrats had suddenly discovered that they were short over 410 poll-watchers. Of course, the PAC would supply the missing manpower. In other developments, Anne Mason reported that plans were already being made to have at least 10,000 union members on hand as Truman addressed a mid-October Philadelphia rally. Everything from banners along the route of his caravan (which had been planned to go by as many CIO plants as possible) to the rental of all the available sound equipment in the city had been taken care of by the PAC.[49] In short, Philadelphia was the epitome of a well-organized city.

The election results were ample proof of the efficacy of PAC organization. Of the six Philadelphia congressional districts, PAC-endorsed Democrats managed to unseat incumbent Republicans in four. PAC Democrats were successful in the first (William Barrett), second (William Granahan), fourth (Earl Chudoff), and fifth (William Green, Jr.).[50] Yet, even with the successes enjoyed by the PAC in Philadelphia and West Virginia, the question of PAC effectiveness on a national scale remains.

Perhaps the best way to analyze the success, or failure,

48. Andrew J. Biemiller, Notes on Political Situations in Various States, August 14, 1947, Folder 2–34–9, Box 34, Series 2, Americans for Democratic Acton Papers, WSHS.
49. Anne Mason to Jack Kroll, October 8, 1948, CIO–PAC Miscellaneous Folder, Box 202, CIO Secretary–Treasurer's Papers, ALH.
50. Pennsylvania, *The Pennsylvania Manual, Vol. 89* (1949).

of the PAC in 1948 would be to examine the returns of the presidential and congressional races, comparing PAC success with Democratic success. However, in a year when Truman's remarkable campaign upset all the experts' predictions, separating the impact of Truman's lonely campaign from that of the CIO electoral machine seems particularly difficult.

Among the first indicators of the direction of the labor vote (the vote that was the special province of the PAC and the AFL–LLPE) were preelection opinion polls. The Green–Brodie poll of April, based upon interviews with CIO members in twenty-five cities, showed that CIO voters intended to support the PAC's choice (no matter who he might be) very strongly. Indeed, several cities showed up to ninety-five per cent of the local CIO membership intended to support the PAC candidate sight unseen.[51] However, much happened between April and November; the Green–Brodie poll was hardly to be trusted.

In October, only three weeks before the election, George Gallup's poll revealed that union members were split fifty-five to thirty-eight per cent in favor of Truman. Even more to the point, a survey of CIO members revealed a pro-Truman edge of fifty-eight to thirty-two per cent (with ten per cent supporting Wallace).[52] It appeared in late October as if Truman would sweep most CIO districts, but the election was still weeks away.

When November 5 finally came, Truman found himself the winner by the surprising margin of 24.1 million votes to 21.9 million votes. In terms of percentages, Truman had garnered 49.5 per cent of the vote to Dewey's 45.1 per cent

51. Jack Kroll to James Carey, April 16, 1948, 1948 Political Action Committee Folder, Box 85, CIO Secretary–Treasurer's Papers, ALH.
52. Morris Ernst and David Loth, *The People Know Best: The Ballots Vs. the Polls* (Washington: Public Affairs Press, 1949), pp. 128–29.
In a year when almost every pollster was proven wrong, it is interesting to note that Jack Kroll's published poll was almost completely accurate in forecasting the electoral vote and the states that Truman would capture. His guess was an electoral vote of 297–192 in favor of Truman. See Jack Kroll's Prediction, October 26, 1948, Box 1, Group 2, Jack Kroll Papers, LCMD.

(Wallace and Dixiecrat Thurmond split about five per cent to the popular total). In comparison to the 1944 Roosevelt total of 25.6 million ballots and 53.4 per cent, Truman's victory seemed slim, a conclusion that was buttressed by the fact that a shift of as little as 30,000 votes in such key states as California, Illinois, and Ohio could have given Dewey the Electoral College triumph.[53] Such a close margin was the basis of many an electoral analysis.

The decline in the national Democratic total, according to the most perceptive of the electoral analysts, Samuel Lubell, was because of the changes that the Truman candidacy had wrought in the Democratic constituency. Lubell, in his famous *Future of American Politics,* defined such changes threefold. First, Jewish voters had defected to the Republicans and Wallace. Second, Irish and German Catholics had returned to the Democratic fold after a flirtation with the Republicans. Finally, the Republicans and the Democrats had exchanged constituencies as farmers had voted Democratic and urban dwellers had forsaken the New Deal coalition to vote for Dewey. The explanation of these shifts, wrote Lubell, could be found in the schisms within the Democratic party. Wallace's candidacy attracted urban Jewish voters, while it painted Truman's campaign with the mark of anticommunism. However, the anti-Communist label appealed to the strongly anti-Communist Irish and German Catholics, who had disapproved of Roosevelt's close relations with Russia. Furthermore, a rapid decline in farm prices separated the farm vote from the Republican party, whose congressional bloc had promised an end to all farm price supports. Finally, the feared shift of Negro voters back to the Republican party (a shift that had worried Clark Clifford in November, 1947) had been averted by the anti-Truman, anti-Negro Thurmond candidacy.[54] In short, much of the credit for Truman's victory, according to Lubell, was owed to the very schismatic elements within the Democratic party that had made victory seem so improbable. It would be interesting

53. Svend Peterson, *A Statistical History of the American Presidential Elections* (New York: Frederick Ungar Publishing Co., 1968), pp. 99–105.

54. Samuel Lubell, *The Future of American Politics* (New York: Harper and Brothers, 1952), pp. 132–78, 198–226.

to note the impact of the PAC in this year of political turmoil.

One of the best ways to separate the impact of the Truman campaign generally from the CIO–PAC campaign specifically would be to compare the returns of CIO districts (counties and congressional districts in which the CIO–PAC was the major campaign organization) to non-CIO districts. By comparing the two kinds of districts over the time span of several elections a pattern would emerge that would reveal the effectiveness of the 1948 PAC campaign. Signs of PAC effectiveness would be a stronger than normal Democratic vote in PAC districts in 1948 and an increase in CIO district Democratic vote that was not reflected in non-CIO districts.

The simplest comparison would be between the presidential vote in CIO counties and the country as a whole. The ten strongest CIO counties (See Appendix), those counties in which the CIO–PAC campaigned hardest and supplanted the efforts of the regular Democratic organization, supported Truman much more strongly than the nation as a whole, but their Democratic totals slipped from their 1944 high.[55] However, using Lubell's analysis, the most significant element in the Democratic slip in CIO counties would be the six-percentage-point drop in Democratic strength in Wayne County (Detroit), Michigan. Because Wayne County was a Jewish, as well as a CIO, stronghold, the drop in the Democratic vote and the significant Progressive vote (almost equal to the six per cent Democratic loss) could have been an illustration of Lubell's belief that the strongest defections from the Democratic party were those of the Jews who fled to Wallace.[56] Otherwise, the Democratic fall-off nationwide was not reflected in the CIO counties' continuing support of the Democratic party.

A more precise comparison of Democratic and PAC campaign effectiveness could be found in a comparison of CIO and non-CIO congressional district votes. Once again, PAC effectiveness should be revealed in a stronger than normal Democratic vote (derived from viewing the district

55. Presidential Vote Table in 1948 Appendix.
56. Ibid.

over a four-election time span) that would not be seen in non-CIO districts (districts in which the Democratic party and Truman were the chief campaign factors). Such a comparison should show voter reaction to a PAC campaign gauged against voter reaction to the Truman campaign.

A comparison of CIO and non-CIO congressional districts indicated not only that Democratic support was stronger in CIO districts, but also that such Democratic support was a new phenomenon. Compared to past congressional elections, CIO districts supported the Democrats much more strongly in 1948. Moreover, the increase in Democratic support in CIO districts was much greater than the increase of Democratic percentages in the strong Truman areas of the West and rural Midwest.[57] It would seem that some factor was operating in CIO districts to increase the Democratic vote that was not operating in the non-CIO districts. The PAC may have been that factor.

The high level of Democratic support in labor districts led some analysts to conclude that Truman's urban victories were indeed the work of organized labor. Moreover, because Truman's margins were usually less than those of labor-endorsed congressmen, many viewed the Truman triumph as a case of labor-engineered "reverse coattails." After all, the AFL and the CIO had been campaigning for Congress long before the PAC had jumped on the Truman bandwagon. The CIO itself had not been universally pleased with Truman. Obviously, labor voters should have reflected this in their preference for prolabor congressmen. For this and other reasons, analysts such as R. Alton Lee concluded that labor's congressional campaign may have indeed dragged Harry Truman into the White House.[58] While district-level returns seemed to support this thesis, a closer examination of labor voting tends to discount the labor "coattails" theory, at least partially.

As Lee pointed out in *Truman and Taft–Hartley,* most labor-endorsed congressmen did outpoll Truman in 1948. However, at least in several cases, the excess margin did

57. Comparison of two Congressional Vote Tables in 1948 Appendix.
58. R. Alton Lee, *Truman and Taft–Hartley* (Lexington: University of Kentucky Press, 1966), pp. 145–52. The theory was originally advanced by Moos, p. 14.

not come from those labor wards in which PAC appeals should have had most influence. Labor wards in at least four CIO areas (Chicago, Milwaukee, Pittsburgh, and Hartford) revealed that blue-collar voters supported Truman at least as strongly as CIO-backed local candidates. In addition, labor voters in Milwaukee and Hartford seemed much less prone to desert the Democratic standard in the presidential election than in the various local races.[59] If the 1948 election was an example of the "reverse coattails" phenomenon, it was not evident in those wards.

Regardless of the coattails theory, labor did play an important part in the Truman victory. Only the day after the election, President Truman himself said that "labor did it."[60] Analysts from Irwin Ross to Richard Kirkendall agreed. Labor did play a special part in the 1948 victory.[61] Perhaps the best way to view that part would be to examine the labor vote itself.

In order to facilitate such an investigation, the 1948 Appendix compares labor wards in strong CIO cities with nonlabor wards in the same area. The comparison also extends to a measurement of labor ward voting for presidential (where the personality of the candidate often plays an important role) and nonpresidential offices (usually congressional elections). Once again, PAC impact would be seen as unusually high 1948 Democratic totals in labor wards as compared to nonlabor wards and previous elections, and a Democratic propensity in nonpresidential elections as well (assuming that a Democratic vote in a nonpresidential election would be more the work of a campaign machine than the candidate's personality).

Observing the presidential vote comparison in the Appendix, it is noticeable that the decrease in the Democratic totals in labor wards in 1948 was much less than the nonlabor ward Democratic loss. Possibly, this could be a sign that PAC propaganda for Truman paid off. However, it is important to note that the Truman vote of 1948 actually increased over the Roosevelt vote of 1944 in heavily

59. Ibid. See also, Appendixes 1948D and 1948E.
60. *New York Times,* November 4, 1948, p. 1.
61. Irwin Ross, *The Loneliest Campaign* (New York: The New American Library, 1968), pp. 254–55. Richard Kirkendall, "Election of 1948," Schlesinger, Israel, and Hansen.

Catholic wards in Pittsburgh (wards eight, sixteen, seventeen, nineteen, and twenty-one). This phenomenon was notable in both labor and nonlabor wards. Such an ethnic shift (which Lubell emphasized) should be balanced by its occurrence in both kinds of wards. If such were the case, PAC ward work may have been the difference between the huge Democratic declines in nonlabor wards and the moderate Democratic decrease in labor wards.[62]

In the nonpresidential elections, the difference between labor and nonlabor wards was not so marked. Although again the nonlabor ward Democratic total suffered a greater loss than the labor ward total, the difference in the loss was only two percentage points. Especially notable in the 1948 labor ward total was the Democratic decline in the Milwaukee Catholic wards (wards five, eight, and fourteen). According to Lubell, these wards should have shown an increase in their Democratic percentages. They did not.[63] Looking at the labor ward totals, the assumption would have to be that PAC activity may have been the crucial factor that kept the Democratic vote from declining as much as it did in nonlabor wards.

What, then, can be said about the 1948 PAC effort? First, the CIO and its PAC realized early in the campaign that the Communist issue would be very important in a negative sense. Analyses of the failures of 1946 had revealed that the CIO–PAC's identification with the Communist party had done nothing but hurt its electoral efforts. Therefore, the CIO decision to avoid Wallace at all costs had been a good one. Using Lubell's analysis, the anti-Communist stance may have been responsible for drawing Catholic voters into the PAC vanguard who would certainly have bolted from the Wallace banner.

Second, Kroll's use of polling techniques and informal cooperation with the ADA spelled a political sophistication that was entirely lacking in Sidney Hillman's 1944 crusade. Whereas Kroll avoided identification of the CIO–PAC with other liberal groups (whose credentials might be suspected by the public), Hillman had wholeheartedly launched him-

62. Labor Ward Table in 1948 Appendix.
63. Comparison of Labor and Nonlabor Ward Tables in 1948 Appendix.

self into the National Citizens PAC, a group that had helped to paint the CIO–PAC red in the public's eye.[64]

Finally, from what little evidence the returns themselves yield, it would seem that the 1948 PAC effort was indeed a victory. CIO counties led the country in their Democratic vote. CIO congressional districts were notable in their margins of Democratic support. Labor wards in CIO cities also followed the pattern. Although none of these would be conclusive evidence, they would tend to indicate that a common factor was operating for the benefit of the Democrats in all these areas. A strong assumption would be that the common factor was Kroll's refurbished CIO–PAC.

As the November elections came and went, CIO President Philip Murray could look back on 1948 as a year of memorable accomplishments. Although he had lost the support of some of the CIO's radical unions, he had increased his following among the ranks of the CIO's anti-Communists. Perhaps of even more importance, the purging of the Communists had helped transform the CIO's Political Action Committee into a truly effective campaign machine. It was a year of victory, not defeat.

64. As important as avoiding bad publicity, in the eyes of Irwin Ross, was the PAC's tactic in 1948 of avoiding all publicity. As long as the PAC was not in the limelight, communism could not be used as an issue by the Republicans as it was in 1944. Ross, pp. 222–24.

7

PAC Almost Victorious: 1950

After the exhilarating victory of 1948, the leaders of the CIO and the Political Action Committee were ready to challenge the devil himself. Although their readiness and eagerness were praiseworthy, their fixation on battling demons would prove to be a serious shortcoming during the first two elections of the 1950s. Still fighting the lost battle of Taft–Hartley, the CIO's politicians devoted more time to exorcising their personal congressional demons than to exploring new ways to mobilize the labor vote effectively. For example, more time was spent in the futile attempt to purge Senator Robert Taft than in polling CIO members on their political preferences. Indeed, the overconfidence brought about by the 1948 Democratic victory could be viewed as one of the causes of the CIO–PAC's political setbacks in the 1950 elections.

Preparations for the 1950 campaign took on an unusual flavor in the CIO camp during the fall of 1949. Americans for Democratic Action, the organization that had provided a most convenient and effective banner under which to assemble the CIO anti-Communist contingent, began to worry about the imminent departure of its labor members and their money now that the CIO Communist crisis was over. When Emil Rieve, ADA board member and president of the Textile Workers Union, let it be known that he was planning to withdraw his union and its funds from the ADA, the crisis came out in the open. Because a third of the ADA's operating expenses were provided by various labor unions, a mass withdrawal of unions from the ADA would leave the organization virtually bankrupt. Moreover, many ADA leaders had reason to believe that the departure of such groups as the Textile Workers Union of America would lead to the resignation of many other ADA units and individuals. Labor was the financial and political buttress that supported the ADA's slim hopes of political power.[1]

When Al Barkan, Rieve's assistant, officially announced Rieve's withdrawal in mid-December, the ADA board was so shocked that it suspended normal business to discuss the matter. Instead of improving matters through discussion, the interchange brought out the fact that both CIO Secretary–Treasurer James Carey and UAW President Walter Reuther were planning similar disengagements.[2] Indeed, despite the shocked reaction of the ADA board, the CIO attitude seemed to be that CIO–PAC was more important than the ADA would ever be.[3] The ADA was but an impediment to prompt and effective PAC action.

The abandonment of ADA was only one sign of PAC Director Jack Kroll's new outlook for the 1950 electoral campaign. The days when Sidney Hillman spent as much time with his National Citizens Political Action Committee as with CIO–PAC were gone. Kroll, the practical politician,

1. The importance of the CIO to the ADA can be easily ascertained by an examination of ADA correspondence in the 1948–1950 period. For example, both Hubert Humphrey and Charles LaFollette felt that it was necessary to clear their respective campaigns for the ADA presidency with President Philip Murray of the CIO, even though Murray was neither an ADA member nor an active participant in ADA affairs. See, Hubert Humphrey to Philip Murray, March 30, 1949, Folder 2–30–4, Box 30, Series 2, Americans for Democratic Action Papers, WSHS. Humphrey was also quite explicit about the amount of money that the CIO donated to the ADA.

2. Al Barkan to Emil Rieve, December 19, 1949, Political Action Department, 1949 Folder, Box 12, Series 1A, Textile Workers Union of America Papers, WSHS.

This was the second letter to Rieve on the subject of TWUA withdrawal from ADA. The first (December 7, 1949, same location) noted that Chester Bowles, an ADA politician of some note, had also contemplated withdrawal, especially after word circulated about the TWUA pullout.

3. Emily Ehle to Joseph Rauh, Jr., December 29, 1949, ADA 1949 Folder, Box 147, CIO Secretary–Treasurer's Papers, ALH.

Emily Ehle, Study Director of ADA, wrote that much of the ADA's grief over the probable loss of the CIO members of the organization could have been averted if some of the ADA's prima donnas, such as Hubert Humphrey, had taken more time to consult CIO leaders such as Philip Murray and James Carey over ADA policy decisions.

realized that PAC objectives could be met only through hard work and single-minded action, not by alliances of liberals. The PAC would be a full-time venture in 1950.

Before jumping into the 1950 campaign, Kroll sent a quick memorandum to President Murray regarding methods of assuring the success of a full-time PAC. To Kroll, one of the best means of achieving such success would be for the PAC to adopt a long-term approach to politics. A long-term approach, Kroll wrote, would mean that the CIO would adopt a list of long-term goals that could keep member interest from flagging even during those long months between electoral contests. Projects that could inspire this kind of political loyalty were abolition of the Electoral College, abolition of southern-dominated congressional seniority, and the enactment of uniform voting laws. Moreover, with the CIO on record as supporting such ends, the third-party supporters in the CIO would be disarmed, the disenchanted liberals of both parties might rally to its cause, and the two major political parties might be persuaded to move in more liberal directions.[4] It was an optimistic plan, indeed, and Murray assured Kroll that he would let his assistant, David McDonald, review it in detail.[5]

In the meantime, plans were being made for the 1950 elections. The PAC campaign began in early October, 1949, with a preliminary assessment of the political situation in the western states. Kroll and his associates realized that the battle of 1950 would be fought at the state level, and a necessary prerequisite for such a battle was good local reconnaissance. With this in mind, the CIO's Research Department was given the task of discovering local voting

4. Jack Kroll to Philip Murray, September 28, 1949, PAC Folder, Box A4–67, Philip Murray Papers, CUA.

CIO strategists had felt that one reason that many CIO members had followed the PCA in 1948 was that body's emphasis on long term liberal goals. If the PAC and CIO were to adopt similar goals without joining a liberal coalition whose loyalty was suspect, they could probably win back many CIO third-party supporters.

5. Philip Murray to Jack Kroll, October 11, 1949, PAC Folder, Box A4–67, Philip Murray Papers, CUA.

McDonald served as Murray's personal advisor on political action as well as being secretary of the United Steel Workers of America.

trends. The western report was the first fruit of the department's labors.[6]

The report that lay on Kroll's desk on October 4, 1949,
contained a number of interesting observations. First,
trends seemed to indicate that the PAC could expect a net
increase of eleven liberal congressmen from the western
states. Such an optimistic estimate was followed by the
prediction that at least two reactionary senators would be
defeated in western elections. Thus, the CIO could look forward to a promising year politically in the far West. One
note of caution followed the report. In the two most populous of the eight western states, California and Washington,
the initial Democratic advantage in voter registration might
not help liberal candidates. It was a particularly well-known
fact that Democrats usually stayed home in off-year elections.[7] The PAC's job might be more difficult than originally
envisioned.

The October report on the western states was the first in
a long series of CIO research directives. On January 19,
CIO researchers submitted their views on the nationwide
chances for PAC (and Democratic) liberals in November,
1950. The January report began realistically by noting that
the chances of seven PAC-endorsed senators were quite
slim. Liberals such as the PAC's 1948 presidential candidate, Claude Pepper, were very likely to be defeated by
their conservative rivals. Only the most inspired PAC legwork could prevent the likes of George Smathers of
Florida, Everett Dirksen of Illinois, Strom Thurmond of
South Carolina, and James Duff of Pennsylvania from entering the Senate in place of an outstanding group of liberal
incumbents.[8]

From the initial note of pessimism, the report soon
passed to more pleasant prospects. Eight "reactionaries"
(in PAC nomenclature) were seen as vulnerable in 1950.
Among this group, which included Iowa Senator Bourke

6. Report of Political Situation in Western States, October
4, 1949, Political Action Committee, 1950 Folder, Box 85,
CIO Secretary–Treasurer's Papers, ALH.

7. Ibid.

8. Confidential Report on 1950 Elections, January 19, 1950,
Political Action Committee, 1950 Folder, Box 85, CIO
Secretary–Treasurer's Papers, ALH.

Hickenlooper, Indiana's Homer Capehart, and Wisconsin's Alexander Wiley, was the CIO's ultimate enemy, Robert Taft of Ohio. The discovery that Taft was beatable could have been the beginning of the PAC's downfall in 1950. It was all too easy to gloat over the imminent defeat of so important an enemy and ignore the Research Department's warning on the following page: "In California, the CIO is supporting Helen Gahagan Douglas . . . [who] will face Richard Nixon, a strong campaigner." [9]

The happy prospect of defeating Ohio's "Mr. Republican" may also have obscured the importance of the conclusion of the January report. After having outlined the probable races in twenty-seven states, the Research Department staff concluded with the important warning that the 1950 elections were much more crucial than they outwardly appeared. Whichever party won the state battles in 1950 would be in a fine position to reapportion election districts. The reapportionment made by the 1950-elected state legislatures would stand for another decade. Indeed, a strong PAC campaign might spell the difference between a fair redistricting and a gerrymander.[10]

By mid-February, the PAC began to reassess its position with a bit of alarm. Although its January goals had been limited to only twenty-two senatorial contests and 159 marginal congressional races (not to mention legislative races in labor states), it found itself with only fourteen full-time staff members to organize the CIO legions for the coming battle. All the political expertise and sophistication in the world could not overcome such a handicap. Yet, because 1950 was a nonpresidential year, the CIO powers had not granted the PAC funds for more than fourteen political workers. What was needed was money—by the Research Department's most modest estimate, at least 750,000 dollars.[11] The PAC had reached its first obstacle of the campaign.

While finances proved to be an early and crucial problem in the 1950 PAC campaign, other issues proved just as

9. Ibid.
10. Ibid.
11. Elections 1950 (Revised), February 13, 1950, Political Action Committee, 1950 Folder, Box 85, CIO Secretary–Treasurer's Papers, ALH.

crucial and substantially more troublesome. While the money problem could be cured by the established PAC practice of the dollar drive (voluntary fund-raising drives among CIO members), these other problems were much less easily dismissed.

The first, and perhaps greatest, problem that the PAC faced in 1950 was the massive change in labor voting sympathies. As Samuel Lubell noted in his 1952 study of American politics, the CIO political machine of the 1950s was dealing with a substantially different electorate than was Hillman's crude apparatus of 1944. The days were gone when CIO members really believed the barricade rhetoric of their leaders, and when memories of the depression were sufficient to keep the wavering CIO voters in line. The days were gone also when workers feared revision of the Wagner Act as sincerely as did their leaders. In the 1950s, the PAC would have to call upon more than rhetoric to get out the pro-CIO vote.[12] Perhaps the best example of the changing role of PAC was demonstrated by PAC's attempted purge of Ohio's Senator Robert Taft.

Senator Taft, as the cosponsor of the hated Taft–Hartley Act of 1947, was one of the CIO–PAC's prime targets in the 1950 elections. To the CIO, Taft was made particularly vulnerable by his Ohio constituency, which included an impressive number of CIO and other union members. It was the PAC belief that these unionists would end the senatorial career of Robert Taft—an assumption that proved to be a major error.

The purge–Taft drive had been underway since August, 1949, when Philip Murray and Jack Kroll had formulated a basic strategy for retiring the Ohio senator. As Kroll had seen the situation, CIO–PAC could be successful if it only could utilize the raw Democratic potential of populous Cuyahoga County. The county, which included Cleveland, had always voted Democratic, but in 1944 Taft had cut his losses in Cuyahoga to only 9,600 votes. Surely, Kroll wrote, a good PAC registration drive should yield more than enough Democratic votes there to offset Taft's 1944 state-wide margin of 17,000 votes. Even though there was some talk of changing the Ohio ballot to discourage the kind of

12. Lubell, pp. 190–209.

party-line voting the PAC would need, a good registration drive should overcome even that handicap. CIO political workers should begin making preparations for such a campaign at once.[13]

The CIO–PAC's Taft campaign was not particularly distinguished by any great CIO–PAC innovations. The only new feature of the Ohio campaign, which pitted PAC–Democrat Joseph Ferguson against Taft, was PAC's issuance of a speaker's "fact book" denouncing Senator Taft. Although the book drew praise from Democrats ranging from Roy Reuther (brother of the UAW president) to President Truman, it did not succeed in electing Joseph Ferguson.[14] Indeed, CIO leaders should have listened less to the praise showered upon their fact book than to the important criticism levelled against their campaign by James Carey's assistant, George Weaver. Weaver saw the real state of affairs in Ohio.

Weaver addressed his complaints to the head of the PAC, Jack Kroll, in a June 15, 1950 letter. He noted three weaknesses in the Ferguson campaign, weaknesses that everyone else in the anti-Taft camp ignored. First, considering that he was a labor candidate, Ferguson was incredibly weak in Ohio's cities, especially the strong CIO cities of northern Ohio (Canton, Cleveland, and Toledo). The primary vote showed that Taft was much stronger in these areas than was the Democratic contender. Second, Ferguson's major source of strength was central and western Ohio, where the CIO–PAC would be nothing but a liability. There was no way that the CIO could boost Ferguson's totals in that area. Finally, both Michael DeSalle, the Democrat who

13. Jack Kroll to Philip Murray, August 23, 1949, PAC Folder, Box A4–67, Philip Murray Papers, CUA.

14. Roy Reuther to Jack Kroll, May 18, 1950, Box 1, Group 5, Jack Kroll Papers, LCMD.

Also, see Harry S. Truman to Jack Kroll, May 17, 1950; George Harrison to Jack Kroll, June 27, 1950, Box 1, Group 5, Jack Kroll Papers, LCMD.

The "fact book" that Truman and others praised (the *Speakers Handbook*) was so unfairly anti-Taft that James Patterson believed that it may have helped Taft in the long run. Although it bore a "United Labor League of Ohio" label, it was really produced by the national CIO–PAC. James T. Patterson, *Mr. Republican* (Boston: Houghton–Mifflin Co., 1972), pp. 458–59.

would challenge Republican Senator John Bricker in 1952, and Henry Miller Bush, a Cleveland college professor and darling of the ADA, had done better than Ferguson in nine of the ten Ohio industrial counties during the May primary. There was some question as to whom the DeSalle and Bush supporters would back in November. The best that the PAC could do was to make a determined bid for Ferguson in those crucial counties.[15] Taft's chances appeared better and better.

Fay Calkins, who worked with the PAC in Ohio, noted other weaknesses in the Ferguson effort. The worst of PAC's problems was Ferguson himself. Although, as state auditor, Ferguson had control over a number of patronage positions, his political apparatus was considerably weakened by the covert opposition of Ohio's Democratic governor, Frank Lausche. It was rumored that Lausche had agreed with the Republicans not to support any determined bid to unseat Taft if they would put up only token opposition to his reelection in 1950. Moreover, Ferguson, whose political acumen was not equal to Taft's in any way, was the choice of neither the CIO nor the Democratic liberals. The CIO had supported the candidacy of Murray Lincoln, a farm bureau liberal who had withdrawn before the primary; the liberals (and the ADA) had backed Henry Miller Bush. Ferguson had defeated Bush in the May primary, leaving himself as the only alternative to Taft.[16] Ferguson's candidacy helped doom the anti-Taft drive from the start.

In its frenzied attempt to upset Robert Taft, the CIO reluctantly decided to back Ferguson rather than to put up a third candidate. Although the CIO was strong in Ohio, its electoral strength was simply not equal to the task of electing a statewide candidate.[17] In fact, the Ohio PAC

15. George Weaver to Jack Kroll, June 15, 1950, Box 1, Group 5, Jack Kroll Papers, LCMD.
16. Calkins, pp. 14–22.
17. Ibid. When it became obvious that Lincoln would not be able to compete successfully with Ferguson, Ohio PAC leaders told their followers that the Democrats had chosen "unusually qualified" candidates for the fall election. Such inspired selections made the choice of a separate PAC candidate unnecessary.

As Patterson and others have pointed out, one of Taft's

contingent soon found that it was not even equal to the task of assisting a Democrat to victory.

On May 12, after his decisive primary victory, Joseph Ferguson had written to Jack Kroll asking for his advice on the final campaign push. The invitation provided an opening for PAC workers to penetrate the Ferguson campaign apparatus. Even though they were desperately needed, however, PAC workers were not unanimously welcomed. Chief among the critics of the PAC in the Ferguson campaign was Ferguson's campaign manager, Clarence Doyle. Doyle objected to the "aboveboard" operations of the PAC. Noting that voters saw union labels on Ferguson campaign literature, union workers ringing doorbells for Ferguson, and union leaders closeted with the candidate, Doyle feared that many voters would accept Taft's charges that he was being persecuted by "outside labor agitators." However, Ferguson's immediate need for PAC financing seemed to outweigh such criticism. The CIO–PAC remained a prominent and public part of the Ferguson camp.[18]

Although labor worked long and hard for Ferguson, Taft was reelected by a margin of 1,645,643 to 1,214,459, literally burying Ferguson. For the first time in his political life, the Republican Senator had carried Cuyahoga County, and he had carried it with a remarkable 23,000 vote edge. As political observers began to pick over the ruins of the Ferguson campaign, one of the more prophetic warnings of Kroll was recalled. In the excitement of the campaign, both the PAC and the United Labor League had forgotten about the Republican-sponsored ballot reform. The effect of the reform had seemed uncertain before the election, but not

---

greatest assets in the 1950 campaign was Ferguson (or Jumping Joe as he was known in Ohio). The Ohio Republican press had a field day comparing Ferguson, the crude, unsophisticated state auditor, to Taft, the Republican pillar of the Senate. Patterson, pp. 456–58.

18. Ibid. The CIO alone supplied over one–third of Ferguson's campaign funds in 1950. The CIO, AFL, and miners and railroad unions donated about eighty-five per cent of Ferguson's funds. Thus, even the complaints of a publicity manager would hardly have warranted censure of such important backers.

after. The new Massachusetts ballot had resulted in a record number of split tickets. The average Ohio voter had supported both Democratic Governor Frank Lausche and Republican Senator Taft. Ballot reform had done exactly what the Republicans had hoped; labor's efforts had seemingly done for naught.[19] Yet, as Samuel Lubell noted, it was not as much a failure in effort (or even in the ballot) as a failure in voter attitude.

While the PAC was taking an active and public role in the campaign, its leaders did not realize how perceptive were the criticisms of Clarence Doyle. Lubell's analysis, which was made in 1952, was in many ways merely an elaboration on Doyle's theme. Thus, he spoke of PAC failures in terms of PAC militancy creating a backlash among nonlabor voters. He noted the strong mutual suspicion between the labor members of the Ferguson alliance and the nonlabor Democrats. He even raised the important point that union members also entertained fears that the PAC was becoming too large and too powerful politically. He concluded with the generalization that the PAC was really able to deliver the vote only to candidates whom unionists already favored (namely Roosevelt).[20] It was not that the PAC had failed to devote enough effort to the campaign, but rather that its massive effort had caused an antilabor, anti-Ferguson backlash among Ohio's voters. As in 1946, the PAC had proved to be a potent weapon in the hands of the opposition.

While the Taft purge was failing in Ohio, a number of other important PAC campaigns were underway. In many of these contests, the PAC would also find that its backing was not an unmixed blessing to many marginal candidates.

In California, the PAC began the campaign with a number of advantages that it had not enjoyed in the Ohio race. Perhaps the most important advantage was Helen Gahagan

19. Ibid. pp. 23–36. Although the PAC dominated the anti-Taft movement, it was but one constituent element of the United Labor League that united the CIO, AFL, UMWA, and Railway Workers behind Ferguson. The PAC was the noisiest (in terms of publicity) and most vulnerable (in terms of its "socialist" reputation) group in the United Labor League.

On the vote and the ballot question see, Patterson, pp. 469–71.

20. Lubell, pp. 201–9.

Douglas, an attractive and intelligent two-term congress-woman, who proved to be the antithesis of Ohio's Joe Ferguson. She had won a decisive primary victory with the help of the CIO-PAC that many felt gave her a distinct advantage in the race for retiring Senator Sheridan Downey's seat. Indeed, Downey had been a liberal Democrat, just as Douglas was.[21] Another advantage that the PAC enjoyed in California was the caliber of the opposition. Whereas Ferguson had to challenge the most famous Republican senator in the country, Douglas had only to face a two-term congressman from Southern California, Richard M. Nixon. Although he had proven himself an able campaigner in both 1946 and 1948, he was seen as much less of a threat than an incumbent senator.[22] Finally, the PAC had a financial advantage in California that it had not had in Ohio. Ferguson's campaign had been run on a shoestring compared with Taft's funding. In California, the Nixon campaign was plagued with financial difficulties in comparison to the well-financed Douglas drive.[23] Victory should have been easy.

As in Ohio, hopes of victory for the PAC were dashed when the returns finally were tallied. Douglas, the favorite in July and August, had been beaten by the largest margin ever recorded in a California senatorial race.[24] What had gone wrong?

21. Statement of Policy on United States Senatorial Campaign, n.d. (1950), California CIO–PAC Executive Board Minutes Folder, Box 26, Irwin L. DeShetler Papers, ALH.

22. Senatorial Elections, 1950, August 28, 1950, Political Action Committee Folder, Box 85, CIO Secretary–Treasurer's Papers, ALH.

23. Although there was little question that Mrs. Douglas had good financial backing in 1950, Richard Nixon's claim concerning his lack of funds was questionable. Although most of Nixon's biographers note his financial problems in 1950, their objectivity is open to question. Those biographies that were based upon more than newspaper accounts are almost unanimously vigorously pro-Nixon (and anti-Douglas) tracts. For several good examples see, Bela Kornitzer, *The Real Nixon* (New York: Rand McNally and Co., 1960), pp. 179–87. Also, Ralph de Toledano, *Nixon* (New York: Henry Holt and Co., 1956), pp. 88–101.

24. Ibid. For the exact size of the Nixon victory see California, *Manual*, 1950.

From the start, the PAC had sadly underestimated Nixon. As he had proven in his 1946 campaign and in the Alger Hiss case, he was an able manipulator of the Communist issue.[25] Moreover, Nixon's political manager, Murray Chotiner, proved to be a master of political prestidigitation whose skill was exemplified in the famous "pink sheet" affair.

Chotiner had a candidate, in Nixon, whose anti-Communist stance was above question. His candidate's opponent had the misfortune to be endorsed by the Communist *Daily Worker*. The problem, as far as Chotiner was concerned, was to stress his candidate's relative purity on the Communist issue without risking accusations of slandering Douglas, a member of Congress and a woman. The solution that occurred to Chotiner was the "pink sheet" campaign. "Is Helen Douglas a Democrat?" asked the headline on Chotiner's masterpiece, a Nixon broadside printed on shocking pink paper. "The record says *no.*" What followed was a Chotiner-devised comparison of the voting records of Helen Douglas with Vito Marcantonio, the American Labor party's left-wing congressman. Although the pink sheet legally avoided slandering Douglas, the message was clear. For the rest of the campaign, Helen Gahagan Douglas was on the defensive against implied charges that she was not completely loyal. After all, would a loyal American vote the same way that Marcantonio did? Chotiner never revealed that Nixon's votes also paralleled Marcantonio's on occasion; he never felt that it was necessary. Nixon's campaign was off to a flying start.[26]

The Nixon camp also gained a good deal of political mileage out of the carpetbagging charge. While "poor"

25. In 1946, Nixon had linked his opponent with the "red" CIO–PAC. During his service on the House Un-American Activities Committee, Nixon rose to national fame as the skilled cross examiner who seemingly exposed a State Department official, Alger Hiss, as a Communist spy. For a brief summary of the Hiss case and its ramifications see, Eric Goldman, pp. 100–135.

26. For two of the most intriguing stories of the pink sheet affair, see the two pro-Nixon accounts of Chotiner's ploy. The most interesting thing about the accounts is that neither author tried to ignore the affair and downplay Nixon's role in it. Kornitzer, pp. 183–84. Toledano, pp. 94–95.

Richard Nixon was campaigning largely on his own, his opponent made use of such important non-Californians as Eleanor Roosevelt, Vice President Alben Barkley, and Labor Secretary Maurice Tobin. In addition, Nixon charged that his opponent was making use of UAW–CIO money and campaign workers imported from Michigan and elsewhere. Interestingly enough, this was the same charge that had demolished PAC candidates' chances in Pennsylvania during the 1946 election.[27] The CIO–PAC proved to be a scapegoat once again.

In Maryland, the CIO–PAC figured negatively in the defeat of Senator Millard Tydings. Although labor traditionally had opposed Senator Tydings, the ADA and other liberal groups associated with labor felt that Tydings was certainly a better candidate in 1950 than his Republican opponent, John Butler. Even after hearing the arguments of the ADA, PAC officials refused to come to the aid of the beleaguered Democrat. When Democratic senators met to organize the Eighty-second Congress, Tydings was not among them. Although Tydings had a number of weaknesses in 1950, the ADA concluded that lack of CIO and liberal support was the key to his defeat.[28]

Ohio, California, and Maryland were all examples of varying degrees of PAC electoral defeat. Yet, the story of the CIO–PAC in 1950 was not one of unmitigated failure; the elections in Michigan and New Jersey were striking PAC successes.

The 1950 Michigan elections were an important test of the recently-consummated PAC–Democratic alliance, which survived the victorious 1948 campaign. However, could such a fragile alliance weather the promised political storms of 1950?

Since so much depended upon the outcome of the 1950 contest, the PAC–Democrats began the campaign early in 1949. By September, 1949, the state Democratic chairman could boast that county campaign committees had been formed in thirty-three Michigan counties, counties

27. Toledano, pp. 92–93. Kornitzer, pp. 182–87.
28. Analysis of State Results, n.d. (1950), Folder 6–3–4, Box 3, Series 6, Americans for Democratic Action Papers, WSHS.

that held over eighty-one per cent of the state's voters.[29] The establishment of such county committees, an activity hardly worth mention in most states, was particularly important in Michigan, where the PAC–liberal elements in the Democratic party were fighting to retain their tenuous control of the state organization. Thirty-three county committees pledged to the PAC–Democrats would help their cause at the state convention.[30] Organizing county committees, however, was but the first step.

The next step for the alliance was to win enough precinct delegate contests to control the state convention. This part of the alliance's plan proved to be more difficult than anticipated because of the determined opposition of the old guard–Teamsters' Union. Fortunately for the liberal alliance, the number of UAW–CIO delegates was sufficient to keep the resurgent old guard under control at the district and state Democratic conventions.[31]

While the PAC and its allies were battling to retain control of the Michigan party, the state PAC chairman, August Scholle, was beginning to plan for November. Scholle first had to find a solution to the persistent racial problem in Detroit; specifically, some formula to keep CIO members in line when the opposition resorted to racial propaganda. Both in 1945 and 1949, strong PAC candidates had been soundly defeated by racist campaigns that drew attention to the CIO's liberal stance on civil rights. Although such a campaign inevitably pulled the Negro vote into the PAC camp, it also pushed the more important CIO–Polish vote toward the enemy. When Scholle's problem came to the attention of the national CIO–PAC, its officers, for once, were as perplexed as Scholle.[32] The CIO–PAC answer,

29. Status of County Committee Organization, September 20, 1949, PAC 1949 Folder, Box 105, Michigan AFL–CIO Papers, ALH.

30. Calkins, pp. 120–23.

31. Ibid.

32. While the CIO–PAC and liberal elements (the ADA and others) had firm control of the Michigan Democratic party, the Michigan AFL–LLPE remained aloof from such practical politics. The state LLPE set up its own separate organization at the state, the congressional district, and the local union level. See, Suggested Method of Organization of

when it came, was an excellent example of both the strongest and weakest points of PAC political thinking.

While the Michigan CIO had been immersed in the practical task of controlling a party, many of the PAC's national leaders were still refighting the battles of 1944. Thus, when Scholle's very practical problem came to their attention, they reacted with the liberal rhetoric of Sidney Hillman. When George L-P Weaver, the CIO's expert on racial matters, replied to Scholle, the best advice he could offer was to make a forthright stand on the principles of civil rights at the beginning of the campaign. Although a stand in favor of civil rights and open housing may have been eminently praiseworthy, it could not have eased the fears of the Polish–CIO voters. Indeed, one of the reasons the Polish vote had been so easily stampeded in the past had been Polish CIO members' fears of a PAC "sellout" in favor of Negroes. What was needed was a temporary soft-selling of the civil rights line, not a more forthright and militant civil rights stand.[33] After receiving Weaver's solution, Scholle apparently decided to ignore the whole civil rights issue during the campaign. Civil rights was a rallying cry for neither side in 1950.

Scholle's other problem was a bit more pedestrian; he had to get out the vote. In this endeavor, he fell back upon a tried PAC practice, the registration drive.

The 1950 Michigan PAC registration drive was noteworthy in at least one respect, the praise that it drew. Perhaps the most impressive compliment paid to the PAC in 1950 was a comment of G. Mennen Williams, the Democratic governor. When Williams, the candidate of the PAC–

Congressional District Leagues, n.d. (1950), LLPE 1950 Folder, Box 200, Michigan AFL–CIO Papers, ALH.

On the Scholle problem see August Kroll to Jack Kroll, April 17, 1950, CIO–PAC Miscellaneous Folder, Box 203, CIO Secretary–Treasurer's Papers, ALH.

33. Weaver's reply, completely naive as it was, would have been an excellent example of the "union voter" rhetoric of the PAC during its Sidney Hillman period. It is somewhat unusual to see such naivete during the tenure of the practical Jack Kroll.

George L–P Weaver to Tilford E. Dudley, May 11, 1950, CIO–PAC Miscellaneous Folder, CIO Secretary–Treasurer's Papers, ALH.

liberal bloc both in 1948 and 1950, was looking for voter registration lists in June, 1950, he wrote to the PAC, not the Wayne County Clerk. He noted that the Michigan PAC probably had the most accurate list of voters in the state of Michigan.[34] Although compiling an accurate registration list was but one aspect of a registration drive, the governor's comment was indicative of the respect that Michigan Democrats had for the thorough PAC registration program.

When the test of PAC registration and the liberal alliance finally came in November, the Democrats won a surprising victory in Michigan. Though a Democratic gubernatorial victory was not unusual in Michigan (Democratic governors had won in 1932, 1936, 1940, and 1948), the election of G. Mennen Williams in 1950 marked the first off-year victory of a Democrat in decades. Moreover, in a year when such Democratic–PAC candidates as Douglas and Ferguson were losing, the Michigan PAC managed to sweep the entire Democratic congressional delegation back into office.[35]

To some extent, the Michigan pattern was repeated in New Jersey. In the ADA's analysis of the 1950 elections, New Jersey was an example of the successful aspects of the campaign. As in Michigan, the entire Democratic congressional delegation returned to office. Moreover, since 1948 had been marked by an unusually high Democratic vote in New Jersey, the retention of the entire slate in an off-year was a remarkable achievement.[36] However, there was some question as to the role of the PAC in New Jersey's Democratic triumph.

34. G. Mennen Williams to Barney Hopkins, June 8, 1950, PAC 1950 Folder, Box 106, Michigan AFL–CIO Papers, ALH.
Williams's confidence in the PAC would have been bolstered even further if he had known the scope of the PAC commitment in Wayne County. Not counting the thousand-odd precinct captains, the PAC had over 1,300 precinct workers active in Detroit's approximately 950 precincts. See, Barney Hopkins to Jack Kroll, November 3, 1950, PAC 1950 Folder, Box 106, Michigan AFL–CIO Papers, ALH.
35. Calkins, pp. 129–45.
36. Analysis of State Results, n.d. (1950), Folder 6–3–4, Box 3, Series 6, Americans for Democratic Action Papers, WSHS.

The New Jersey CIO–PAC began its campaign in late 1949, when state CIO leaders decided to concentrate PAC efforts in eight (first, second, fourth, and tenth through fourteenth) congressional districts. Yet, before the drive had even emerged from the planning stages, the state CIO discovered that its major problem would be registration. When 1950 census figures were checked against registration rolls, it became clear that voter registration was abnormally low. Over thirty per cent of New Jersey's adult population was unregistered; almost fifty per cent of the state's CIO members were among these.[37] A registration drive was the first order of business.

Starting in February, 1950, and continuing until late September, the CIO-sponsored drive netted some impressive results. First, the statewide percentage of unregistered voters declined from over thirty-two per cent to less than thirty per cent. More importantly, the percentage of CIO members who remained unregistered declined from almost fifty per cent to under forty per cent in most areas, and to less than thirty per cent in certain key congressional districts. Although over thirty per cent of the CIO electorate remained ineligible even after the drive, a good deal of the blame could go to the quadrennial purge of inactive voters. In many areas, almost as many voters were declared ineligible due to their failure to use their franchise since 1946 as were newly registered by the PAC. A number of CIO members who the PAC had assumed to be registered were declared ineligible by election boards for just such a reason.[38] Even with such oversights, however, the PAC registration drive had proven to be successful.

The next step of the New Jersey campaign was to convince CIO members to vote for PAC-endorsed candidates. At this stage, the state PAC judiciously decided to run a campaign that would stimulate CIO members while not arousing non-CIO members. The idea behind such a decision was that, in many areas, PAC endorsement would do more to provoke voters against an endorsed candidate than

37. The Effectiveness of PAC in New Jersey, January 8, 1951, pp. 1–5. A copy of this report, authored by the New Jersey CIO, was borrowed from Professor Maurice Neufeld of the New York State School of Industrial and Labor Relations, Ithaca, N.Y.

38. Ibid., pp. 5–16.

to help him. Thus, most of the direct PAC campaigning was done through the mail. At least four mailings were sent to each registered CIO member. Three of the mailings were various PAC pamphlets emphasizing everything from the negative voting records of Republican congressmen to the massive amount of money being spent by Republican candidates. The final mailing was simply a penny postcard that displayed the name and the picture of the PAC–endorsee. In heavily Negro districts, a fifth mailing was directed to Negro voters that emphasized civil rights issues. The mail campaign was backed by a series of nonpartisan radio announcements by movie stars urging people to vote. The PAC itself made only one radio announcement, a call by the PAC chairman for a strong liberal vote.[39] All in all, it was a very cautious campaign publicly.

While the mail and radio campaign was in progress, the PAC organized blockworkers in every voting district that had large numbers of CIO members. One blockworker was assigned fifty CIO members, and that blockworker's job was to make sure that every eligible voter in each CIO member's family voted on November 7. No blockworker would be paid until he, or she, presented signed statements from the Democratic poll-watcher noting that all CIO members assigned to the worker had voted. It was a somewhat cumbersome process, but it guaranteed that most CIO members would vote.[40] The results made all the extra bother seem well worthwhile.

As previously noted, all of the incumbent Democrats supported by the PAC were reelected. In the three marginal Republican districts where the PAC was also active, the Democratic candidates managed to narrow the Republican plurality, although not enough to ensure election. The most impressive result of the election was both the increased CIO vote and the increased Democratic percentage in wards where CIO members comprised a sizeable majority of the electorate. For example, in the heavily-CIO first, ninth, and thirteenth wards in Newark, blockworkers managed to turn out a CIO vote (a figure that included CIO relatives) that ranged from ninety-four to 144 per cent of the CIO member registration figure. This was a

39. Ibid., pp. 17–18.
40. Ibid., pp. 19–21.

substantial increase over the estimated 1948 turnout. Moreover, in the same three wards, the Democratic percentage rose from seventy-one per cent in 1948 to over seventy-five per cent in 1950. The rise in the first ward was even more dramatic. There, the Democratic percentage rose from a 1948 figure of sixty-six per cent to a 1950 total of over eighty-five per cent. Similar tales were told in the other large CIO cities, such as Trenton and Jersey City. The CIO vote was up, as was the Democratic total. At the same time, the urban vote in nonlabor wards and the rural vote were decidedly more Republican than in 1948. As the New Jersey CIO noted, "the election results confirm the effectiveness of PAC." [41] Unfortunately, results in other states outweighed such outstanding successes.

In Indiana, where the PAC had proudly captured the Third Congressional District in 1948, Congressman Thurman Crook blamed his 1950 defeat on "labor apathy." [42] Since the third district had only one strongly Democratic industrial county, St. Joseph County, Crook had to carry that county by a huge margin in order to make up for the heavily Republican vote in the rural areas. In 1948, Crook, with impressive PAC support, carried St. Joseph County by over 13,000 votes, a total that allowed him to capture the district by a 7,000 vote margin. Crook carried St. Joseph County by only 1,000 votes in 1950, a margin that doomed him to a 10,000 vote defeat.[43] As a matter of fact, the number of CIO union members in St. Joseph County (42,000) was actually greater than Crook's county total (39,000).[44] In both of the Indiana congressional districts where the CIO had a substantial portion of the electorate (the first and third districts), the story was the same. The Democratic vote declined by from six to eight per cent, a decline that was sufficient to push such marginal districts as the third into the Republican camp.[45]

41. Ibid., pp. 22–45.
42. Paul C. Bartholomew, *The Indiana Third Congressional District, A Political History* (South Bend: Notre Dame University Press, 1970), pp. 171–77.
43. Ibid.
44. Loren Houser to Herbert McCreedy, April 18, 1954, Folder 12, Box 53, Michigan AFL–CIO Papers, ALH.
45. Richard Scammon, *America Votes* (New York: The Macmillan Co., 1956), p. 98.

The ADA's analysis of the 1950 elections was also barren of praise for PAC. It noted that of the thirty seats lost by the Democrats in 1950, almost half were lost in the strong labor states of Illinois, Ohio, and Indiana. Interestingly enough, about half of the districts lost in these three states were lost in areas with strong labor concentrations. For example, the Democrats lost races in Canton, Cincinnati, and Toledo, Ohio, all areas of high labor (and CIO) concentrations. The same could be said for the seats lost in Chicago, Illinois and South Bend and Indianapolis, Indiana. Yet, since the PAC almost invariably backed liberals, could the 1950 election be viewed as a purge of liberals? The ADA report concluded quite the opposite. Of the nineteen Democrats who had consistently and vociferously opposed the McCaren–Wood bill (a key anti-Communist measure whose opponents were unanimously viewed as liberals), only four had been defeated at the polls. However, the report continued, the sweeping nature of Republican successes in Ohio, California, and Indiana made the outlook for future elections particularly doubtful.[46] In short, though the Democratic reverses were confined neither to marginal Democratic labor districts, nor to liberal Democrats' districts, failures in Ohio and elsewhere indicated that a good deal more work had to be done by both liberals and labor for the coming elections. The outlook was not bright.

One last factor remained to be considered as far as the 1950 election was concerned. Although the PAC and the ADA had scrupulously avoided mentioning the fact, there was a war in progress. What effect did Korea have on the CIO's electoral efforts?

Considering that the election took place during a period of United Nations offensives in Korea, it would be hard to analyze the impact of the fighting on the elections. After all, the series of reverses that marked the beginning of

46. The information used in this paragraph was taken from three ADA reports on the 1950 elections. They were as follows: House of Representatives, 1950 Election Analysis, December 7, 1950; Analysis of State Results, n.d. (1950); Analysis of the 1950 Federal Elections, n.d. (1950), Folder 6–3–4, Box 3, Series 6, Americans for Democratic Action Papers, WSHS.

Chinese intervention during early 1951 had not yet occurred. The United States was winning the war in early
November, yet, only months before, the allied forces had
been huddling around Pusan on the edge of total defeat.[47]
What would the voter remember, Pusan or the Inchon
landing?

Samuel Lubell, in his study of American voting trends,
came to the conclusion that the war had a profound effect
on certain voting groups. For instance, among a number
of isolationist midwestern farmers, the war seemed to have
reinforced the latent belief that the Democratic party invariably brought war. A number of farmers interviewed
by Lubell said that they had voted for Truman in 1948,
but that the war had made them Republicans. As far as the
unionist was concerned, however, Lubell provided no specific data.[48] As campaigns as diverse as the Taft purge and
the New Jersey drive indicated, the 1950 elections in
unionist areas were decided by a number of factors. The
war was but one of these factors; it was not the most decisive issue.

What, then, was the PAC's role in the 1950 elections?
In a phrase, it was almost victorious. Although far too
many key candidates had suffered defeat to call it a victory,
the PAC defeat was neither as universal, nor as resounding, as that of 1946. Indeed, there were a number of bright
spots for the PAC in 1950.

The PAC's role in Michigan and New Jersey was especially noteworthy. In Michigan, the PAC won an important
double battle. Although it had not been able to solve its
persistent Detroit race problem, it had strengthened its
hold on the state Democratic party and had elected the first
off-year Democratic governor in decades. In New Jersey,
the PAC had successfully pioneered political techniques
that promised to overcome some of the PAC's most pressing problems. As the New Jersey PAC had demonstrated,
the CIO could carry on a successful campaign without all
of the noise and publicity it had used in the past. The

47. For a summary of American actions in Korea during
1950 see John W. Spanier, *The Truman–MacArthur Controversy and the Korean War* (New York: W. W. Norton and
Co., 1965), pp. 65–134.
48. Lubell, pp. 160–61, 177–78, 260–61.

quiet campaign had the added advantage of not offending the independent voter who had come to fear the machinations of big labor. It promised to be the PAC's weapon of the future. In the meantime, the Political Action Committee would have to settle for being almost victorious.

8

Defeat Becomes a Habit: 1952

Although the CIO had ended the 1950 electoral campaign on a note of optimism, this optimism would prove to be inappropriate for the coming battle with General Dwight D. Eisenhower. The Political Action Committee had developed an excellent political machine in its nine years of existence, but the machine would be no match for the charismatic Eisenhower. In previous presidential contests, the PAC had the incumbent, and the charisma, on its side. In 1952, the CIO Political Action Committee would discover that it had backed a losing presidential candidate for the first time in its brief history.

Late in 1951, an introspective PAC looked back on its first eight years. Noting the accomplishments and failures of the period, the PAC staff drew an interesting picture of the exact state of the CIO's political committee in the new decade. Their findings, published in a confidential report, filled twenty-four pages and covered five major points.

The first observation that the CIO–PAC staff made concerning the status of PAC was a note on precinct level organization. Admitting that complete nationwide precinct organization was beyond the capabilities of their organization, the staff proudly declared that the PAC had managed to penetrate most of the nation's industrial precincts. Assuming that at least four workers were required for each electoral precinct, PAC had recruited blockworkers from among the CIO membership at almost every local and regional union meeting. By 1951, such cities as Detroit could boast that they had fulfilled their four blockworkers per precinct obligation.[1] The hoped-for network of CIO

1. Confidential Report of the CIO–PAC for 1951, Copy of James Carey, n.d. (1951), p. 1, Political Action Committee 1950–1951 Folder, Box 85, CIO Secretary–Treasurer's Papers, ALH.

blockworkers had already begun to spread throughout the industrial strongholds of the nation.

While PAC representatives were busily recruiting block-workers, the national office had initiated a number of organizational innovations within its own bailiwick. The PAC comptroller's office, the personal domain of George Rettinger, had grown from the makeshift operation of the 1944 campaign to a full-time service employing three staff members. Constantly working over PAC contributions and expenditures, Rettinger and his assistants were trying to systematize the national PAC's financial role in the hundreds of local CIO political campaigns. Sidney Hillman's staff had only to divide the substantial endowment of the 1944 PAC (the 700,000 dollar donation of the CIO unions) into parcels that PAC projects could utilize. The comptroller of 1951 had both to campaign for union contributions (including the ever-present dollar drives) and to dole out his gleanings to the most worthy of the potential PAC efforts.[2] It was not a glamorous job, but it was the key to all of the CIO–PAC's activities.

The PAC Research Department was another departure from 1944 practice. Whereas Sidney Hillman felt that a man like Thomas Amlie could handle the PAC's research chores, Jack Kroll's PAC had a full-time staff whose duties ranged from the compilation of voting statistics to the selection of campaign propaganda. The prime job of the Research Department staff was to aid the PAC in determining where, when, and how the CIO could best support its political allies. Raw material such as CIO membership by voting units, election returns by precinct, and surveys of public opinion were collated so as to give Kroll and his assistants a single picture of where the CIO voter lived, how he voted, and when he would respond to what political pitch. Although the Research Department did not determine where the PAC would campaign, its reports helped shape the content and concentrations of a CIO campaign. Even during such nonelection years as 1951, the five members of the department were collecting and collating voting statistics from previous years as well as keeping close tabs on the doings of Congress.[3] While the main Political Ac-

2. Ibid., p. 3.
3. Ibid., pp. 3–8.

tion Committee was in a state of off-year hibernation, the research staff collected the raw data that would guide the Committee once the electoral effort was underway.

The final administrative department that had undergone extensive changes since the Hillman days was the Public Relations and Publications Department. Originally the realm of Joseph Gaer, the department had taken on a number of new duties since Gaer had single-handedly written most of the PAC's press releases. In 1951 alone, the PAC public relations staff had distributed 1,948,000 speeches, broadsides, and press releases to both CIO officials and members of Congress who had sought CIO aid on specific problems. Moreover, the department had become a magazine publisher, having brought out the bi-weekly *Political Action of the Week,* which it distributed to over 12,000 local unions and to congressmen and libraries. At the same time that the Public Relations Department worked on these projects, it also made certain that every state and national convention of a CIO union would be fully supplied with PAC publications and exhibits. Everything from maintaining a news service for CIO and affiliated newspapers to devising new PAC pamphlets was the special realm of the Public Relations and Publications Department, which had a permanent staff of but two people.[4]

As the precinct organizing drive and PAC reorganization was proceeding, the Political Action Committee had also begun to work successfully with minority groups by 1951. In 1944, Henry Lee Moon was the PAC's one and only contact with the black and minority community. Seven years later, the PAC had organized minority group electoral operations in seven states. In Indiana, the black community, organized by the PAC, had proven to be an important supplement to the CIO contingent in the 1950 elections.[5] The CIO–PAC looked forward to even closer political cooperation between blacks and labor in the future.

4. Ibid., pp. 8–9. The Public Relations Department had to prepare speeches for incumbent congressmen on twenty-six occasions in 1951. That is an interesting comment on the respect that those congressmen held for the PAC.

5. Ibid., pp. 10–11. Work with minority groups gave the PAC electoral strength in the Indianapolis area that it would not have had if it had worked only with CIO members.

Although establishing closer relations with various minority groups had been one of PAC's prime goals during 1951, that operation had not obscured CIO–PAC participation in a number of special congressional elections. Of the four special elections in which the PAC participated in 1951, two (West Virginia's fifth and Pennsylvania's thirty-third district) were won by Democrats with strong CIO backing and a third (Texas' thirteenth) resulted in a working agreement between PAC and the winning candidate.[6] The CIO–PAC had established an enviable (and hard to duplicate) track record in 1951.

The year 1951 had also marked the beginning of a PAC subsidy program, whereby marginal CIO districts (districts with only a small number of CIO voters) were reimbursed by the national PAC for their political activities. The idea behind the program was that a PAC registration and propaganda campaign might be quite effective even in a non-CIO area if some means could be found to fund the drive. A marginal district might have the raw manpower, but it would not have enough money to keep paid workers in the field. The solution would be to send national PAC organizers and cash into the marginal district to direct and pay for such a program.[7] Although it had not yet been tested, such a program might prove very successful in 1952.

The CIO–PAC in 1951, then, was a political action organization that seemed trimmed and ready for the campaign ahead. The first step toward preparation for that campaign was necessarily an assessment of the task.

Late in 1951, the PAC's Research Department prepared its first estimate of the political situation for the coming year. Because 1952 would be a presidential campaign year, the PAC's task was somewhat complicated. Not only would the Committee be called upon to deliver the labor vote in the various congressional and senatorial races, but it would also have to invest time and money in promoting a strong Democratic presidential vote in the wards and precincts where it was active. As the Research Department noted,

6. Ibid., pp. 11–13. The key loss occurred in St. Louis, where the PAC was feuding with the local Democratic machine.

7. Ibid., pp. 14–17.

there were nine states in which the Republicans would surely concentrate their efforts in 1952; all nine were states with strong CIO concentrations.[8] If the PAC were to repeat its 1948 victory, it would have to do everything in its power to deliver the labor vote in those crucial nine states.

Delivering the labor vote to an unnamed Democratic presidential nominee may have been one of PAC's chief goals for 1952, but of equal importance was the necessity of keeping Congress in friendly hands. In those same crucial states, six senators who were seeking reelection were considered vulnerable. Among these were such antilabor men as Ohio's John Bricker, Wisconsin's Joseph McCarthy, and California's William Knowland. If the CIO could but replace these three, the Senate would be much more inclined to consider such prolabor legislation as revision of Taft–Hartley. Moreover, the CIO–PAC would have certain advantages in purging the three. All three had been elected by slim margins, margins that could be easily changed in favor of the Democrats. Each came from states with significant numbers of labor voters. Indeed, California, Ohio, and Wisconsin were all strongholds of organized labor. Finally, a strong Democratic presidential contender could easily carry the three states; Roosevelt and Truman had both won them.[9]

In the campaign to keep Democratic control of the House of Representatives, the CIO–PAC task would not be so easy as it had been in previous elections. In Pennsylvania and California, for instance, extensive reapportionment following the 1950 census had weakened a number of traditionally Democratic districts. As the Research Department noted, Pennsylvania reapportionment would be done by an overwhelmingly Republican legislature. There, the question would be "not whether the Democrats will lose, but how much they lose."[10] The Democrats' crucial

8. Elections 1952, November, 1951, Folder 13, Box 38, Michigan AFL–CIO Papers, ALH. The states were California, Illinois, Michigan, Massachusetts, New Jersey, New York, Ohio, Pennsylvania, and Texas.

9. Ibid. The CIO was also hopeful of defeating Senator Edward Martin of Pennsylvania and retaining Blair Moody in Michigan. Both were considered to be defeatable.

10. Ibid.

losses in 1950 state elections were coming back to haunt the PAC in 1952. Before the Political Action Committee would be allowed the privilege of debating its chances in the various House races, however, it would have to face the problem of choosing the Democratic standard bearer.

Early in 1952, the leading candidates for the Democratic presidential nomination began courting organized labor, which they believed might well hold the key to what promised to be an extremely close race. By May, Senator Estes Kefauver's Midwest coordinator was working as hard as he could to deliver the key Michigan PAC–Democratic delegation to the Kefauver camp. Significantly, Kefauver's coordinator operated out of the law offices of the firm of Griffiths, Williams, and Griffiths, a firm controlled by PAC candidates Martha Griffiths (Democratic nominee in the Seventeenth Congressional District) and G. Mennen Williams (the incumbent governor).[11] Although Kefauver appeared to be the early favorite, other candidates also tried to swing the Michigan PAC into their respective camps.[12] Franklin D. Roosevelt, Jr., long a favorite of the CIO, used his influence in behalf of the candidacy of Averell Harriman, an honored diplomat who had served as special assistant to President Truman. Senator Robert Kerr of Oklahoma, another of the candidates, made his plea to the PAC as a "friend of labor." To prove his labor sympathies, Kerr accompanied his plea with the endorsement of the president of the Oklahoma State Federation of Labor.[13] Yet, while the various candidates pleaded with PAC, both CIO President Philip Murray and PAC Director Jack Kroll had apparently decided to back a completely different man.

David McDonald, the secretary–treasurer of both PAC

11. Hicks Griffiths to Barney Hopkins, June 12, 1952, CIO–PAC Ohio Folder, CIO Secretary–Treasurer's Papers, ALH.

12. Kefauver won all the Democratic primaries in 1952. Perhaps his best performance was in New Hampshire, where he soundly defeated President Truman. For a good, although pro-Stevenson, view of the 1952 campaign see, Kenneth S. Davis, *A Prophet in His Own Country* (Garden City: Doubleday and Co., 1957), pp. 380–96.

13. Franklin D. Roosevelt, Jr. to Barney Hopkins, May 23, 1952; Robert S. Kerr to Barney Hopkins, June 5, 1952, PAC 1952 Folder, Box 108, Michigan AFL–CIO Papers, ALH.

and the powerful United Steel Workers of America, later recalled that Kroll and Murray both had jumped on the bandwagon of Adlai Stevenson, the governor of Illinois.[14] Although Stevenson was not a declared candidate, a number of prominent Democrats, including Congressman Sidney Yates of Illinois; Governor Henry Schricker of Indiana, and virtually the entire executive board of the Independent Voters of Illinois, the Americans for Democratic Action affiliate in that state, had formed a Draft Stevenson Committee early in 1952. The exact role of the CIO in the draft of Stevenson is uncertain, but both Kroll and Murray were known to be Stevenson sympathizers. Yet, according to Walter Johnson, the chairman of the Draft Stevenson Committee, the only labor leaders who were really deeply involved in the early Stevenson campaign were not the two CIO leaders, but rather David Dubinsky of the AFL International Ladies Garment Workers' Union and Alex Rose of the Millinery Workers.[15] Although Dubinsky and Rose, the leaders of New York's Liberal party and antagonists of Sidney Hillman in 1944, were the earliest labor leaders on the Stevenson bandwagon, Kroll of the PAC was instrumental in blocking a Harriman–Kefauver attempt to bundle up labor's votes into an anti-Stevenson coalition. It was Kroll, not Dubinsky, who convinced the numerous labor delegates at the Democratic National Convention that Stevenson was indeed a prolabor candidate.[16] Regardless of Kroll's role in deciding the Stevenson nomination, a number of key CIO leaders were clearly dissatisfied with Adlai Stevenson.

Perhaps the chief anti-Stevenson voice in CIO–PAC circles was that of David McDonald. McDonald, a college graduate and a power in the United Steel Workers of America, found the urbane charms of Averell Harriman infinitely preferable to the personality of the governor of

14. David McDonald, *Union Man* (New York: E. P. Dutton and Co., 1969), p. 225.

15. Walter Johnson, *How We Drafted Stevenson* (New York: Alfred A. Knopf, 1955), pp. 18–23, 168–69. Johnson, as chairman of the Draft Stevenson Committee, bent over backwards to disprove any charges that the Stevenson nomination was masterminded by any political group or labor organization.

16. Ibid., pp. 124, 147.

Illinois. Whereas disagreement among CIO leaders concerning the choice of candidates was not uncommon, never before had such a prominent figure as McDonald differed with the PAC's choice. McDonald was especially important because he personally controlled the Steel Workers' political action program.[17] Inasmuch as the Steel Workers were responsible for getting out the CIO vote in such important Pennsylvania cities as Pittsburgh, Bethlehem, and Philadelphia, McDonald's opposition to, or even lukewarm acceptance of, the CIO presidential choice could have serious consequences for PAC hopes.

Although McDonald's was the loudest voice raised in opposition to Stevenson, other labor leaders also were unhappy with the party's choice. By 1952, CIO leaders expected their candidates to be opposed to Taft-Hartley as a matter of course. Stevenson, on the other hand, came quite close to endorsing the hated labor law. Yes, he had stated, he was against the ban on closed shops, but he was for some restriction on the unfair practices of unions. Labor leaders could hardly believe their ears—perhaps McDonald was right.[18]

While the CIO and the Democrats were still arguing over the choice of a presidential candidate, the Republican bandwagon had rolled into Chicago. There, a partial rematch of the 1948 contest pitted conservative Senator Robert Taft of Ohio against the political unknown who had inherited the Dewey faction of the party. The unknown was none other than General Dwight D. Eisenhower, a war hero who almost had been nominated by the Democrats in 1948. As the Eisenhower train pulled into the Windy City, Taft's fortunes seemed to be at a high point. Having won the bulk of the state primary contests (the

17. McDonald, p. 225.
18. In its report for 1951, the CIO–PAC emphasized that all Pennsylvania (and especially Pittsburgh) elections were left to the jurisdiction of the Steel Workers. See, Confidential Report of the CIO–PAC for 1951. Copy of James Carey, n.d. (1951), p. 12, Political Action Committee 1950–1951 Folder, Box 85, CIO Secretary-Treasurer's Papers, ALH.

For Stevenson's often contradictory comments on Taft-Hartley and their effect on labor leaders see Barton Bernstein, "The Election of 1952," Schlesinger, Israel, Hansen, Vol. 4, pp. 3251–52.

General had won only New Jersey and Oregon), Taft entered the convention with 530 delegates pledged to his cause; only 604 were needed for victory. Eisenhower, by contrast, had but 427 votes, and twenty-one of these were contested. Yet, even with such a seemingly insurmountable lead, Taft was the loser. The twin keys to his loss were the contested delegations of Georgia, Louisiana, and Texas and the political expertise of Ike's floor managers, New Hampshire Governor Sherman Adams and Massachusetts Senator Henry Cabot Lodge.[19]

Eisenhower, the people's man, was running a rather unusual popular campaign by this time. Neglecting the primaries, he had allowed most primary states to fall to his opponents by default. For a man whose memoirs were filled with pious references to democracy, his 1952 hopes lay primarily with the delegates chosen by strictly-controlled state party conventions. The climax came as the convention voted on his "Fair Play" amendment to the rules, an amendment that forbade the contested (Taft) delegations from voting upon their own credentials. Once the Adams–Lodge duo had drummed up enough backroom support for the amendment to ram it through the convention, a substantial portion of the Taft vote was erased. Thus, when the convention finally got around to judging the southern delegations, Eisenhower's forces controlled the floor. The General easily won the first round, but his victory was not the sort to endear him to democrats.[20]

The actual balloting came as an anticlimax. Eisenhower had opened up a 595 to 500 vote lead on the first ballot. The only drama of the convention came as Minnesota Senator Edward Thye transformed this margin into a majority by climatically switching his state's nineteen Stassen votes to Eisenhower. Ike tossed the Taft conservatives a bone by selecting conservative Senator Richard Nixon, the PAC's old California nemesis, as his running mate.[21]

19. Dwight D. Eisenhower, *The White House Years,* Vol. 1: *Mandate for Change* (Garden City: Doubleday and Co., 1963), 36–43.

20. Ibid., p. 43.

21. Ibid., pp. 43–47.

With an ideologically balanced ticket, the Republicans launched their campaign.

After the July nominations of Stevenson and Eisenhower, CIO–PAC leaders began to prepare for the campaign in earnest. The first fruit of their labors was the *1952 Speaker's Book of Facts.*

The *Speaker's Book* was the Political Action Committee's attempt to reduce the often complex issues of the campaign into a series of easily understood PAC policy positions. Every policy statement was accompanied by a series of arguments whereby the CIO blockworker could convince the labor voter of the rightness of the PAC position. In essence, the *Speaker's Book* concentrated upon four basic areas: the candidates and their respective platforms, foreign policy, domestic policy, and the McCarthy menace.

After drawing a glowing portrait of Governor Stevenson, the *Speaker's Book* wholeheartedly condemned General Eisenhower as a political incompetent. Although nobody would question the General's sincerity, or his obvious military qualifications, the PAC was quick to point out that Eisenhower had been trained as an army officer, not a politician. Moreover, his decades of service to the country as a military man had succeeded in cutting him off from the political realities of the postdepression United States. Indeed, had it not been the General himself who had remarked in 1948 that any man who had spent his entire adult life in the military had no competence to serve in the White House? [22] This was just the beginning of the PAC barrage against the Republican candidate.

As if to prove the political naivete of the General, the *Speaker's Book* quoted a number of his public remarks on controversial issues. It was with obvious relish that the PAC reprinted the classic Eisenhower comment on social security (a "mule's sort of heaven"), especially because

22. CIO, *A Speaker's Book of Facts, 1952* (Washington, D.C.: CIO–PAC, 1952), pp. 1–20, 25–26. The statement concerning an officer being unqualified for the presidency was taken from a 1948 Eisenhower letter to a Mr. Kindler in which Eisenhower disclaimed any desire or qualification to run for the presidential nomination. See, *New York Times,* January 24, 1948, p. 2.

it could be pointed out that his benefits under the army's retirement system were infinitely superior to even the best enjoyed by citizens on social security. On the controversial tidelands oil issue, the PAC could gleefully report that Eisenhower had favored giving the oil lands to the states, hardly a position that would win him votes in northern industrial cities. Finally, concerning Taft–Hartley, the General had gone on record as favoring the Taft–Hartley Act because it had given labor relations a "better climate." [23] Almost every one of Eisenhower's remarks seemed to have been potentially offensive to one voting bloc or another. It was the PAC's job to get the various blocs outraged at the General.

When it came to foreign policy, the CIO–PAC was treading on dangerous ground. In trying to sell the people a Democratic presidential candidate on the basis of the incumbent's record, it had to take cognizance of the fact that Truman was under fire for a number of alleged security lapses within his State Department as well as for the firing of a nationally-popular military leader. Moreover, Truman was a war President, a man held responsible for getting the country into an unpopular and seemingly interminable war.[24] Truman's was a hard record to defend in the political climate of 1952.

Although most of the charges against the Truman Administration would later be proven groundless, the PAC *Speaker's Book* repeated all the arguments against the anti-Truman charges almost as a matter of course. Truman was portrayed as the man who had single-handedly saved Greece, Turkey, and western Europe. He was the President who had made the North Atlantic Treaty Organization work. Under his regime, the Communists had been purged from the labor unions and other critical positions. His was the Administration that had pushed through the Marshall Plan, and his was the Administration that had stemmed

23. *Speaker's Book,* pp. 29, 30, 34. *New York Times,* March 24, 1950, p. 4. *Washington Post,* June 19, 1952, p. 2; June 14, 1952, p. 7.

24. Perhaps one of the best sources on this phase of the Truman Administration would be Spanier, *The Truman–Mac-Arthur Controversy and the Korean War.*

the Communist menace in Korea.[25] As the PAC portrayed him, President Harry S. Truman was the very epitome of American anticommunism. It was Truman, not the Republicans, who could rest on his laurels.

When the *Speaker's Book* turned to domestic policy, it began to deal with the favorite issues of the CIO. Again, the PAC found itself defending a number of Administration failures. The inflation that accompanied the Korean War, the high taxes that paid for the war, and the economic squeeze in which the average worker found himself, were all blamed on Truman in one way or another. As with foreign policy, the PAC had an answer for each of the Republican charges.

Inflation was the result of congressional activity, not presidential policy, noted the *Speaker's Book*. Starting with the Taft Amendment to the 1946 Price Control Extension Act, an amendment that had cut the heart out of price control, Congress had consistently opposed effective price control legislation.[26] When the PAC spoke of effective price control legislation, it meant nothing less than a return to the rigid standards of World War Two. Therefore, such congressional measures as the Defense Production Act of 1950, which allowed neither policing of commodity speculation nor effective food price controls, were simply not acceptable to the CIO–PAC.[27] When Congress amended the Defense Production Act in 1951 and 1952, its efforts, in the eyes of CIO–PAC, were even less acceptable than the 1950 measure. For instance, the 1951 measure reinstituted the Taft Amendment policy of allowing manufacturers to raise prices in direct relation to increased costs, costs being defined so broadly as to include plant expansion. The 1952 measure actually lifted controls on a number of agricultural products as well as almost all credit transactions. In the PAC's words, what was needed was "honest

25. On the Communist controversy and the Truman Administration, see Earl Latham, *The Communist Controversy in Washington* (Cambridge: Harvard University Press, 1966).

26. The Taft Amendment essentially allowed business to raise its prices in proportion to any increase in costs. See U.S., *Statutes at Large,* 60, Part 1, 664–78.

27. For the complete provisions of the price control section of the 1950 Defense Production Act, see U.S., *Statutes at Large,* 64, 803–12.

and equitable price controls," controls that were clearly understandable and took into account the problems of quality control.[28]

The second domestic issue that the Political Action Committee used to berate the Republicans and Congress was taxes. The PAC's argument was not that taxes were too high (even though they stood at record levels in 1952), but rather that Congress, led by the conservative coalition of Republicans and Dixiecrats, was taxing the American people in the wrong way.[29] One of the PAC's prime arguments on the tax issue was that while millions of dollars in revenue were escaping due to tax loopholes, Congress was talking not of closing the loopholes, but rather of shifting more of the burden of taxation upon lower income groups. The key exhibit in the PAC case was the conservative call for a national sales tax. When southern senators Henry Byrd and Walter George called for a sales tax, the PAC eagerly reprinted the call in its *Speaker's Book*.[30] CIO–PAC reprinted the sales tax proposal as a preview of what taxation might be like under a Republican regime.[31] Blaming the Republicans for the sales tax may not have been fair, but the move had political potential.

The final issue that PAC chose to dramatize was the so-called McCarthy menace. Ever since a prolabor senator had been defeated by Joseph McCarthy in 1946, the CIO had actively been working for McCarthy's defeat. When McCarthy discovered communism in 1950, he was no immediate threat to the CIO. However, when his charges seemed to loose a wave of national hysteria concerning domestic threats to the nation's security, a wave that threatened to engulf both organized labor and the Demo-

28. U.S., *Statutes at Large*, 65, pp. 134–38; 66, pp. 296–306. *Speaker's Book*, p. 216. Inflation was a very real issue in 1952 as the Consumer Price Index indicated. The Index, which had stood at an inflated 139.5 in 1946, was up almost forty-two per cent by early 1952. The April, 1952, Index stood at 189.6. See, U.S. Bureau of Labor Statistics, *Monthly Labor Review*, 74 (1952), 747.

29. *Speaker's Book*, pp. 253–58.

30. Ibid., p. 258. For the views of George and others, see *New York Times*, January 10, 1951, p. 1.

31. *Speaker's Book*, p. 253.

cratic party, the CIO launched a counteroffensive.[32] Noting McCarthy's smear tactics and continued resorts to character assassination, the *Speaker's Book* called for the Senate expulsion of Joseph McCarthy, "whose pretended crusade against subversive activities has in fact been an effort to subvert our great democratic principles." [33]

As the PAC continued to campaign on the basis of the issues set forth in the *Speaker's Book,* a number of special problems began to slow the CIO drive. By October, a note of worry began to creep into CIO–PAC correspondence. PAC problems were due to two factors: Stevenson's slipping popularity and Eisenhower's apparent capture of the female vote.

While the Adlai Stevenson of August seemed clearly superior to the blundering and often misinformed Eisenhower, the Stevenson of late October no longer appeared to be a winner. After the Republicans had talked their way out of the Nixon fund scandal, a scandal capped by the brilliant television performance of Eisenhower's young running mate, the General's campaign began to gain momentum.[34] An important factor in Eisenhower's newfound appeal was the continuing deadlock in the Korean conflict. When the war still raged on in mid-October, a number of voters apparently decided that a General was needed in the White House. The climax of this phase of the campaign was Eisenhower's October 24 Detroit speech, in which he promised to "go to Korea." [35] To the Stevenson camp, another important factor in Eisenhower's new popularity was the "egghead" campaign of the Republican party. Because the General was no match for Stevenson as a public speaker, the Republican strategy seemed to have

32. Ibid., pp. 155–57. Perhaps the best available work on labor and McCarthy is David M. Oshinsky, "Senator Joseph McCarthy and American Labor," M.S. thesis, New York State School of Industrial and Labor Relations, 1968. Although Oshinsky hits most of the key points, a number of important items, such as the CIO preparation and national distribution of a huge anti-McCarthy brochure, are overlooked. See McCarthy File, Box 4, Series B, AFL–CIO C.O.P.E. Papers, WSHS.

33. *Speaker's Book,* p. 163.

34. *New York Times,* September 24, 1952, p. 1.

35. *New York Times,* October 25, 1952, p. 1.

been to picture Stevenson as an "egghead," a professorial type who was distant from the people.[36] By early October, Eisenhower's speeches began to ridicule Stevenson's famous wit. After all, was it not improper to joke about the war, communism, inflation, and all the other serious issues of the campaign? [37] By the end of October, Adlai Stevenson was no longer the favorite.

As Stevenson's popularity slipped, Jack Kroll became increasingly concerned about PAC's ability to deliver the labor vote. In a hasty memorandum to the various state PAC headquarters, he warned that the Republicans seemed to be doing an excellent job of selling Eisenhower to America's housewives. Kroll attributed Republican successes to matronly fears of war and communism, fears he believed could be overcome by a hard sell of the campaign's economic issues. If wives were reminded that Republicanism meant unemployment and breadlines, perhaps they could be coaxed back into the Democratic fold. However, Kroll wrote, only an all-out effort by the PAC's legions of blockworkers could hope to reverse the Republican trend.[38]

On the very day that Kroll sent out his warning to the state PAC's, he also sent a confidential letter to Philip Murray. While he publicly was concerned with the female vote, privately he worried that even the male CIO vote might be in jeopardy. The heart of the letter was a market research analysis of CIO members' voting preferences in Cleveland, Philadelphia, Chicago, Detroit, Columbus, and Los Angeles. As expected, the report showed CIO voters following the PAC endorsement of Stevenson in overwhelming numbers, but that was not all. Even though the raw figures showed CIO Stevenson support at between two and three times the strength of the Eisenhower following, the private comments of the researchers revealed that such figures may have been far from accurate.[39]

36. The "egghead" campaign is emphasized by pro-Stevenson historian Eric Goldman. See Goldman, pp. 222–26.

37. Ibid. See also, Davis, pp. 424–27.

38. Jack Kroll to All State and Local PAC's, October 16, 1952, Folder 13, Box 53, Michigan AFL–CIO Papers, ALH.

39. Jack Kroll to Philip Murray, October 16, 1952, PAC Folder, Box A4–104, Philip Murray Papers, CUA.

According to those private comments, a chief factor operating to invalidate the findings was the very group pressure that the PAC counted as its secret weapon. The few unionists who did admit they favored Eisenhower always hesitated to reveal their feelings until they were certain they were not being overheard. Willard Porter, the researcher in Columbus, wrote that the Eisenhower voters he counted invariably either whispered their preference, or waited until no other workers were around. All of them had been very conscious of overt group pressure.[40] Thus, the optimistic findings shown by the raw figures could easily have been in error. Perhaps as many as ten to twenty per cent of those interviewed may have privately been Eisenhower, not Stevenson, supporters.[41]

It was hard to pinpoint the exact date when the Democrats began to sense that all was lost. President Truman, with the benefit of hindsight, felt that the trouble started with two incidents, the August move of the national campaign headquarters to Springfield, Illinois and the September refusal of Stevenson to face the Communist bogey squarely. By moving his headquarters to Illinois, Stevenson split the Democrat effort into Springfield-led and Washington-led campaigns. As far as the Communist issue was concerned, Truman believed that if it had been quashed early in the campaign, it would never have gotten out of hand.[42] Truman may have had a point.

When Governor Stevenson finally confronted the issue of creeping Communist infiltration, his address seemed too intellectual, too moderate to scotch the rumors that had been building since Yalta. While Nixon and the Republicans had been hammering on the issues of Hiss, of Yalta, and of the loss of China, Stevenson could only say that "to imply that the Government is crawling with Com-

40. Willard Porter to Jack Kroll, October 10, 1952, PAC Folder, Box A4–104, Philip Murray Papers, CUA.

41. "Results of Poll," October 16, 1952, PAC Folder, Box A4–104, Philip Murray Papers, CUA.

The reason for this possible error was the large number of "no comment" responses in Detroit and Los Angeles in particular.

42. Harry S. Truman, *Memoirs by Harry S. Truman,* Vol. 2: *Years of Trial and Hope* (Garden City: Doubleday and Co., 1955), pp. 498–501.

munists today is to say that the F.B.I. does not know its business." In answer to charges of a Yalta sell-out of Poland, he could only reply, "If these were mistakes, let us discuss them." Such answers may have satisfied a college seminar, but they hardly served to quiet public fears.[43]

As Kroll had warned in October, such fears were very real to large segments of the public. When the votes were counted, the PAC and the Democrats realized the enormity of their error. The election proved to be a Republican landslide.

PAC hopes of capturing the Senate through victories in its six key industrial states were shattered. Not only did Eisenhower sweep the North, but he even cracked the solid South by winning Tennessee and Texas. The massive anti-McCarthy campaign mounted by the Wisconsin CIO Industrial Union Council came to nothing. Ohio's Bricker and California's Knowland returned to the Senate, Knowland to take up the majority leadership after the 1953 death of Robert Taft. Surprisingly, the Democrats lost only two seats in the Senate, the results of five Republican victories (including that of Barry Goldwater in Arizona and Frank Barrett of Wyoming) and three Democratic triumphs (most notably John Kennedy and Henry Jackson) over incumbent opponents. On the other hand, the Republicans were very successful in the various House races. Picking up over twenty seats, they were able to win a comfortable House majority.[44] The question that baffled the experts for months was, how had the GOP done it?

Among the more interesting analyses of the election was Samuel Lubell's study entitled *The Revolt of the Moderates,* a study that dwelled at length upon PAC failures. Noting that many unionists voted Democratic out of fear of

43. Adlai Stevenson, *Speeches of Adlai Stevenson* (New York: Random House, 1952), p. 99. Stevenson did not squarely face the Communist issue until a September 12, 1952 speech in Albuquerque, New Mexico.
An excellent treatment of the Republican Yalta campaign can be found in Athan G. Theoharis, *The Yalta Myths: An Issue in U.S. Politics, 1945–1955* (Columbia: University of Missouri Press, 1970).
44. Congressional Quarterly Service, *Congress and the Nation, 1945–1964* (Washington, D.C.: Congressional Quarterly Service, 1965), pp. 3a–63a.

Republican antiunionism. Lubell stated that the wives of these very unionists voted Republican out of fear of Democratic war policies. Far from increasing Democratic sentiment, the PAC emphasis on economics had virtually forced voters into choosing between Democratic good times and Republican peace. Because times were good, most voters felt that the only moral vote would be for peace. It was only because of Truman's success in avoiding recession that the luxury of such a choice was granted to the electorate.[45] It was indeed an ironic twist.

While Lubell concentrated upon the general electorate, Arthur Kornhauser and his Wayne State associates delved into the mysteries of the 1952 labor vote. In a book entitled *When Labor Votes,* he minutely examined the preferences of Detroit members of the CIO United Automobile Workers. The study that Kornhauser and his associates made of the 1952 elections revealed three interesting facts. First, even among the heavily-indoctrinated UAW members, women had a greater tendency to favor Eisenhower in preelection polls than men. Although the difference was slight, it bore out Jack Kroll's contention that women were the weak link in the PAC's chain of committed voters. Second, the study concluded that the two leading issues in the campaign were Korea and prosperity. The seventy-five per cent of the surveyed auto workers who supported Stevenson felt that the prosperity issue, which the PAC had emphasized, was the key issue; the Eisenhower voters felt that the war was the key. Finally, an overwhelming majority of union voters expressed complete support of the CIO's political action program. Not only did the unionists feel that union political action was proper, but most of them implicitly trusted and supported union political endorsements.[46] In Detroit, it would seem that the PAC did an excellent job.

The CIO–PAC's own analysis of the 1952 campaign

45. Samuel Lubell, *Revolt of the Moderates* (New York: Harper and Brothers, 1956), pp. 40–43, 149, 258. Lubell noted that one of his sources of voting statistics for 1952 had been the CIO–PAC.

46. Arthur Kornhauser, Harold Sheppard, and Albert Mayer, *When Labor Votes: A Study of Auto Workers* (New York: University Books, 1956), pp. 42, 46, 55, 332, 334.

made a number of the same points as the Kornhauser study. However, the PAC concluded that the results of the 1952 election were caused by two voting shifts that both Lubell and Kornhauser minimized.

Jack Kroll's report, submitted to the CIO Executive Board only weeks after the election, emphasized four points. First, the Eisenhower landslide was due to a decided shift in the voting preferences of rural, not urban, Americans. Citing the returns from the fourteen major industrial states as well as those from a number of large cities, Kroll showed that Stevenson's margin in all of the industrial areas actually increased over that of Truman. In comparison, the returns from twenty-three farm states showed a distinct Stevenson loss. On the local level, Kroll cited a study of voting patterns in Indiana that revealed that Stevenson's urban vote matched that of Truman, but his support in rural counties was markedly less than that of the President. This section of Kroll's report emphasized that the Stevenson loss occurred in areas well outside the PAC's jurisdiction.[47]

The second point that Kroll made paralleled some of the findings of the Kornhauser study. Basing his statements upon voting returns in CIO wards in Pennsylvania, Ohio, and New Jersey, Kroll maintained that the vote of CIO members was just as pro-Democratic as ever. A New Jersey poll had found that over sixty-five per cent of the CIO's members in that state had followed PAC recommendations. The PAC's own preelection poll at factory gates in Los Angeles, Chicago, Cleveland, Columbus, Detroit, and Philadelphia had shown that over seventy per cent of the membership would support the CIO's choice. The Stevenson vote in Detroit, Akron, and Youngstown had come close to matching the 1948 Truman vote. Considering that the British Labor party never expected more than seventy-five per cent of British workers to support its candidates, Democratic support among CIO voters was indeed extraordinary.[48]

47. Election Results, a Report submitted by Jack Kroll to the CIO Executive Board, November, 1952, Political Action Committee 1952 Folder, Box 22, Irwin L. DeShetler Papers, ALH.
48. Ibid.

The third point that Kroll emphasized was the female vote. In Kroll's estimate, most of the votes of women went to the General. Kroll felt that the Republican campaign was most effective in bringing out many women who had never exercised their franchise before. This was one of the signal failures of the Democratic campaign. The PAC and the Democrats had managed to hold the loyalty of the traditionally Democratic voter, but the Republicans had captured a whole new section of the voting populace.[49]

Kroll's conclusion was mildly optimistic. He felt that the 1952 defeat had been due primarily to the personal appeal of Eisenhower the man. Hopefully, the PAC and the Democratic party would not have to contend with the General in future electoral campaigns. Noting that Eisenhower had barely managed to carry enough Republicans into Congress to assure his control of that body, Kroll was particularly optimistic about Democratic chances for the 1954 campaign.[50]

In examining the voting returns themselves, it is interesting to note that Kroll's optimism was hardly reflected in Democratic percentages. While the nation as a whole had given Stevenson almost three million more votes than it had Truman, Stevenson's percentage of the total vote dropped almost six points from Truman's 1948 total.[51] As far as the CIO's ten strong counties were concerned, the story was much the same.

During the eight years since 1944, the ten counties with the highest concentrations of CIO voters had supported Democratic candidates with less and less vigor. In 1944, Roosevelt had received about fifty-nine per cent of the vote of these counties. By 1952, Stevenson could command but fifty-three per cent of the vote of the same counties.[52] Such a trend hardly boded well in 1956.

The vote in labor wards of five major CIO-dominated cities showed an even more alarming trend. Although the labor wards had given Roosevelt almost seventy-three per cent of their votes in 1944, a figure that had risen to seventy-four per cent for Truman, these same wards turned

49. Ibid.
50. Ibid.
51. Appendix, 1952 Table.
52. Ibid.

out only sixty-seven per cent of their votes for Stevenson. At the same time, the more affluent wards in the same cities were giving Stevenson almost the same amount of support they had given Truman. While the labor wards had seen their Democratic total slip by over seven per cent, the Democratic percentage in affluent wards had dropped by only two per cent.[53] Although labor wards still supported the Democrats very strongly, Kroll's optimistic account of the continuing strength of the Democratic labor vote was at best misleading.

When all the fireworks had finally been expended, the CIO–PAC of 1952 could be viewed in only one light. It was not a success. Its major candidate had been trounced by the Republican nominee; its source of political strength had begun to erode; and its political future remained remarkably uncertain. It had run a well-organized campaign in the CIO tradition, but the presence of a national hero had frustrated its carefully laid plans. The year 1952 was a difficult year for the Political Action Committee; it was the year in which defeat became a habit.

53. Ibid.

9

1954: A CIO Victory?

The 1954 election marked the end of era in labor history. In 1954, the CIO Political Action Committee, once a threat to every antilabor lawmaker, ran its last campaign before disappearing in the merger of its parent organization with the American Federation of Labor. Although it was its last, it was not the PAC's least significant campaign. In many ways, the Political Action Committee's last campaign may have been its most successful.

By 1954, the Political Action Committee had weathered a number of political crises with varying degrees of success. The overwhelming defeat of Adlai Stevenson, the Democratic–PAC presidential candidate in the 1952 elections, had been its most recent and most traumatic political experience. Never before had a PAC-backed presidential candidate been defeated. Admittedly, until Stevenson, the PAC had always backed incumbents, but the crushing defeat still provided the conservative press with a fitting subject for gloating editorials. *Fortune,* having reported the defeat in detail, accompanied the story with a glowing report of the outlook for business–labor relations under the incoming Eisenhower Administration. The only consolation left to the PAC's Jack Kroll, noted the article, was that the labor vote had shifted less dramatically to Eisenhower than had the votes of other groups.[1] However, while *Fortune* was prematurely laying PAC in its grave, the national CIO convention, meeting in Atlantic City, was approving a resolution that stated, "In the basic conviction that the entire program of the CIO is the program that provides the hopes and needs of the American people, we rededicate ourselves to our program of political action."[2]

1. "Picking up the Pieces," *Fortune,* 46 (December 1952), pp. 83–84.
2. *Proceedings of the Fourteenth Constitutional Convention*

The dramatic defeat of 1952 was but a temporary setback, a prelude to 1954.

The drive for a labor victory in 1954 began amid the shambles of the 1952 defeat. Almost before the votes had been counted, the PAC began a campaign to discredit the "reactionary" elements in the Eighty-third Congress.[3] The first order of business in this campaign was to discover which of the "reactionaries" was most vulnerable.

Kroll and his staff had decided early in 1953 that the best place to concentrate the CIO–PAC effort in the coming year would be in the so-called "marginal" districts. The marginal districts, those electoral areas in which the incumbent had won no more than fifty-five per cent of the vote, were logical choices for two reasons. First, anti-PAC incumbents in these areas could be unseated by a shift of only about five per cent of the vote, a shift that Kroll and his staff felt the PAC was capable of producing. Second, PAC-endorsed incumbents in marginal districts deserved extra support. They were the pro-PAC incumbents most likely to fall in case of a determined Republican offensive. With this in mind, Kroll's staff had drawn up a list of the marginal districts by February, 1953.[4]

Perhaps the most noteworthy aspect of the list was the preponderance of PAC-endorsees among the marginal incumbents. Senators Hubert Humphrey, Estes Kefauver, Paul Douglas, and Matthew Neely were prominent among the list of PAC-backed liberals who would have to run for reelection in 1954. All of the group had been elected in the 1948 Democratic sweep and there was serious doubt in the PAC camp concerning their chances in what appeared to be a Republican year.[5] Regardless, the PAC began to plan both for the defense of these candidates and for the political demise of anti-PAC marginal incumbents.

The first task that faced PAC leaders in winning the marginal districts was to discover what had gone wrong in 1952. What had made working wards turn from the PAC–

of the Congress of Industrial Organizations, Atlantic City, N.J., December 1–4, 1952, p. 412.

3. Ibid., p. 419.

4. Marginal Elections 1954, February, 1953, Folder 5, Box 46, Michigan AFL–CIO Papers, ALH.

5. Ibid.

Democratic standard bearer and support Eisenhower? In their preliminary studies, PAC workers came up with one answer to this vexing problem. The answer was the CIO woman.

In a PAC study of over one hundred CIO steel workers' families in Baltimore, the overwhelming conclusion had been that CIO women were tipping the scales in Eisenhower's favor. Although the CIO male was voting for the PAC–Democratic choice, his wife, a voter whom the CIO had previously ignored, was casting her ballot for the Republican candidate.[6] If the CIO–PAC were to return to its winning ways in 1954, it would have to find some means of luring the CIO woman voter into the PAC–Democratic fold. The problem was a monumental one.

While PAC experts were considering the CIO–wife question, Kroll and his associates were proceeding with campaign business as usual. By September, 1953, the PAC drive was well underway throughout the country. The official commencement of the CIO–PAC campaign took place in Detroit, where ex-President Truman entertained an appreciative union audience with a stinging castigation of the Republican Administration. At the same time, the CIO introduced its own news commentator, John W. Vandercook, who was to bring the CIO message to the nation nightly. The CIO executives Walter Reuther, James Carey, and Jack Kroll issued Labor Day messages urging the membership on to battle with the reactionary Republican regime. By the end of the same month, the fight at the local level was joined, as even such peripheral PAC areas as Tennessee began to start dollar drives for 1954. Already, the intensity of the PAC effort differentiated this campaign from previous efforts.[7]

After the Labor Day cheers had died down, the PAC began to contemplate seriously the problems raised by the Baltimore study. Because union wives and other women had been chiefly responsible for Eisenhower's six million

6. 1952 Baltimore Study, n.d. (1953), Maryland–1954 Folder, Box 4, File A, Committee on Political Education Section, AFL–CIO Papers, WSHS.

7. *CIO News,* September 14, 1953, p. 3; August 31, 1953, p. 3; September 7, 1953, p. 2. *Textile Labor,* September 19, 1953, p. 3.

vote margin, some means had to be devised to bring women into the Political Action Committee campaign. The American Federation of Labor, also aware of the problem, began to take steps to negate the adverse effects of the female vote. The AFL Labor's League for Political Education set up a special women's division to carry the union message to the federation's members' ten million wives. The PAC reached women through the "family conference," a special union meeting for the member and his spouse that was devoted to giving both the latest political pitch from PAC. The 1952 election had proven the power of the woman voter; PAC would not forget the lesson in 1954.[8]

The CIO campaign to recruit women voters began in January, 1954, when the CIO–PAC called a national "family participation conference." One hundred and fifty-two union women representing some twenty-three CIO unions and twenty-six states met in Washington, D.C., on January 14 to lay concrete plans for a PAC female campaign during the coming electoral battle. Their first task, after going through the usual convention preliminaries, was to define the political problem that confronted PAC. They stated the problem in three parts. First, after noting that union wives were usually not politically active in a positive manner, the delegates decided that one of the major PAC shortcomings was its failure to relate household problems to political problems. Although economic questions had a very real bearing on household crises, the wives of CIO members too often saw little connection between national economic problems and the household money squeeze. Second, most of the delegates felt that women had not been active in CIO campaigns because many of them were timid about entering a new and strange situation. Some method would have to be devised to make women feel welcome in a PAC campaign. Finally, the delegates decided that social ridicule played an important part in discouraging female participation in PAC activities. Most women did not want to face the ridicule of their neighbors if they were working for an unpopular PAC-endorsed candidate.[9]

8. Sam Stativisky, "Labor's Political Plans for '54" *Nation's Business,* 42 (April 1954), pp. 25–27.

9. Summary of Conference on Family Participation in Political Action, Washington, D.C., January 14–15, 1954, n.d.

The delegates then had to discover means of overcoming these problems. A number of suggested programs came out of the Washington conference, among which were several minor changes in PAC techniques that the assembled women felt would be effective in encouraging wives to support PAC candidates. First, the PAC was encouraged to hold a series of local family conferences, each to concentrate on a specific issue of interest to the union wife. Second, in each state and local PAC, the delegates called for the assignment of one permanent staff member to the task of guiding family participation in the PAC campaign. Third, and probably of most importance, the conference asked that the PAC campaign on a year-round basis. Every adult member of a CIO family should be constantly informed of political events and their relevance. If CIO families were informed about politics, they surely would have more interest in the PAC's political campaigns. A special women's political leaflet mailed to CIO homes, the Vandercook radio program, and the formation of CIO-sponsored community service clubs (a CIO version of the Rotary Club) would keep union members and their wives interested and active in politics.[10] An active and informed membership was the first step to political success.

Although much conference time was devoted to proposing new PAC programs, delegates did not hesitate to criticize existing PAC political techniques. For instance, the delegates universally condemned the PAC for sending its political broadsides only to local union leaders. Part of membership (and wife) apathy was due in no small part to lack of knowledge of current CIO concerns. In addition, what little material did trickle down to the membership was too often written in a pedantic style that relegated it to the family wastebasket virtually unread. The PAC should return to the "punchy" style that it had used in the 1944 campaign. Finally, the participants noted that no existing PAC program attempted to interest the woman CIO member in PAC activities. Even a plant or union newspaper that mixed a bit of gossip with the PAC pitch would help

(1954), California Political Action Committee, Family Participation Program Folder, Box 26, Irwin L. DeShetler Papers, ALH.
    10. Ibid., pp. 2–3.

to interest the woman unionist in her union and the PAC.[11]

When the conference adjourned on January 15, it was clear that the PAC would have to put forth a monumental effort in order to enact the delegates' recommendations. The first step in this effort would be to carry out the conference's resolution that "the CIO Political Action Committee . . . conduct throughout the country a series of regional conferences of employed women and homemakers for the purpose of integrating the family voter into the CIO political action program." [12]

While these conferences were being sponsored throughout the nation in even such normally antiunion states as Arkansas, Iowa, and Oklahoma, PAC was making other changes in its campaign apparatus as well. Women were assigned the task of writing special columns that would appear regularly in CIO and affiliated union newspapers. By September, CIO national headquarters was publishing a pamphlet entitled "New Look," which was a lively propaganda bulletin aimed specifically at the woman voter. On the eve of the election, the PAC made one last try for the distaff vote with an appeal entitled "Why Women Should Vote," which stressed the high cost of running a household under the Republican Administration. If the female vote went to the Republicans in 1954, it was not due to PAC inattention.[13]

Besides the increased emphasis on women voters, the PAC initiated several other changes in its campaign effort. The two most obvious of these were the early start for the campaign and the nationwide Vandercook radio broadcasts. In previous years, a PAC campaign would usually begin no earlier than eleven months before the election. As the February, 1953 report on marginal districts showed, Jack Kroll was working on the 1954 campaign long before the eleven month point. The Vandercook broadcasts were another mark of the same trend. Vandercook's news program

11. Ibid., pp. 4–6.

12. Women's Role in Political Action, California Political Action Committee, Family Participation Program Folder, Box 26, Irwin L. DeShetler Papers, ALH.

13. *CIO News,* August 8, 1954, p. 10; September 6, 1954, p. 9; September 13, 1954, p. 10. *United Automobile Worker,* October 1954, p. 5.

with a PAC pitch began on Labor Day, 1953, more than a year prior to the 1954 elections. Another change, which with the two above could be considered tuning of the campaign machine, was a new method of defining electoral issues. The *CIO News* publicized the trend in an article entitled "Jersey PAC Has a Machine." For 1954, the New Jersey PAC had decided that the best way to keep in touch with its membership concerning issues, registration, and candidates was to employ data processing machines. New York's Political Action Committee followed the trend by commissioning the famous pollster Elmer Roper to survey political attitudes in the Empire State. Even little Connecticut possessed a modern PAC that used the latest and most advanced polling techniques to gather issues for its "fact book." [14]

Although the Political Action Committee had initiated several changes in its 1954 campaign approach, certain emphases remained the same; basic political techniques, such as registration, were still a part of the CIO–PAC effort. Jack Kroll went so far as to state in an interview, "An unregistered member anywhere is a political scab. He is as much danger to our organization as a man who crosses a picket line." [15] In addition to registration, PAC maintained its emphasis on the importance of hard-hitting issues that would really motivate the union voter. Two years without an ally in the White House had furnished labor with several solid economic issues upon which to base its bid to overthrow the Republican Congress.

The principle issues that the PAC exploited in its 1954 fight were unemployment, high taxes, lack of housing, and inflation. During March, 1954, unemployment reached such a high level, having passed the five per cent mark in the estimates of the Bureau of Labor Statistics, that the union press began to hint about the return of 1929. During April, unemployment rose again, this time nudging six per cent in Pennsylvania and Michigan, but the Administration still displayed no sign of being able to cope with the recession.

14. *CIO News,* January 4, 1954, p. 9; September 20, 1954, p. 8. *Labor Union Political Expenditures* (Washington, D.C.: Senate Republican Policy Committee, 1955), p. 4.

15. Strativisky, "Labor's Political Plans," p. 26.

The Political Action Committee was quick to exploit the situation.[16]

In June, the PAC sent out the first copies of its *1954 Handbook,* a book that dedicated thirty pages to what it called "recession from the bottom up." The *Handbook* outlined the situation in simple words and figures that even the least educated voter could understand. Indeed, it took little education to realize that a situation in which almost four million persons were unemployed was not praiseworthy, especially if one counted oneself in the unemployed category. As the *Handbook* stated, there were many parallels between 1929 and 1954; to a generation that still remembered the real terrors of depression, such parallels could easily shift some voters into Democratic ranks. Moreover, the three pages of reprinted Eisenhower denials of the reality of recession were not likely to ease the minds of wavering voters. The *Handbook,* combined with a constant barrage from the labor press, would try to keep the issue of unemployment before the union voter until the November elections.[17]

The PAC's second issue, the Eisenhower tax policy, was not exactly one that would endear the Administration to labor. The basis of labor's discontent was the very nature of the Administration's Internal Revenue Code of 1954. Although the law gave almost two and one half billion dollars worth of tax relief to corporations, the workingman's plea for an increase in the personal exemption was ignored by the Republican-dominated Congress. In a year of tight money, the average unionist could well sympathize with the baby on the cover of *Steel Labor* who was saying, "I think I'm worth more than $600 to Pop! Don't You?" [18]

16. U.S., Bureau of Labor Statistics, *Monthly Labor Review,* 88 (June 1955), 711–13. Typical reactions of the CIO press can be seen in the following: *Advance,* March 1, 1954, p. 1; *United Automobile Worker,* March 1954, p. 3.

17. Congress of Industrial Organizations Political Action Committee, *1954 Handbook* (Washington, D.C.: CIO–PAC, 1954), pp. 214–17, 234.

18. *Steel Labor,* April, 1954, p. 1. The Internal Revenue Code of 1954, when it was finally enacted, had a number of provisions that materially benefitted businessmen. For instance, Congress allowed a four per cent tax relief from income earned from dividends (down from Eisenhower's more liberal

The Republican defeat of the George Amendment, which would have raised the personal exemption to 800 dollars, meant a real loss to the unionist, a loss that was not sweetened by "trickle down" tax relief to large corporations. Neither the PAC nor the labor press were likely to let the voter forget his loss—the labor press greeted the defeat with headlines; PAC added twenty-three more pages to the *Handbook*.[19]

The Eighty-third Congress was no more favorable to an expanded public role in housing than it had been to lower income tax relief. Although the Consumer Price Index for rent stood at a record high of twenty-nine points above the 1947–1949 base years, the Republican Congress defeated even the nominal housing measure that the Administration had proposed.[20] While the public was forced to pay almost one-third more rent, Congress virtually ended the public housing program. As for the affluent worker who sought government financing for private home construction, the Republicans' deflationary monetary policy made home loans difficult and costly to procure. The *Handbook* summarized the situation in the following words, "At best, the Administration housing proposals barely hang on to the wholly inadequate rate of new home building achieved in 1953." [21]

---

relief proposal), the allowance of the double-declining balance form of computing depreciation on plant and equipment for business, and several changes in the computation rules that liberalized methods for determining operating losses. U.S., *Congressional Record*, 83rd Cong., 2nd sess., 1954, 190, Part 9, 12399, 12436, 12525.

19. The final version of the George Amendment that appeared before the Senate (and was defeated by a vote of 49 to 46) would have only raised the personal exemption to 700 dollars. See, U.S., *Congressional Record*, 83rd Cong., 2nd sess., 1954, 190, Part 7, 9300. Also, see *United Automobile Worker*, May, 1954, p. 12. *CIO News*, March 29, 1954, p. 6. CIO, *Handbook*, pp. 162–85.

20. The Eisenhower public housing proposal called for 35,000 new units of public housing for four consecutive years. This measure was defeated by the House, 176–211, and another bill substituted. U.S., *Congressional Record*, 83rd Cong., 2nd sess., 1954, 190, Part 4, 4489–4490.

On the rise in rent see, *Monthly Labor Review*, 76 (December 1954), 1418.

21. CIO, *Handbook*, p. 22.

Inflation had been one of the Republicans' tools for discrediting the Truman Administration. The PAC grasped at the issue by trying to argue that Eisenhower seemed no more capable of handling the situation than had his predecessor. However, the Administration had succeeded in reducing the Consumer Price Index from an October, 1953 high of 115.4 to a July, 1954 reading of 115.2. The index for food had risen only one-half of one per cent, and the bread index, upon which the CIO based its cry of inflation, had barely crept up two points.[22] Still, even such a minor degree of inflation seemed incongruous in a period of major recession. As Walter Reuther stated in his 1954 Labor Day address, there seemed to be more of those "fifty-cent dollars," which Eisenhower had decried, in circulation during the Truman years.[23] The Eisenhower Administration had created a situation that the average union voter, with a little persuasion from PAC, could see was in need of change.

The Political Action Committee viewed one other failure of the Eisenhower Administration with alarm, the failure to revise Taft–Hartley. Eisenhower had promised, during the campaign, to change the most onerous sections of the act and, upon his election, had even instructed Labor Secretary Martin Durkin to submit a detailed revision plan. However, when the President had refused to act favorably upon his recommendation, Durkin, the only labor member of the cabinet, had resigned.[24] As the *CIO News* saw it, the only "working man" in the Administration's "millionaire's club" had finally seen the true nature of his associates.[25] With the resignation of Secretary Durkin on September 20, 1953, labor's last hope of favorably revising Taft–Hartley died.[26] Eisenhower's only public concession to labor proved to be no more reliable than his denials of the reality of recession. The *Handbook* summed up the position of the CIO

22. *Monthly Labor Review,* 77, pp. 1418–19.
23. *CIO News,* August 30, 1954, p. 2.
24. *New York Times,* September 11, 1953, p. 1.
25. *CIO News,* September 14, 1953, p. 2.
26. For a summary of the labor movement's attempts to revise Taft–Hartley after Eisenhower took office see, Gerald Pomper, "Labor Legislation: The Revision of Taft–Hartley in 1953–1954," *Labor History,* 6 (Spring 1965), 143–58.

in the words of Walter Reuther, "Justice and fairness in the law are what President Eisenhower has promised to labor. Justice and fairness are all we ask." [27]

By election day, CIO–PAC had endorsed candidates in forty-two states. The PAC had given active support to 256 candidates seeking seats in the House of Representatives, twenty-four senatorial candidates, and sixteen gubernatorial aspirants.[28] To the endorsed candidates, PAC support meant more than just a few registration drives and free publicity in union publications. PAC support to many lonely Democrats meant the one sure source of campaign funds. In 1954, the national PAC, alone, spent over one million dollars in support of its endorsed candidates. In addition, the affiliated political committees of the United Steel Workers of America and the United Automobile Workers spent about half that amount on essentially the same candidates. Total labor spending, including the half million dollar expenditure of the AFL and the railroad unions, was in excess of two million dollars for the non-presidential year of 1954.[29]

What PAC support and spending really meant could be seen in the Michigan and California elections. Although the Michigan PAC effort was somewhat atypical because of the formal alliance between the state Democratic party and the PAC, the California PAC campaign was typical of PAC efforts in many large industrial states. Preparations for the campaign in Michigan involved a number of duties quite outside the realm of other state PACs. For instance, a good part of early 1953 was spent in choosing PAC nominees for various state patronage jobs.[30] Moreover, as the most affluent member of the Michigan Democratic coalition, the PAC was expected to support a number of marginal party organizations in rural sections of the state.[31] While these petty matters kept the Michigan CIO office

27. CIO, *Handbook,* p. 159.
28. *CIO News,* November 8, 1954, p. 3.
29. *Labor Union Political Expenditures,* pp. 3–12.
30. For example, see Lawrence L. Farrell to Barney Hopkins, April 14, 1953, 1953 PAC Folder, Box 110, Michigan AFL–CIO Papers, ALH.
31. Neil Staebler to August Scholle, April 23, 1953, Folder 18, Box 42, Michigan AFL–CIO Papers, ALH. Staebler was the head of the Michigan Democratic party.

busy, a number of potential candidates were already asking PAC leaders for CIO endorsement.[32] Indeed, in Michigan, CIO–PAC endorsement was as important as Democratic party endorsement in other states.

PAC leaders set their strategic goals in the state well before the August, 1954, primary. Essentially, the PAC's job was to retain all of the incumbent Democratic congressmen, the Democratic governor, and the Democratic state officers. In addition, PAC tacticians believed that an inspired PAC effort should be capable of picking up both of the two additional House seats and the Senate post being contested in the 1954 elections. Specifically, the House seats would have to be wrested from Republican incumbents in the sixth (Flint) and the new seventeenth (Detroit) congressional districts. The Senate post that the PAC wanted to capture was held by Homer Ferguson, a conservative Republican who the CIO–PAC believed to be quite vulnerable.[33] As in previous elections, PAC hopes would ride on the ability of CIO blockworkers to turn out a sufficiently large vote in Detroit labor wards to offset the rural Republican tendencies of the rest of the state.

Using the arguments set forth in the *Handbook,* PAC blockworkers saturated Detroit, Flint, and other CIO strongholds with political broadsides, doorbell-ringing volunteers, and determined registration workers. The result of all this activity was a resounding victory in November. As state CIO Secretary–Treasurer Barney Hopkins announced after the campaign, the recession, along with effective local political action, was responsible for sweeping the entire PAC slate into office. The incumbents, the two marginal congressional candidates, and Homer Ferguson's Democratic opponent all won at the polls.[34]

32. Congressman Alvin Bentley to Thomas Burke, November 20, 1953, 1954 PAC Folder, Box 111, Michigan AFL–CIO Papers, ALH. The request from Bentley for CIO help was particularly interesting since he was a Republican incumbent from a non-CIO congressional district (district eight, located in the Saginaw area).

33. Marginal Districts, House of Representatives, 1954, January, 1954, Folder 13, Box 53, Michigan AFL–CIO Papers, ALH. Also, Marginal Elections, 1954, February, 1953, Folder 5, Box 46, Michigan AFL–CIO Papers, ALH.

34. Barney Hopkins, For Immediate Release, November 3,

In California, the PAC effort was less broadly-based and a good deal less successful. The California CIO controlled neither the state Democratic party nor a major portion of the vote in any of the state's cities. Thus, the California campaign was necessarily limited to supplementing Democratic campaigns in areas where the CIO was strong.[35]

Although the national PAC felt that the California CIO should concentrate on four marginal congressional districts (the third, sixth, thirteenth, and fourteenth), the state PAC leaders felt that their chances would be improved if they concentrated on ten (the same plus seven, eleven, twelve, seventeen, twenty-one, and twenty-six) districts.[36] Henry Santiesteven, the California CIO's congressional expert, believed that a number of these districts would go to the Democrats if labor's resources could be used efficiently. The problem was that a number of the most promising Democratic districts were in areas of small CIO concentrations and, conversely, the district with the highest CIO concentration (the sixth district) had the most unpromising Democratic candidate (incumbent Robert Condon).[37] The most promising race in the entire California CIO region (which encompassed Washington and Oregon) was not even in the state of California. The PAC had an excellent chance to win a Democratic congressional seat in Portland, Oregon.[38]

When the election was finally over, California Regional CIO Director Irwin L. DeShetler had few victories with which to console himself. Of the four seats that the National CIO had felt to be most important, the Democrats had managed to retain only two of their three incumbents, while the Republican incumbent actually increased his

1954, 1954 PAC Folder, Box 113, Michigan AFL–CIO Papers, ALH.

35. John Despol to Irwin DeShetler, May 11, 1954, Political Action Committee 1954–1955 Folder, Box 22, Irwin L. DeShetler Papers, ALH.

36. Henry Santiesteven to Irwin DeShetler, n.d. (1954), Political Action Committee 1954–1955 Folder, Box 22, Irwin L. DeShetler Papers, ALH.

37. Ibid.

38. Marginal Districts, House of Representatives, 1954, January, 1954, Folder 13, Box 53, Michigan AFL–CIO Papers, ALH.

margin. However, the Democrats had managed to pick up one of the Republican seats in the California–PAC list of target districts. Moreover, such endangered incumbents as PAC–Democrat Cecil King managed to retain their seats, even in the face of determined opposition (which in King's case was Vice President Nixon's protegé, Robert Finch). The Portland, Oregon PAC-endorsee had done quite nicely, winning a congressional seat from a Republican incumbent.[39] Although DeShetler had few victories to savor, he also had few defeats to regret. California did not furnish the PAC with a clearcut victory, but, more importantly, it did not brand the CIO with the onus of defeat. Was this the national situation?

On the morning after the election, CIO–PAC discovered that its endorsed candidates had been successful in 126 congressional districts, fifteen senatorial contests, and eight gubernatorial battles.[40] Both the House and the Senate were now in Democratic hands. Yet, was the Democratic triumph really a PAC victory, or merely a return to a Democratic norm after the aberrant election of Eisenhower? Could the Democratic upsurge of 1954 be credited to a typical off-year loss for the party in power, or was it, at least partially, the handiwork of the PAC?

The Eighty-fourth Congress had a composition of 232 Democrats and 203 Republicans in the House, and forty-nine Democrats and forty-seven Republicans in the Senate. This Democratic margin was the result of the election of twenty-one Democratic congressmen from formerly Republican districts and the victories of two Democrats who defeated incumbent Republican senators. At the same time, the Republicans were able only to defeat one Democratic senator and three incumbent congressmen.[41] Thus, the victory of 1954 was really won in twenty-one congressional districts and two Senate races.

A closer examination of the twenty-one congressional districts and the two Senate contests reveals more than a

39. Election returns from Richard Scammon, *America Votes* (New York: The Macmillan Company, 1956), pp. 31–32. The Portland PAC victor was ERA's Edith Green.

40. *CIO News*, November 8, 1954, pp. 2–3.

41. Scammon, pp. 22–305. Also, Morse (Oregon Senator) turned Democratic after 1954 elections.

return to the pre-1952 Democratic norm, or an off-year shift. Far from merely winning back seats that the Republicans had seized in 1952, the freshman Democrats had won most of their victories in traditionally Republican areas, such as Portland, Oregon; Union County, New Jersey; and Milwaukee, Wisconsin. As the Appendix shows, most of the twenty-one districts were either in urban centers, such as Chicago or Boston, or else in areas most likely to be unionized. The crucial Senate races were in states with similar electorates. In Michigan, Patrick McNamara, an AFL official, defeated the conservative Republican incumbent, Homer Ferguson. The other critical Senate race occurred in Oregon ,where active PAC volunteers supplied much of the campaign machine which enabled Richard Neuberger to defeat incumbent Senator Guy Cordon.[42] The CIO–PAC had endorsed all but one of the successful Democratic candidates.[43] Such a series of correlations would seem more than mere coincidence. The likelihood of coincidence is even further strained when one considers that eighteen of the twenty-one races were won in those states that *Fortune* called, "States Where Labor Has Political Strength," states such as Illinois, Indiana, Massachusetts, Michigan, Minnesota, Missouri, New Jersey, New York, Pennsylvania, West Virginia, and Wisconsin.[44]

A sampling of CIO districts, as shown in the Appendix, in the years 1946, 1950, 1952, and 1954 reveals that while the 1952 vote was smaller than that of the control year, 1950, the 1954 Democratic vote in labor districts was abnormally large. Some factor was in operation during the 1954 elections that made the Democratic vote over five per cent greater than the corresponding Democratic vote in the normal year, 1950.[45] Assuming that the difference between

42. Ibid. Also see, Richard Neuberger to Irwin DeShetler, November 12, 1954, Political Endorsements, 1954 Folder, Box 29, Irwin L. DeShetler Papers, ALH. Edith Green to Irwin DeShetler, November 10, 1954, Political Endorsements, 1954 Folder, Box 29, Irwin L. DeShetler Papers, ALH.
43. *CIO News,* November 8, 1954, pp. 2–3. See also, Appendix.
44. "States Where Labor Has Political Strength," *Fortune,* 53, p. 226.
45. 1954 Table in Appendix.

1950 and 1952 was Eisenhower, there still remains the un-explained extra Democratic vote of 1954.

Examining the total vote, in the Appendix, of the ten most heavily unionized states in 1950, 1952, and 1954 further dramatizes the abnormally large Democratic vote of 1954. However, the increase in Democratic support is most obvious in those states where unemployment was most serious, namely Michigan, Pennsylvania, and New Jersey.[46] It would seem that the very issue that PAC chose to publi-cize did, in fact, have some bearing on the Democratic vote.

In 1953, Doris Mersdorf studied the problem of motivat-ing the union member to take an active part in union-endorsed political action. Her conclusions, after having observed Chicago Local 222 of the Oil Workers Inter-national, were that the average member felt politically motivated for only two reasons. These were his own eco-nomic demands and a high degree of personal involvement in his union.[47] Thus, if PAC could claim any amount of responsibility for the Democratic victory of 1954, it would have to be demonstrated that it stimulated membership activity in the local, or dramatized the members' economic stake in a Democratic triumph.

The CIO–PAC used every facility at its disposal to show the average unionist that there were concrete economic reasons for voting Democratic in 1954. The *CIO News* and the organs of the CIO affiliates had been trumpeting the unemployment message since early January. The spe-cialized CIO publications, those monthly bulletins of the standing committees, also reflected the intensity of the cru-sade against Eisenhower unemployment. *Economic Out-look,* the publication of the CIO Department of Education and Research, devoted its entire June issue to "Collective Bargaining and Full Employment in 1954." The issue de-picted, in vivid prose and forbidding graphs, the sorry prospect for an economy run on the "trickle down" theory.[48] *Political Action of the Week,* the PAC's insiders'

46. 1954 Table in Appendix.
47. Doris E. Mersdorf, "Local 222; A Study of Factors Associated with the Willingness of its Membership to Define Political Action as a Union Function," M.A. thesis, University of Chicago, 1953, pp. 75–79.
48. *Economic Outlook,* June 1954, pp. 41–48.

publication, consumed several issues with diatribes against the recession that the Administration so persistently denied.[49] Even the *Handbook,* with its simplistic arguments and definitive-looking figures, based its message upon the premise that the Republicans were deflating the worker's wallet.

The PAC goal in 1954 was to involve both the unionist and his family in the campaign. If family conferences, dollar drives, registration, and get-out-the-vote campaigns did not accomplish such an end, it is doubtful that any organized activity could rouse the worker from his apathy. By election day, some PAC program or publication should have reached every voting CIO member.

The actual test of CIO effectiveness would be a concrete count of the votes of union members and their wives both in 1954 and preceding elections. Since such absolute information is not available, the next best test must necessarily be opinion polls and union district votes.

The polls showed an interesting correlation between increased PAC activity and increased union vote. While Kroll claimed about seventy-five per cent of union men voted for Stevenson, the polls showed only a fifty-seven per cent union Stevenson vote. Yet, in 1954, the same polls showed an increase in the union Democratic vote to over sixty-four per cent. The same situation occurred among union wives, for which the polls showed an increase in the Democratic percentage from forty-one to forty-six per cent.[50] Considering the supposed off-year apathy, there must be some explanation of the increase in the Democratic percentages.

Could the 1954 elections be considered merely a resurgence of the Democrats' waning fortunes, or a standard off-year loss by the party in power? If either were the case, why would only the PAC candidates fare so well? An examination of the 1954 tables in the Appendix shows that while PAC endorsed Democrats were winning even greater

49. *Political Action of the Week,* February 1, 1954; February 22, 1954; August 16, 1954.
50. Angus Campbell and Homer Cooper, *Group Differences in Attitudes and Votes: A Study of the 1954 Congressional Election* (Ann Arbor: Institute for Social Research, 1956), pp. 21, 32.

victories than in 1950, the nonendorsed Democrats were doing only slightly better than in 1950 and actually worse than in 1952. At the ward level, strong labor wards in four CIO cities were showing a dramatic increase in Democratic strength when compared with both 1950 and 1952. Yet, in the very same cities, nonlabor wards that received only slight attention from the PAC were showing a much less dramatic rise in Democratic support. In Hartford, for instance, the nonlabor areas actually displayed a loss in Democratic strength in comparison to former years, while labor areas showed a five percentage-point gain.[51]

The evidence would seem to point to 1954 as a labor victory. The Democratic victories were won in labor areas by labor-endorsed and financed candidates. Democratic margins were consistently increased in union areas. In Cook County, Illinois, for instance, the Democratic margin of Senator Paul Douglas could be traced strictly to increased Democratic strength in working-class areas. The PAC was proud to point out that the Douglas vote in non-working class suburbs actually decreased from the level of his 1948 victory.[52] In highly-unionized Milwaukee, Henry Reuss attributed his Fifth Congressional District win over a Republican incumbent to the "great efforts" of the Milwaukee CIO.[53] However, the triumph did not belong to labor in general, but to the CIO and PAC in particular. It was CIO–PAC that made the bulk of labor's political expenditures.

51. 1954 Table in Appendix.
52. *Chicago Sun–Times,* November 7, 1954, p. 24. This clipping was found in Illinois-1954 Folder, Box 2, File A, AFL–CIO C.O.P.E. Papers, WSHS.
53. *Wisconsin CIO News,* November 5, 1954, p. 5. Reuss was repeatedly attacked by state AFL President George Haberman during the 1954 campaign. *Milwaukee Journal,* July 11, 1954, p. 1, clipping in Wisconsin–1954 Folder, Box 8, File A, AFL–CIO C.O.P.E. Papers, WSHS.
Along these same lines, it is interesting to note that the new Democratic representative from the Ninth Wisconsin Congressional District also credited his victory to PAC. Lester Johnson, the winner, noted that his victory was because of his carrying thirteen of Eau Claire's sixteen wards (usually Republican strongholds). In his words, "Much of this was the result of efforts by organized labor." See PAC 9th District Folder, Box 4, Wisconsin State Industrial Union Council Papers, WSHS.

While the AFL, with twice the potential resources, was spending only half a million dollars on the campaign, the CIO unions spent three times that figure on a well-coordinated drive.[54] While the AFL was not even bothering to use its publications to publicize its candidates, the *CIO News* dedicated almost every issue to some aspect of the political campaign.[55] Finally, while the AFL was still remembering its Eisenhower honeymoon under AFL leader and Labor Secretary Martin Durkin, the CIO was grinding out reams of condemnations of Eisenhower, his recession, and his party.

Although the CIO helped the Democrats win a victory in 1954, it was not a typical PAC campaign. The 1952 defeat changed the PAC's preconceptions about the political role of labor drastically. No longer would a campaign mean simply a delivery of registered unionists to the polls. The union member could not be depended upon to vote as directed unless he was given a concrete economic justification for such a vote. His wife was even less dependable. What the PAC did in its last campaign was to involve the unionist and his wife in a movement based upon sound economic motives. It seized upon the Eisenhower Administration's economic failures and inflated them into prophecies of another 1929. With the extra spur of economic motivation, labor's votes helped nudge enough mar-

54. The AFL–LLPE records for 1954 reveal again and again that LLPE turned down requests for funds from Democrats who later won with PAC financing. See, James McDevitt to Roy Hill, May 17, 1954, Oregon–1954 Folder, Box 6, File A, AFL–CIO C.O.P.E. Papers, WSHS. McDevitt was turning down aid for Edith Green, the eventual winner in Oregon's Third Congressional district.

55. Neither the *American Federationist* nor the *International Teamster* displayed any interest in the campaign, especially in their October, November, and December, 1954 issues.

It is also interesting to note that after both LLPE–PAC cooperation in the 1952 campaign and the signing of the AFL–CIO No Raid Pact in 1953 that PAC and LLPE did not cooperate to any unusual extent in the 1954 elections. For instance, even in late 1956, Jack Kroll was complaining about lack of unity in the merged (AFL–CIO) organization's political drive. See Memorandum: Preliminary Analysis of 1956 National Election, November 19, 1956, pp. 6–7, Box 4, Group 2, Jack Kroll Papers, LCMD.

ginal Republican districts into the Democratic column to ensure a Democratic victory in 1954. As Jack Kroll said in summing up the election, "The workers voted their economic interests." [56]

56. Statement on 1954 National Election, n.d. (1954), p. 6, Box 4, Group 2, Jack Kroll Papers, LCMD.

10

The Dilemma of Partisan Politics

Only twelve years after the July 7, 1943, meeting in the CIO's Washington headquarters, the CIO Political Action Committee was swallowed whole by the newly-organized AFL–CIO. The PAC and its counterpart in AFL ranks, the LLPE, were no more. In their place stood a new super organization, the Committee on Political Education, that promised to exert powers undreamed of by its predecessors. However, the merger of labor's two political committees left a number of important problems unsolved. Prime among these was the difficult question of the proper role of labor in the political arena. Would labor continue to be the favorite mistress of the Democratic party, or would it chart its own political course? This was the dilemma of partisan politics.

In August, 1955, Jack Kroll sent a letter to CIO President Reuther explaining the details of the PAC–LLPE merger. As he noted, he expected little trouble merging the two organizations. Both he and his AFL counterpart, James McDevitt, had been on friendly terms for a number of years. Although there had been little significant cooperation between the two organizations since the 1950 elections, when a few joint AFL–CIO political ventures had been initiated, both the national offices and the two field organizations expected to be working together by the 1956 elections. However, there were two minor problems that might slow complete amalgamation. The first of these, financing, could be solved by allowing the two organizations to continue their existing financial arrangements. The second problem might prove more difficult to ameliorate. What, Kroll asked, should be done about existing political commitments? [1]

1. Jack Kroll, Memorandum on the Merger of PAC and LLPE, August 18, 1955, Political Action Committee 1952–1955 Folder, Box 85, CIO Secretary–Treasurer's Papers, ALH.

The problem of political commitments was one that plagued the PAC since the days of the Cowan–Brophy–Walsh report. It will be recalled that in December, 1942, President Murray's three political advisors stressed the importance of working within the Democratic party. "We recommend," the three had written, "that work be carried on largely within the Democratic Party. . . . Our influence in the Democratic Party is already large and can be increased greatly if the proper methods are followed." [2] Unfortunately, the report's recommendations were based less upon political realities than upon the authors' naivete. Regardless of the political qualifications of Murray's advisors, the CIO cast its lot with the Democrats for the next ten years. The partnership was not always a happy one.

Perhaps the most important shortcoming of the PAC–Democratic alliance was that it severely restricted the CIO's political horizons. A case in point would be the Wayne Morse affair. Late in 1949, Wayne Morse, Oregon's liberal Republican Senator, loosed a bitter barrage of criticism against the CIO and its Political Action Committee. In a letter addressed simply to "Kroll," Morse made the following point:

> I think you people in the CIO are going to have to make up your minds in respect to my candidacy for reelection as to whether or not you want any liberals in the Republican Party. The attitude of your CIO critics in Oregon leads me to the opinion that, apparently, at least some of you in the CIO want liberals only in the Democratic Party. If and when that ever comes, I respectfully suggest to you that the best interest of American Labor will then be more seriously jeopardized than it is at the present time.[3]

Continuing his letter with a pointed reminder that the CIO–PAC's stated purpose was to win a Congress that was sympathetic to the CIO, he suggested that at least part of the blame for enacting the Taft–Hartley Act must be borne

2. Nathan Cowan, John Brophy, and J. Raymond Walsh to Philip Murray, December 30, 1942, p. 21, CIO Political Programs Folder, Box 25, Wayne County AFL–CIO Papers, ALH.

3. Wayne Morse to Jack Kroll, December 10, 1949, Political Action Committee 1949 Folder, Box 85, CIO Secretary–Treasurer's Papers, ALH.

by the PAC, which refused to give Robert LaFollette, Jr., its undivided support in the 1946 Wisconsin senatorial contest. In Morse's words, "If Bob LaFollette had received united CIO support in 1946, he would have been reelected. If Bob LaFollette had been reelected, our chances of blocking the passage of the Taft–Hartley bill would have been greatly improved." [4] Morse's words brought back echoes of Thomas Amlie's 1944 warning to PAC concerning the Progressive party.[5] Would one-party loyalty help or hinder the PAC's ultimate objective? Morse obviously felt that dogmatic partisanship was the PAC's greatest mistake.

The Morse affair did not end with his blast at Kroll concerning the 1950 election. In 1953, as Morse was contemplating a switch to the Democratic party, the Senator suddenly found himself relieved of his responsibilities on the Senate Labor Committee. Because he had been an honored guest at the 1952 CIO convention, he addressed a letter to James Carey asking why the CIO had not even raised a whimper in his defense. Why, he wrote, should a senator with a fine labor record go undefended merely because he was not a "liberal Democrat?" More pointedly, he noted that the very senators who refused to help him, "that group of so-called liberal Democrats in the Senate, who in my book are spineless wonders," were men whom the PAC had elected and who should take advice from the CIO.[6] As in 1949, Morse was questioning the political principles of the labor organization. Did the CIO and the PAC really want a liberal Congress, or did they support Democratic candidates regardless of ideology? At the same time, Morse's complaint about the CIO's failure to exercise control over its congressional contingent highlighted an even more critical failure of the CIO's political action program.

While Wayne Morse continued to badger CIO officials about their political commitments, the PAC's Jack Kroll began to question the very foundation of the PAC's politi-

4. Ibid.
5. *Wisconsin,* n.d. (1944), CIO–PAC Campaign Plans Folder, Box 58, Thomas R. Amlie Papers, WSHS.
6. Wayne Morse to James Carey, January 24, 1953, Senate Correspondence Folder, Box 45, CIO Secretary–Treasurer's Papers, ALH.

cal program. Ever since the Cowan–Brophy–Walsh report had committed the CIO to the Democratic party, the CIO and the PAC had found that their influence in the party had not increased greatly, as the report had prophesied. As Wayne Morse had unwittingly pointed out, the PAC's power over Democratic candidates had often ended the moment that the candidate had been elected.[7] Even this was but a symptom of the increasing dissatisfaction that the CIO–PAC felt toward its ten-year marriage to the Democratic party.

Kroll set forth his bill of particulars against the Democrats in a post-1952 election memorandum to Walter Reuther. In a four point summary, he blasted the Democrats for everything from refusing to give the CIO an official position on the national committee to allowing too many conservative congressmen the use of the party's name.

Kroll's first complaint was that the CIO was essentially an outside agent as far as the Democrats were concerned. In Jack Kroll's words, the CIO was bargaining with the Democratic party "much as it would with an employer."[8] The CIO was not a party to the day-to-day operations of the Democratic National Committee. Although such a position had certain advantages, among them the technical maintenance of the CIO's political freedom of action, the avoidance of the party's financial responsibilities, and the reduction of a threat of political splits within the ranks of the CIO, the outside position had a number of disadvantages that outweighed any number of advantages. Because the CIO was outside the Democratic pale, Democratic politicians did not see the work and time the PAC had invested in Democratic candidates. Not realizing how active the CIO–PAC had been, Democratic politicians invariably underestimated the contributions that the CIO made to Democratic victories. Moreover, the outside position excluded CIO spokesmen from the inner councils of the

7. Ibid.
8. *Memorandum,* n.d. (1955) Box 4, Group 2, Jack Kroll Papers, LCMD. Another copy of this report (each copy was numbered) was found in CIO Secretary–Treasurer Papers and was dated November 4, 1955. See *Memorandum,* November 4, 1955, Democratic National Committee, 1953–1955 Folder, Box 174, CIO Secretary–Treasurer Papers, ALH.

party. Thus, when the Democrats selected a national chairman, a man with whom the PAC had to work closely, the CIO had not a single vote.[9] This was just the beginning of Kroll's complaint.

"More serious problems arise," wrote Kroll, "with respect to relations between the CIO and Congress." Although the PAC had no official position on the Democratic National Committee, it had some effect on the party's general policies through its representation at the quadrennial Democratic convention. Such was not the case in Congress. In the halls of Congress, the power rested not with the northern liberal branch of the party, but with the southern conservatives. Thus, the congressional branch of the party could be completely opposed to prounion legislation, even though the national convention, the democratically-chosen voice of the party, had gone on record as favoring such legislation. Indeed, though the Democratic convention officially condemned right-to-work laws in 1952, the Democratic congressional leadership represented twelve of the eighteen states that supported such laws. The PAC alone could do nothing about such conservatives; they invariably lived in districts where the CIO had absolutely no electoral strength. Considering the CIO's troubles even with liberal congressional leaders, Kroll found the congressional situation completely intolerable.[10]

What were the alternatives to the existing political relationship? Kroll noted six alternate courses of action, all dependent upon one factor—the necessity that the CIO initiate some changes soon. It was quite clear that the Democrats were satisfied with the existing situation; only the CIO was the loser.[11]

Kroll's first alternative was simply to abandon politics. Considering that the PAC spent almost a million dollars in every national campaign, the monetary savings alone would justify such a course. Moreover, the spending of a million dollars in a congressional campaign guaranteed neither electoral success nor the cooperation of candidates who were elected with PAC help.[12] It is questionable, how-

9. Ibid.
10. Ibid.
11. Ibid.
12. Ibid.

ever, whether Kroll really felt that this suggestion was a viable alternative.

Kroll's second course was a return to strict voluntarism. The CIO would endorse neither party, but rather would extend aid to only a few selected "friends." Although Kroll noted this alternative, it seemed clear that this course also went against his political inclinations.[13]

While abstinence and strict voluntarism seemed out of the question, there were several ways of increasing the CIO's strength within one of the existing political parties. The CIO could intensify its bargaining with the Democrats and the Republicans and raise the level of its demands. Such a course might yield the kind of success that the CIO and the PAC sought. An even better means of influencing the two parties might be to encourage the membership to join the respective parties and run for party office. This course had been followed in Michigan and the Michigan CIO virtually ran the state Democratic party. Such a course also had the advantage of keeping membership interest in politics at a high level all year long. Finally, the CIO leadership could go directly to the Democratic party and demand an official place on the national committee. Thus, the CIO would be in much the same position as the British Trade Union Congress, an official partner in a major political party.[14] All of these suggestions seemed to have Kroll's full backing.

Jack Kroll ended his memorandum with a call for a national meeting of state and local CIO leaders to decide which political alternative to pursue. Before the meeting could take place, however, the CIO became involved in merger negotiations with the AFL.[15] Kroll's suggestions were lost in the excitement as the CIO rushed to rejoin its parent federation. Amidst the flurry of activity, the PAC disappeared. After twelve years of faithful service, the Committee faded away.

What can be said about the PAC in retrospect? Perhaps the most striking thing about the Committee was its public image. Almost from the day of its birth, its critics saw it

13. Ibid.
14. Ibid. See also Chapter 5 for a more thorough discussion of the Michigan Democratic party.
15. See Kroll merger memorandum, Footnote 1.

as a grave threat to the American Way. After all, was the PAC not a cynical sell-out of the nonpartisan tradition? Was it not a political juggernaut designed to trample its foes both within and without the labor movement? Had it not sold labor's bargaining power in politics for the dross of Rooseveltian Democracy? Had it not brought the socialist state to Michigan, where it had subverted the state Democratic party? In short, PAC critics found it much more important and dangerous than cooler observers and political realists. In many ways, the mythical PAC of the critics was as important as the real organization.

In its first year of existence, the CIO's political committee was little more than an amateur organization. Yet, its amateur status did little to deter its critics from inflating its powers and pernicious nature. Thomas Girdler, chairman of Republic Steel, did much to set the tone of the critics. Standing as a staunch defender of the Gompers tradition, Girdler condemned the CIO and Hillman for dragging the labor movement into the political arena where it did not belong. Without actually saying it, he implied that there was something alien and disloyal about a politicized labor movement.[16] The AFL was quick to concur.

In 1944, the *American Federationist,* official organ of the AFL, was filled with condemnations of the CIO's political move. The climax came in a September, 1944, article by R. J. Watt. Watt called the CIO move nothing but a crude bundling-up of the labor vote and the delivery of same, strings free, to the Democrats. Certainly, this was a dangerous and serious departure from established, traditional method.[17] Although a closer examination of Samuel Gompers's political practice revealed that the bundling-up of the labor vote had been an ancient and honored art in American labor history, the Girdler–Watt charge became facet one of the PAC myth.

An equally important facet of the mythical PAC was the legend of its incredible political power. Probably the one man most responsible for this bit of fabrication was Arthur Krock, political analyst of the *New York Times.* Although Philip Murray, Sidney Hillman, and other CIO leaders

16. *New York Times,* September 17, 1944, p. 18.
17. R. J. Watt, "Labor and Politics," *American Federationist,* 51 (September 1944), p. 5.

had placed their bets on Henry Wallace's 1944 campaign for the vice presidential nomination, Krock publicly maintained that the selection of Harry Truman was "cleared" with Hillman before it had been presented to the Democratic convention.[18] As the 1944 primaries began to thin the ranks of Republican and Democratic conservatives, it was the PAC that was most prominently credited with the pruning process. Such nationally-known conservatives as Martin Dies and Champ Clark spurred on the mythmakers with their tales of being "done in" by Hillman's band of "Communists." [19] After a number of PAC candidates managed to win their way into office, the juggernaut myth grew and expanded. Indeed, entire congressional hearings were devoted to means whereby the PAC might be shackled.[20] Strangely enough, this facet of the myth lent itself particularly well to pro-PAC fantasies.

Once PAC partisans were armed with the supposed knowledge that the Committee was a major power in American politics, they began to weave the PAC into their fantasies of third parties and massive political realignments. Even before the creation of the Committee, CIO leaders had been particularly prone to such fantasies. The PAC's union voter concept, a plan that saw CIO voters as the base for a New Deal political party, traced its origins from the Textile Worker's utopian plan of 1943, "Toward a New Day." By 1948, the infectious new-party virus had spread from PAC leadership circles to outside liberals. In that year, University of London professor Harold Laski published a study of American politics that viewed the CIO Political Action Committee as the potential savior of American Democracy. Because the established political parties were faced with a seemingly insoluable problem, that of balancing demands for an equitable distribution of

18. *New York Times*, July 25, 1944, p. 18. After Krock's editorial, "Clear it with Sidney" became the battle cry of the Republican campaign, Dewey and his cohorts viewed the "dangerous" influence that Hillman had over Roosevelt with exaggerated alarm.

19. *Washington Post*, May 17, 1944, p. 8; August 4, 1944, p. 15.

20. U.S., House, Committee on Military Affairs, *Hearings on H.R. 3937 to Repeal the War Labor Disputes Act,* 79th Cong., 1st sess., 1945, pp. 1–7.

income with equally persuasive calls from their corporate backers to resist such demands, a new progressive force untied to corporate power would surely come to the fore. This force, in all likelihood, would be the CIO–PAC, the only major political organization in the United States not bound by corporate ties. If the existing Republican and Democratic parties continued to follow the counsels of their conservatives, the PAC would be forced to offer the public a liberal alternative, an alternative that would closely follow the Jeffersonian tradition. In this sense, the founding of the PAC in 1943 was as important an event in American history as the creation of the Populist alliance of the 1890s. The PAC would be to America what the Co-operative Commonwealth Federation was to Canada, or the British Labour party was to the mother country. "The trade-unionist of urban America has an abstract sense of the need for solidarity with the poor farmer and agricultural labourer," wrote Laski, and it would be the PAC that would weld these disparate blocs of the New Deal alliance into a permanent, liberal alternative to the existing party system in the United States.[21] American labor was on the verge of a brave new world, a world that would be made possible by the CIO Political Action Committee.

When such distinguished social analysts as Harold Laski swallowed the PAC myth, it was little wonder that less perceptive politicos were misled by PAC publicity. Consider, for instance, the case of Leonard DeCaux.

DeCaux was the first of the CIO's Communists to be given the axe by the Murray–Carey–Brophy faction. A New Zealander educated at Harrow and Oxford, DeCaux had gotten into the American labor movement through the International Workers of the World (his first love) and the Brookwood Labor College (which he found a bit too tame). After a mid-1920s stint on *Industrial Solidarity,* the New York-based Wobbly newspaper, he returned to England as a reporter for the leftist *Federated Press* and joined the Communist party. The next milestone was a brief job for the *Illinois Miner,* a job important chiefly because of DeCaux's ultimate employer, John L. Lewis of the United

21. Harold J. Laski, *The American Democracy* (New York: The Viking Press, 1948), p. 241; also, pp. 134–37, 200–223, 238–49.

Mine Workers of America. As depression descended upon the country, DeCaux viewed the situation from the security of the Brotherhood of Locomotive Engineers' Cleveland office. While the world came tumbling down, he managed to put out the BLE's monthly *Journal*. Even the coming of the New Deal did little to faze the Cleveland labor editor. Indeed, he had utter contempt for the "bliss-was-it-in-that-dawn boys" of both the Communist and non-Communist camps who fled to Washington to remake America.[22] However, when John L. Lewis began the push for the CIO, Len DeCaux wanted in.

Serving as editor of the *CIO News* from 1937 to 1947, DeCaux was in the CIO but was never a trusted leader like Hillman, Brophy, or even Jack Kroll.[23] Thus, his vision of the CIO and, particularly, the CIO–PAC was more typical of the far left than of CIO leadership. As a genuine labor radical, DeCaux was as much ensnared in the trap of the PAC myth as Harold Laski.

What was the PAC to Len DeCaux? It was a vision, a dream come true, an all-pervasive excitement, and most of all, the foundation of the brave new world that the IWW had seen in 1905. While many impatient dreamers had turned to the Communists and the New Deal to speed the worldly attainment of nirvana, DeCaux saw salvation in the CIO and the PAC. To him, CIO–PAC had that certain "spark," or as he wrote:

> By spark I mean an emotional plus factor conspicuous in mass movements, in revolutions, in wars deemed to be just—the exuberance of being one of many sweeping on united against the foe, through immediate gains, through glowing if vague and distant goals.[24]

Without defining it, DeCaux saw the PAC as the kind of popular movement that would surpass even Laski's vision in accomplishments. It was the superbly emotional mass movement that would finally bring a true revolution to America. Yet, was that really the PAC?

In reality, the Political Action Committee was none of

22. Len DeCaux, *Labor Radical* (Boston: Beacon Press, 1970), p. 184; also, pp. 2–27, 94–121, 134–54.
23. Ibid., pp. 219–69.
24. Ibid., p. 441.

the things its mythmakers saw. Although it clearly modified the Gompers tradition, Samuel Gompers himself would probably have been less perturbed by PAC moves than R. J. Watt was. Gompers had never been one to shy away from politics.

The "clear it with Sidney" campaign was also not the kind of creation that should have materially aided Arthur Krock's reputation for omniscience. Hillman and the PAC were neither as brilliant, nor as powerful, as the sage of the *Times* believed. It must be remembered that strategist Hillman was the architect of the incredibly naive 1946 PAC campaign and that the powerful CIO–PAC usually lost as many labor districts as it won. As far as Hillman the power-broker was concerned, none of Roosevelt's close advisors ever credited him with being more than an intimate of the President. Indeed, a number of Kroll's complaints about Democratic unresponsiveness to PAC pressure were as true in Hillman's day as they were during Kroll's tenure.[25]

As far as the visions of Laski and DeCaux, they were simply incredible. Certainly, CIO leaders were fond of dreaming of themselves as champions of a brave new world. Even present AFL–CIO leaders have been known to wax poetic on the subject in unguarded moments. Outside of speechmaking and congressional canvassing, however, neither the CIO nor the PAC did anything that radically altered the political status quo.

The PAC, realistically, was a vehicle through which the CIO had hoped to exert more control on America's political processes. Unfortunately for the CIO and the PAC, Americans in the late 1940s and early 1950s were less susceptible to PAC's political programs than to Cold War rhetoric. In 1945 and 1946, the PAC had been the victim of a number of defeats caused by its wooing an anti-Communist audience with words of world cooperation and radical change. When the PAC finally realized the persuasiveness of the anti-Communist pitch, its new party line

25. *New York Times,* July 25, 1944, p. 18. James Loeb to Mrs. Franklin D. Roosevelt, November 15, 1944, James Loeb Correspondence Folder, Box 18, Series 1, Americans for Democratic Action Papers, WSHS. The UDA threat of liberal reprisals in the event of Byrnes's nomination probably had more effect than Sidney's PAC.

was barely sufficient to keep the House Un-American Activities Committee from its door. The radical purge and the new party line won it few new followers.

While the PAC was not a successful reorganizer of the American party system, it could safely rest upon a number of its accomplishments. Over the years, almost the entire liberal bloc of Congress had received crucial aid from the PAC at one time or another. The list of Senators who had been elected with PAC help sounded almost like a liberal's who's who. John F. Kennedy, Hubert Humphrey, Paul Douglas, Matthew Neely, Estes Kefauver, Henry Jackson, Mike Mansfield, and Albert Gore had all been the recipients of PAC aid in their electoral campaigns. Unfortunately, the list of conservatives elected over PAC candidates was almost as impressive. Richard Nixon, Everett Dirksen, Robert Taft, William Knowland, and Homer Capehart had all humiliated their PAC opponents. Outside of the electoral sphere, the PAC had bravely advanced a number of programs that had excellent prospects. The union voter concept, for example, seemed an outstanding idea in 1944. Liberals had always bemoaned the fact that workers voted economically, not ideologically. The PAC finally tried to change the situation. Among minority voters, the PAC also tried to pioneer new political paths. Even though the Negro–CIO coalition never seemed to materialize outside of Detroit, at least the PAC had tried to make such a coalition work. Yet, PAC programs never more than approached their potential greatness. The PAC's twelve years were years of almost's and maybe's, almost's and maybe's engendered by the basic dilemma of partisan politics.

The dilemma was this: Could the PAC remain a liberal pressure group, a group dedicated to liberals of both parties and to liberal programs regardless of their popularity, or would it seek effective political power with all the compromises such a course involved? As Senator Morse wrote in 1949, "You people in the CIO are going to have to make up your minds. . . ." The CIO never did.

Appendix

Percentage of Presidential Vote in Ten Strongest CIO Counties

County—Area	CIO [1]	Democratic [2]	
		1940	1944
Indiana			
Lake—Gary	47.4	60.8	60.6
Michigan			
Genessee—Flint	40.6[3]	56.3	55.7
Wayne—Detroit	43.4	61.6	63.4
New York			
Schenectady—Schenectady	51.5	45.3	43.9
Ohio			
Lucas—Toledo	32.9	50.5	49.6
Stark—Canton	27.2	56.2	52.7
Summit—Akron	39.0	58.5	58.4
Pennsylvania			
Allegheny—Pittsburgh	24.0	58.0	57.2
Northhampton—Bethlehem	41.0	56.5	54.7
Westmoreland—Vandergrift	48.2	59.9	58.2
Average for Counties		57.9	58.3
Dem. Vote		1,296,000	1,380,000
Total Vote		2,219,000	2,356,000
National Average		54.7	52.8
Dem. Vote		27,243,000	25,603,000
Total Vote		49,766,000	48,026,000

1. CIO membership figures taken from William H. Riker, "The CIO in Politics, 1936–1946," (Ph.D. dissertation, Harvard University, 1948), pp. 205–12. Riker's CIO membership numbers are then divided by 1944 voters in the district; U.S., Bureau of the Census, *Vote Cast in Presidential and Congressional Elections, 1928–1944* (Washington, D.C.: G.P.O., 1946), pp. 38–67.

2. U.S., Bureau of the Census, *Vote Cast*, pp. 38–67.

3. The percentage figure for Genessee County is that for the entire congressional district, which included several other counties. The real Genessee County figure should be much higher since most CIO members in the congressional district lived in the Flint area.

1944B

Vote Percentage in Selected Strong CIO Districts

District			CIO [4]		Democratic [5]	
			1944	1940	1942	1944
Michigan						
1, 13–17		Detroit	43.4	59.2	57.9	59.2
2		Jackson	38.2	37.7	36.5	35.1
6		Flint	40.6	48.8	42.9	44.6
Indiana						
1	Gary		47.5	60.9	53.6	61.7
3	South Bend		26.0	48.7	44.8	47.9
Pennsylvania						
20	Bethlehem		27.2	56.2	53.3	57.3
25	Newcastle		36.7	49.1	41.5	49.6
27	New Kensington		48.2	56.9	53.5	59.7
28	Erie		24.2	45.5	40.6	45.4
New York						
31	Schenectady		25.4	—	34.8	40.0
Ohio						
9	Toledo		32.9	54.7	48.2	48.4
14	Akron		25.4	52.8	48.7	50.3
19	Youngstown		22.9	61.9	56.4	63.4
New Jersey						
1	Camden		24.0	44.4	39.3	49.4
Wisconsin						
1	Kenosha		22.1	44.2	26.6	24.4
Average			35.1	52.0	48.8	50.5

4. Riker, pp. 205–212.
5. U.S., Bureau of the Census, *Vote Cast,* pp. 148–60.

1944C

Vote Percentage in Control Districts: No Active PAC Participation

District	Blue Collar Labor [6]		Democratic [7]	
	1944	1940	1942	1944
Arizona				
AL (At Large)	8.2	71.1	70.8	69.1
Idaho				
1 Lewiston	11.0	62.0	54.1	56.6
2 Boise	3.8	46.9	45.2	47.7
Iowa				
1 Iowa City	15.8	39.6	37.4	43.3
Maine				
2 Lewiston	47.7	33.4	32.4	32.2
Montana				
1 Great Falls	4.4	45.4	59.9	68.6
2 Butte	7.3	62.6	52.8	54.3
Utah				
2 Salt Lake City	10.1	63.3	55.8	62.3
West Virginia				
2 Morgantown	10.8	57.5	50.2	54.1
Wisconsin				
10 Superior	7.8	64.3	51.6	41.8
Wyoming				
1 AL	4.5	53.4	49.3	44.3
Average	10.9	55.0	50.6	53.1

6. U.S., Bureau of the Census, *County and City Data Book,* 1949, pp. 74–337. Blue collar labor is defined as manufacturing and mineral industry operatives only.

7. U.S., Bureau of the Census, *Vote Cast,* pp. 148–60. The 1940 vote is taken from Malcom Moos, pp. 179–215. The Wisconsin vote includes the Progressive party vote.

1944D
The Labor Voter: Presidential Elections
Democratic Percentage in Strong Labor Wards [8]

Area	Labor Wards				Nonlabor Wards			
	Ward	1936	1940	1944	Ward	1936	1940	1944
Chicago	12	83	77	79	5	57	54	65
	21	85	79	80	7	58	50	55
	22	87	82	83	48	61	52	57
	25	80	66	71	50	53	40	44
Average		84	76	79		57	49	55
Hartford								
E. Hartford		59	54	57	Newington	45	45	45
S. Windsor		56	50	51	W. Hartford	38	33	38
Windsor		51	48	50	Wetherfield	33	32	36
Average		56	52	55		37	34	38
Milwaukee	5	90	75	73	1	79	62	62
	8	92	79	77	18	55	38	43
	14	97	93	91	Shorewood	52	35	42
	21	88	68	65	Whitefish Bay	46	24	30
Average		91	79	77		60	43	46
Pittsburgh	3	90	85	84	4	69	63	65
	6	85	85	84	7	56	40	41
	16	87	76	78	8	66	37	52
	17	86	78	78	19	67	52	49
	21	80	70	71	26	61	47	43
Average		83	79	79		64	52	50
Four-City Average		84	76	77		57	47	53

8. Strong labor wards are defined as wards in which over eighty per cent of population belongs to the "operative," "laborer," or "skilled labor" occupational categories of the United States Bureau of the Census' census tracts in cities with strong CIO concentrations. For a detailed breakdown of the census tracts and comparable ward voting, see, U.S., Bureau of the Census, *Sixteenth Census of the United States: 1940. Population and Housing, Statistics for Census Tracts,* Chicago, Hartford, Milwaukee, and Pittsburgh (statistical volumes are arranged in alphabetical order by the name of the city). Ward boundaries were taken from Scammon, pp. 81, 309, and 403. Scammon's boundaries were checked with 1944 sources to see where they differed from 1944 ward borders.

Voting statistics were drawn from the following: *Chicago Tribune,* November 4, 1936, p. 6; November 5, 1936, p. 5; November 6, 1940, pp. 2, 4; November 9, 1944, p. 4. Connecticut, *Register and Manual,* 1937, 1941, 1945. Pennsylvania, *Pennsylvania Manual,* Vol. 83, 85, 87. Wisconsin, *Blue Book,* 1937, 1942, 1946. The cities were originally chosen for their high proportion of CIO members. See, Riker, pp. 205–12.

Nonlabor wards were selected in non-working class areas and were composed of at least eighty per cent "professionals," "proprietors," or "clerical" workers as defined by the U.S. Bureau of the Census. All other statistics were drawn from the same sources used for labor wards.

1944E

The Labor Voter: Non-Presidential Elections
Democratic Percentage in Strong Labor Wards [9]

Area	Labor Wards				Nonlabor Wards			
	Ward	1936	1940	1944	Ward	1936	1940	1944
Chicago	12	70	67	77	*5*	56	46	59
	21	73	71	74	*7*	55	43	52
	22	77	73	79	*48*	57	45	54
	23	76	70	78	*49*	53	40	50
	25	71	59	68	*50*	47	30	41
Average		73	68	75		54	41	51
Hartford								
E. Hartford	59	53	57	Newington	44	41	45	
S. Windsor	57	50	50	W. Hartford	38	31	37	
Windsor	51	46	51	Wetherfield	34	28	37	
Average		56	51	55		38	31	38
Milwaukee	(Democratic/Progressive Percentage)							
	5	34/55	26/53	72/3	*1*	40/38	29/38	58/1
	8	41/51	35/44	73/2	*18*	26/26	16/26	39/1
	14	42/54	45/45	86/2	Whitefish B.	23/21	10/18	27/1
	21	36/50	26/48	63/3	Shorewood	24/25	15/18	34/1
Average		38/53	33/48	73/2		26/25	19/25	41/1
Three-City Average (Democratic + Progressive)		75	69	73		48	41	49

9. The sources for this are the same as for Table 1944D.

Democratic Congressional Vote Percentage in Districts Previously
Republican

District [10]	Labor [11] 1944	CIO–PAC Endorsed?	Democratic [12] 1944	1942
California				
2 Western Mtns.	17.5		—	63.9
4* San Francisco	—	Yes	—	51.0
6* Oakland	27.4	Yes	—	52.0
13* Los Angeles	—	Yes	46.1	55.0
18 L.A. suburbs	—		43.2	55.7
Connecticut				
1* Hartford	42.5	Yes	48.6	54.2
2* New London	24.9	Yes	48.6	51.2
3* New Haven	57.5	Yes	48.3	51.5
AL*	40.1	Yes	47.7	51.6
Delaware				
AL*	23.1	Yes	45.3	50.5
Illinois				
3* Chicago	—	Yes	48.7	52.0
9* Chicago	—	Yes	48.7	52.8
22 Champaign	8.9		44.3	50.8
Maryland				
4* Baltimore	—	Yes	49.1	59.2
Michigan				
12 Houghton	10.8	Yes	46.9	50.6
Minnesota				
4* St. Paul	27.0	Yes	34.3	51.8
Missouri				
8 S.E. Rural	11.2		48.5	50.5
11* St. Louis	—	Yes	49.6	58.9
Ohio				
3* Dayton	51.2	Yes	48.4	52.6
14* Akron	47.0	Yes	48.7	50.3
16* Canton	37.2	Yes	47.3	53.0
Pennsylvania				
1* Philadelphia	—	Yes	—	58.4
5* Philadelphia	—	Yes	—	53.6
Washington				
3* Vancouver	24.3	Yes	42.9	52.0
West Virginia				
1* Fairmont	35.3	Yes	45.3	50.4
3 Clarksburg	13.8	Yes	46.8	52.5

* Denotes that CIO–PAC claimed credit for the victory.

10. Moos, pp. 179–215.

11. U.S., Bureau of the Census, *County and City Data Book,* 1949, pp. 24–337.

12. Blank spaces signify no Democratic candidate during that year or no comparable district during that election. U.S., Bureau of the Census, *Vote Cast,* pp. 148–60.

1948A
Percentage of Presidential Vote in Ten Strongest CIO Counties [13]

County	CIO	Democratic		
		1940	1944	1948
Indiana				
Lake	37	61	61	59
St. Joseph	40	56	54	55
Michigan				
Genessee	47	57	56	53
Wayne	41	62	64	58
Ohio				
Lucas	33	51	50	52
Stark	27	56	53	48
Summit	39	59	58	55
Pennsylvania				
Allegheny	24	58	57	55
Northhampton	41	57	55	55
Westmoreland	48	60	59	58
Average for Counties		59	59	56
Dem. Vote		1,315,000	1,400,000	1,284,000
Total Vote		2,232,000	2,370,000	2,287,000
National Average		55	53	50
Dem. Vote		27,243,000	25,603,000	24,045,000
Total Vote		49,766,000	48,026,000	48,489,000

13. The ten strongest CIO counties and their respective CIO memberships were selected from the following three sources: Local Unions, n.d. (1950), PAC 1950 Folder, Box 105, Michigan AFL–CIO Papers, ALH; Loren Houser to Herbert McCreedy, April 28, 1954, Folder 12, Box 53, Michigan AFL–CIO Papers. ALH; Riker, pp. 205–12.

Voting statistics were derived from George Gallup, *The Political Almanac, 1952* (New York: B. C. Forbes, 1952), pp. 147–62. U.S., Bureau of the Census, *Vote Cast,* pp. 38–67.

1948B
Vote Percentages in Selected Strong CIO Districts [14]

Congressional District	CIO	Democratic			
		1942	1944	1946	1948
Indiana					
1	37	54	62	53	61
3	25	45	48	44	52
Michigan					
1	63	78	81	66	84
6	36	43	45	42	50
13	38	51	58	47	63
14	50	59	57	47	57
15	33	65	64	52	65
16	52	59	62	52	63
Ohio					
9	33	48	48	49	53
14	25	49	50	53	58
19	23	56	63	60	68
Pennsylvania					
20	27	53	57	53	59
25	37	42	50	41	47
27	48	54	60	53	62
28	24	41	45	36	46
Average		52	56	50	59

14. Strong CIO congressional districts were selected in the same manner as strong CIO counties. See Ibid.

Voting statistics for the 1942–1948 congressional races came from U.S., *Congressional Directory*, 79th Cong., 1st sess., 1945, pp. 254–261; 81st Cong., 1st sess., 1949, pp. 244–251.

1948C
Vote Percentage in Control Districts with
No Active PAC Participation [15]

Congressional District	Labor	Democratic			
		1942	1944	1946	1948
Arizona					
AL (1948=1+2)	8	71	69	67	62
Idaho					
1	11	54	57	49	53
2	4	45	48	39	49
Iowa					
1	16	37	43	39	46
Maine					
2	48	32	32	39	33
Montana					
1	4	60	69	58	68
2	7	53	54	45	49
Utah					
2	10	56	62	47	58
West Virginia					
2	11	50	54	49	55
Wisconsin					
10	8	52	42	45	43
Wyoming					
AL	5	49	44	44	49
Non-CIO Average	11	51	53	48	53
CIO Average		52	56	50	59

15. Ideally, non-CIO control districts should have been in northern industrial areas similar to CIO-PAC districts except having no PAC working in them. However, since the PAC was active in every major northern industrial city (and since there were no two-party races in southern industrial areas), I have had to use smaller industrial areas in the West where the PAC was not active. The sources used to determine PAC activity were essentially the same as in Table 1944B. However, certain correspondence proved useful in determining lack of PAC activity. Irwin DeShetler to Joseph Deardoff, January 3, 1955, Nevada State CIO–PAC Folder, Box 29, Irwin L. DeShetler Papers, ALH.

Voting statistics from Ibid.

1948D
The Labor Voter: Presidential Elections [16]
Democratic Percentage in Strong Labor Wards

Area	Labor Wards				Nonlabor Wards			
	Ward	1940	1944	1948	Ward	1940	1944	1948
Chicago	12	77	79	73	5	54	65	49
	21	79	80	73	7	50	55	44
	22	82	83	74	48	52	57	46
	23	80	79	74	49	41	50	47
	25	66	71	77	50	40	44	36
Average		76	79	74		49	55	44
Hartford								
	E. Hartford	54	57	57	Newington	45	45	41
	S. Windsor	50	51	47	W. Hartford	33	38	30
	Windsor	48	50	48	Wethersfield	32	36	32
Average		52	55	54		34	38	32
Milwaukee	5	75	73	69	1	62	62	58
	8	79	77	71	18	38	43	34
	14	93	91	80	Shorewood	35	42	25
	21	68	65	66	Whitefish B.	24	30	16
Average		79	77	72		43	46	36
Pittsburgh	3	85	84	81	4	64	65	63
	6	85	84	84	7	40	41	37
	16	76	78	78	8	37	52	53
	17	78	78	80	19	52	49	51
	21	70	71	73	26	47	43	45
Average		79	79	82		52	50	51
Four-City								
Average		76	77	71		47	53	42

16. Almost the same sources have been used for this as have been used for Table 1944D. Updated voting statistics were drawn from: *Chicago Tribune,* November 3, 1948, p. 2; November 4, 1948, p. 2. Connecticut, *Register and Manual,* 1949. Pennsylvania, *Pennsylvania Manual,* Vol. 89. Wisconsin, *Blue Book,* 1950.

1948E

The Labor Voter: Nonpresidential Elections [17]

Democratic Percentage in Strong Labor Wards

Area		Labor Wards				Nonlabor Wards			
	Ward	1940	1944	1948		Ward	1940	1944	1948
Chicago	12	67	77	72		5	46	59	51
	21	71	74	74		7	43	52	51
	22	73	79	69		48	45	54	47
	23	70	78	68		49	40	50	46
	25	59	68	69		50	30	41	44
	Average	68	75	72			41	51	48
Hartford									
E. Hartford		53	57	57	Newington		41	45	43
S. Windsor		50	50	47	W. Hartford		31	37	34
Windsor		46	51	49	Wethersfield		28	37	32
	Average	51	55	44			31	38	35
Milwaukee	(Democratic and People's Progressive Vote)								
	5	79	75	68		1	67	59	57
	8	77	75	67		18	42	40	39
	14	90	88	77	Shorewood		33	35	28
	21	74	66	62	Whitefish B.		28	28	22
	Average	81	75	68			44	42	38
Three-City									
	Average	69	73	69			41	49	43

17. Ibid.

1952A
Percentage of Presidential Vote in Ten Strongest CIO Counties [18]

County	CIO	Democratic		
		1944	1948	1952
Indiana				
Lake	37	61	59	55
St. Joseph	40	54	55	50
Michigan				
Genessee	47	56	53	48
Wayne	41	64	58	58
Ohio				
Lucas	33	50	52	48
Stark	27	53	48	42
Summit	39	58	55	52
Pennsylvania				
Allegheny	24	57	55	51
Northhampton	41	55	55	49
Westmoreland	48	59	58	58
Average for counties		59	56	53
Democratic Vote (in millions)		1.4	1.3	1.6
Total Vote (in millions)		2.4	2.3	2.9
National Average		53	50	44
Democratic National Vote (in millions)		25.6	24.0	27.2
Total Vote (in millions)		48.0	48.5	61.6

18. Almost the same sources were used to ascertain CIO membership as for Table 1948A. Updated election statistics were drawn from Scammon, *America Votes.*

1952B
Percentage of Presidential Vote in Strong Labor Wards
(Democratic Vote)[19]

		Labor Wards				Nonlabor Wards		
		1944	1948	1952		1944	1948	1952
Chicago	12	79	73	62	7	55	44	44
	21	83	73	64	48	57	46	46
	23	79	74	64	49	50	47	47
	25	71	77	67	50	44	36	44
	Average	78	75	64		52	43	45
Detroit	9	79	81	80	1	69	75	75
	13	84	85	80	2	49	47	42
	15	71	75	72	18	66	71	63
	17	61	63	59	22	50	50	44
	Average	75	78	74		56	57	51
Hartford								
E. Hartford		57	57	50	Newington	45	41	36
S. Windsor		51	47	39	W. Hartford	38	30	31
Windsor		50	48	41	Wethersfield	36	32	30
	Average	55	54	49		38	32	32
Milwaukee	5	73	69	64	18	43	34	31
	8	77	71	64	Shorewood	42	25	25
	21	65	66	53	Whitefish B.	30	16	22
	Average	71	68	60		40	27	27
Pittsburgh	6	84	84	79	4	65	63	57
	16	78	78	71	7	41	37	34
	24	59	62	54	11	56	53	50
	31	62	63	55	14	55	44	45
	Average	73	74	67		55	49	47
Labor Average		74	74	67				
Nonlabor Average		53	47	45				

19. Voting statistics from Scammon, *America Votes;* and Wisconsin, *Blue Book,* 1946–1954. See also Connecticut, *Register and Manual,* 1946–1954.

Labor wards were chosen on the basis of eighty per cent of their population being in the "operative," "skilled labor," and "labor" categories of the census. See, U.S., Bureau of the Census, *Seventeenth Census of the United States: 1950, Population and Housing,* Vol. 3: *Statistics for Census Tracts.*

New Democratic Congressmen from 1952 Republican Districts

District	Area [20]	Labor Vote Percentage [21]	CIO–PAC Endorsed? [22]	District's 1938–1950 Classification [23]
Delaware				
AL	—	22.2	Yes	Marginal Republican
Illinois				
3 *	Chicago	—	Yes	Marginal Republican
12 *	Chicago	—	Yes	Marginal Republican
25 *	Cairo	15.1	Yes	Redrawn 1951
Indiana				
8	Evansville	20.8	Yes	Marginal Democrat
Maryland				
5	Western Shore + Baltimore	8.0	Yes	Redrawn 1951
Massachusetts				
8 *	Boston	—	Yes	Marginal Republican
Michigan				
6 *	Flint	41.4	Yes	Marginal Republican
17 *	Detroit	—	Yes	Redrawn 1951
Minnesota				
9	N-W State	3.1	Yes	Normal Republican
Missouri				
4	Independence	—	Yes	Redrawn 1951
6	St. Joseph	—	Yes	Redrawn 1951
New Jersey				
6 *	Union Co.	37.9	Yes	Normal Republican
New York				
21 *	Upper West Side Manhattan	—	Yes	Redrawn 1951
Oregon				
3 *	Portland	—	Yes	Marginal Republican
Pennsylvania				
11 *	Wilkes-Barre	36.5	Yes	Redrawn 1951
19 *	York	38.8	Yes	Redrawn 1951
25 *	New Castle	45.5	Yes	Marginal Republican
Virginia				
9	Western Tip	3.8	No	Normal Democrat
West Virginia				
4	Huntington	21.4	Yes	Marginal Republican
Wisconsin				
5 *	Milwaukee	—	Yes	Marginal Republican
9	Eau Claire	12.7	Yes	Normal Republican

* Denotes probable CIO–PAC factor in victory.

20. Scammon, pp. 52–410.

21. U.S., Bureau of the Census, *Congressional District Data Book* (Washington: G.P.O., 1961), pp. 2–129. These figures

1954B
Selected CIO Districts: Percentage of Vote for Endorsed Candidate

District [24]	Area	1946	1950	1952	1954
Indiana					
1	Gary	51.9	52.6	56.4	61.4
3	South Bend, Elkart	43.6	46.4	44.9	49.2
Michigan					
1	Detroit	65.9	82.2	84.2	88.3
2	Jackson, Ann Arbor	28.0	39.0	36.3	40.1
6	Flint, Lansing	42.0	46.3	47.0	51.1
13	Detroit	46.9	61.4	64.8	65.8
14	Detroit	46.3	51.5	53.0	58.2
15	Detroit	51.9	64.1	66.7	72.7
16	Detroit	51.9	60.7	60.7	67.9
Average for Nine Districts		47.8	55.2	50.8	60.7
Michigan					
17	Detroit	Redrawn	1951	47.0	52.2
Pennsylvania					
26	Washington, Greene Fayette Counties	Redrawn	1951	59.1	65.3
28	Pittsburgh	Redrawn	1951	58.7	65.1
Average for Twelve Districts		47.8	55.2	53.3	57.4

are drawn from a 1954 census of industry.

22. *Labor Union Political Expenditures* (Washington: Senate Republican Policy Committee, 1955), pp. 3–12. Endorsement is defined as a substantial PAC contribution to the winning candidate.

23. A marginal district is one which is usually won by less than fifty-five per cent of the vote. A normal district is one in which the victor draws at least sixty per cent of the vote. See, Moos, pp. 24–81.

24. All selected districts had CIO membership equal to at least forty-four per cent of the 1944 electorate. See Riker, pp. 205–12. Riker's figures were in turn checked against reliable CIO membership figures as cited for Table 1948A. Voting statistics came from Scammon, pp. 98–319.

1954C
Control Districts with No PAC-Endorsed Candidate;
Democratic Vote Percentage [25]

District	Area	1946	1950	1925	1954	Labor [26]
Illinois	Redrawn					
14	Elgin, McHenry	1947	25.8	28.5	27.6	24.6
		Redrawn				
15	Joliet, Will Co.	1947	36.7	36.4	37.2	31.9
18	Peoria	32.5	38.4	44.8	42.5	25.9
Indiana						
4	Fort Wayne	39.5	43.1	35.4	39.6	25.8
9	Rural Southern Counties	43.3	44.6	43.2	48.3	20.1
Maryland						
1	Eastern Shore	49.1	43.0	38.9	44.5	28.6
Michigan						
12	Western half of N. Peninsula	45.2	38.3	41.8	44.1	21.1
Minnesota						
2	Rural S. Central	31.6	32.9	30.6	39.1	12.9
New Jersey						
2	Atlantic City	32.9	45.7	36.6	36.4	23.3
New York						
28	Newburgh and Orange County	38.4	36.8	33.9	32.7	30.1
Utah						
1	All of state but Salt Lake & Provo	50.1	51.1	39.5	46.6	12.5
Virginia						
9	Western Counties	51.8	58.4	48.3	50.5	3.8
Average		46.1	40.6	42.0	41.1	22.1

25. Election districts chosen by lack of PAC financial support, *Political Expenditures of Labor,* pp. 3–12; voting statistics, Scammon, pp. 98–319.

26. U.S., Bureau of the Census, *Congressional District,* pp. 2–129.

1954D
1954 Congressional Election Vote Percentages in the Ten States
with the Most Unionists [27]

State	Unionists 1954	Endorsed Vote 1950	1952	1954	October Unemployment [28]
1. New York	42.0	Redrawn 1951	41.9	45.8	3.1 4.8 in June
2. Pennsylvania	40.6	53.3	52.6	54.4	5.0 6.6 in April
3. California	37.9	Redrawn 1951	47.9	53.4	2.4 4.8 in March
4. Illinois	41.4	55.0	54.0	60.8	3.1 5.1 in May
5. Ohio	48.0	Redrawn 1951	45.1	43.7	2.7 3.9 in March
6. Michigan	51.6	42.5	44.0	47.0	5.3 6.9 in Sept.
7. New Jersey	36.4	46.4	46.4	53.2	4.0 5.4 in May
8. Indiana	35.9	46.5	43.8	47.9	2.6 5.1 in March
9. Massachusetts	30.8	49.8	50.1	54.7	3.3 4.5 in April
10. Missouri	43.0	Redrawn 1951	54.0	55.1	3.2 3.8 in April

27. "States Where Labor Has Political Strength," *Fortune,* 53 (April 1956), p. 226. Unionists means AFL + CIO + Independents. Voting statistics are from Scammon, pp. 31–319.

28. Unemployment refers only to those workers who had *not* exhausted their state unemployment insurance benefits. U.S., Bureau of Labor Statistics, *Monthly Labor Review,* 78 (June 1955), pp. 711–13.

1954E
Democratic Vote in Strong Labor Wards [29]

City	Labor Ward Percentage					Nonlabor Ward Percentage				
	Ward	1948	1950	1952	1954	Ward	1948	1950	1952	1954
Chicago	12		63.3	61.8	72.5	7		41.7	48.6	54.2
	21		64.3	65.0	79.4	48		47.0	48.9	56.8
	23		65.6	65.7	76.4	49		46.9	51.6	57.8
	25		68.8	67.2	77.3	50		36.7	47.3	57.0
	Average		65.3	64.7	76.3			42.9	49.0	56.4
Detroit	9	85.3	83.9	83.6	87.0	1	77.9	78.0	77.8	81.4
	13	85.4	83.8	84.3	88.7	2	46.1	39.3	46.3	48.1
	15	75.3	73.2	75.9	81.9	18	70.0	66.8	67.3	73.2
	17	63.5	59.5	63.8	70.6	22	49.6	47.3	50.2	55.0
	Average	77.6	75.7	77.5	82.7		56.7	54.1	56.9	60.4
Hartford										
	E. Hartford	57.0	63.0	54.2	59.1	Newington	42.7	48.8	41.5	42.5
	S. Windsor	47.3	49.3	44.5	48.9	W. Hartford	34.2	42.3	38.0	37.7
	Windsor	49.4	55.2	48.0	52.4	Wethersfield	32.0	40.5	35.2	35.3
	Average	54.2	59.5	51.9	56.5		34.7	42.9	38.0	37.9
Pittsburgh	6	83.7	79.7	79.1	83.0	4	63.2	60.5	57.8	64.6
	16	77.6	68.5	71.4	77.4	7	37.3	34.6	35.0	38.9
	24	61.8	54.3	54.3	60.0	11	52.6	49.4	50.2	56.9
	31	62.8	56.4	55.4	63.6	14	43.5	39.8	45.2	50.1
	Average	73.9	66.8	67.2	73.1		49.2	45.8	47.3	52.7
Four-City										
	Average	73.5	69.4	69.9	76.9		52.3	47.8	51.0	55.9

29. Essentially the same sources make up the basis for this table as are used for Table 1952B. Updated voting statistics come from Connecticut, *Register and Manual*, 1956; Wisconsin, *Blue Book*, 1956; Pennsylvania, *Pennsylvania Manual*, Vol. 95.

Bibliography

Manuscript Collections

AFL–CIO Committee on Political Education Papers, Wisconsin State Historical Society, Madison, Wis.

Americans for Democratic Action Papers, Wisconsin State Historical Society, Madison, Wis.

Thomas R. Amlie Papers, Wisconsin State Historical Society, Madison, Wis.

Association of Catholic Trade Unionists, Detroit Branch Papers, Archives of Labor History and Urban Affairs, Wayne State University, Detroit, Mich.

Elmer Austin Benson Papers, Minnesota Historical Society, St. Paul, Minn.

John Toussaint Bernard Papers, Minnesota Historical Society, St. Paul, Minn.

Van A. Bittner Papers, West Virginia University Library, Morgantown, W. Va.

Briggs Local 212 Papers, Archives of Labor History and Urban Affairs, Wayne State University, Detroit, Mich.

John Brophy Papers, Catholic University of America, Washington, D.C.

Charles Chiakulas Papers, Archives of Labor History and Urban Affairs, Wayne State University, Detroit, Mich.

Clark Clifford Papers, Harry S. Truman Library, Independence, Mo.

CIO Secretary–Treasurer's Papers, Archives of Labor History and Urban Affairs, Wayne State University, Detroit, Mich.

Irwin L. DeShetler Papers, Archives of Labor History and Urban Affairs, Wayne State University, Detroit, Mich.

John Edelman Papers, Archives of Labor History and Urban Affairs, Wayne State University, Detroit, Mich.

Neal Edwards Papers, Archives of Labor History and Urban Affairs, Wayne State University, Detroit, Mich.

Katherine Ellickson Papers, Archives of Labor History and Urban Affairs, Wayne State University, Detroit, Mich.

Richard Frankensteen Papers, Archives of Labor History and Urban Affairs, Wayne State University, Detroit, Mich.

Delmond Garst Papers, Archives of Labor History and Urban Affairs, Wayne State University, Detroit, Mich.

Adolph Germer Papers, Wisconsin State Historical Society, Madison, Wis.

Samuel Gompers Letterbooks (film), Labor Management Documentation Center, Cornell University, Ithaca, N.Y.

Oscar F. Hawkins and Family Papers, Minnesota Historical Society, St. Paul, Minn.

Sidney Hillman Papers, Amalgamated Clothing Workers Union, New York, N.Y.

John Melseth Jacobsen Papers, Minnesota Historical Society, St. Paul, Minn.

Jack Kroll Papers, Library of Congress, Manuscripts Division, Washington, D.C.

Labor's Non-Partisan League Papers, Wisconsin State Historical Society, Madison, Wis.

Patrick V. McNamara Papers, Archives of Labor History and Urban Affairs, Wayne State University, Detroit, Mich.

Michigan AFL–CIO Papers, Archives of Labor History and Urban Affairs, Wayne State University, Detroit, Mich.

Philip Murray Papers, Catholic University of America, Washington, D.C.

William Nagorsne Papers, Wisconsin State Historical Society, Madison, Wis.

Harry Cyril Read Papers, Catholic University of America, Washington, D.C.

Monsignor Charles Owen Rice Papers, Pennsylvania State University Archives, University Park, Pa.

Monsignor John A. Ryan Papers, Catholic University of America, Washington, D.C.

Genevieve Fallon Steefel Collection of the Minnesota Progressive Party, Library of Congress, Manuscripts Division, Washington, D.C.

Textile Workers Union of America Papers, Wisconsin State Historical Society, Madison, Wis.

Rolland J. Thomas Papers, Archives of Labor History and Urban Affairs, Wayne State University, Detroit, Mich.

Wayne County AFL–CIO Papers, Archives of Labor History and Urban affairs, Wayne State University, Detroit, Mich.

West Virginia Federation of Labor Papers, West Virginia University Library, Morgantown, W. Va.

West Virginia Labor Federation AFL–CIO Papers, West Virginia University Library, Morgantown, W. Va.

West Virginia State Industrial Union Council Papers, West Virginia University Library, Morgantown, W. Va.

Wisconsin State Industrial Union Council Papers, Wisconsin State Historical Society, Madison, Wis.

Oral History Interviews

Harry Block Interview, Pennsylvania State University Archives, University Park, Pa.

Albert J. Fitzgerald Interview, Pennsylvania State University Archives, University Park, Pa.

James Matles Interview, Pennsylvania State University Archives, University Park, Pa.

Monsignor Charles Owen Rice Interview, Pennsylvania State University Archives, University Park, Pa.

Public Documents

U.S. Bureau of Labor Statistics. *Monthly Labor Review,* Vols. 56–78.

U.S. Bureau of the Census. *Sixteenth Census of the United States: 1940. Population and Housing,* Statistics for Census Tracts.

U.S. Bureau of the Census. *Seventeenth Census of the United States: 1950. Population and Housing,* Vol. 3.

U.S. House of Representatives. Committee on Military Affairs. *Hearings on H.R. 3937 to Repeal the War Labor Disputes Act.* 79th Cong., 1st sess., 1945.

————. Committee to Investigate Campaign Expenditures. *Hearings on H.R. 551.* 78th Cong., 2nd sess., 1944.

————. Labor Committee. *Hearings on Proposed Amendments to the Fair Labor Standards Act.* 79th Cong., 1st sess., 1945.

————. Special Committee on Un-American Activities. *Hearings on H.R. 282.* 78th Cong., 2nd sess., 1944.

U.S. Senate. Committee on Labor and Public Welfare. *Hearings on S. J. Res. 22, A Labor Relations Program.* 80th Cong., 1st sess., 1947.

————. Special Committee to Investigate Presidential, Vice-Presidential, and Senatorial Campaign Expenditures. *Hearings on S.R. 263.* 78th Cong., 2nd sess., 1944.

U.S. *Congressional Record.* Vols. 89–100.

U.S. *Statutes at Large.* Vols. 57, 64–66.

Union Documents

Amalgamated Clothing Workers of America. *Documentary History of the Amalgamated Clothing Workers of America.* New York: Amalgamated Clothing Workers of America, 1920.

————. *Proceedings of the Seventh Biennial Convention of the*

Amalgamated Clothing Workers of America. Montreal, Canada. May 11–15, 1926.

———. *Proceedings of the Sixteenth Biennial . . . Atlantic City, New Jersey. May 10–14, 1948.*

American Federation of Labor. *Proceedings of the First Constitutional Convention of the American Federation of Labor. Columbus, Ohio. December 8, 1886.*

———. *Proceedings of the Sixty-sixth Constitutional Convention . . . San Francisco, California. October 6–16, 1947.*

Congress of Industrial Organizations. *Proceedings of the Sixth Constitutional Convention of the Congress of Industrial Organizations, Philadelphia, Pennsylvania. November 1–5, 1943.*

———. *Proceedings of the Seventh Constitutional Convention . . . Chicago, Illinois. November 20–24, 1944.*

———. *Proceedings of the Eighth Constitutional Convention . . . Atlantic City, New Jersey. November 18–22, 1946.*

———. *Proceedings of the Ninth Constitutional Convention . . . Boston, Massachusetts. October 13–17, 1947.*

———. *Proceedings of the Eleventh Constitutional Convention . . . Cleveland, Ohio. October 31–November 4, 1949.*

———. *Proceedings of the Fourteenth Constitutional Convention . . . Atlantic City, New Jersey. December 1–4, 1952.*

———. *Report of President Philip Murray to the Sixth Constitutional Convention of the Congress of Industrial Organizations. Philadelphia, Pennsylvania. November 1–5, 1943.*

International Ladies Garment Workers' Union. *Proceedings of the Twenty-fifth Convention of the International Ladies Garment Workers Union. Boston, Massachusetts. May 29–June 9, 1944.*

———. *Report of the General Executive Board to the Twenty-Fifth Convention of the International Ladies Garment Workers Union. Boston, Massachusetts. May 29–June 9, 1944.*

Michigan CIO Council. *Proceedings of the Tenth Annual Convention of the Michigan CIO Council, Grand Rapids, Michigan. June 21–23, 1948.*

Textile Workers Union of America. *Proceedings of the Ninth Biennial Convention of the Textile Workers Union of America. Washington, D.C. May 14–18, 1956.*

———. *"Toward a New Day." Report to the Third Biennial Convention of the Textile Workers Union of America. May 12, 1943.*

United Automobile, Aircraft, and Agricultural Implement Workers of America–CIO. *Proceedings of the Special Convention of the United Automobile Workers of America. Cleveland, Ohio. March 27–April 6, 1939.*
————.*Proceedings of the Sixth Constitutional Convention . . . Buffalo, New York. August 4–16, 1941.*
————.*Proceedings of the Tenth Constitutional Convention . . . Atlantic City, New Jersey. March 23–31, 1946.*
————. *Proceedings of the Eleventh Constitutional Convention . . . Atlantic City, New Jersey. November 9–14, 1947.*
United Electrical, Radio, and Machine Workers of America, *Proceedings of the Twelfth Convention of the United Electrical, Radio, and Machine Workers of America. Boston, Massachusetts. September 22–26, 1947.*
United Mine Workers of America. *Proceedings of the Twenty-eighth Consecutive and Fifth Biennial Convention of the United Mine Workers of America. Indianapolis, Indiana. September 20–October 5, 1921.*

Special Union Documents

Congress of Industrial Organizations. *Proceedings of the International Executive Board, CIO.* Complete typed originals from 1940 to 1955. International Union of Electrical and Radio Workers National Offices, Washington, D.C.

Other Primary Sources

Books

Brock, Clifton. *Americans for Democratic Action.* Washington: Public Affairs Press, 1962.
Brophy, John. *A Miner's Life.* Madison: University of Wisconsin Press, 1964.
Byrnes, James F. *All in One Lifetime.* New York: Harper and Brothers, 1958.
Calkins, Fay. *The CIO and the Democratic Party.* Chicago: University of Chicago Press, 1952. (Miss Calkins was a CIO–PAC worker in 1950.)
Cooke, Morris L., and Murray, Philip. *Organized Labor and Production.* New York: Harper and Brothers, 1946.
DeCaux, Len. *Labor Radical: From the Wobblies to CIO.* Boston: Beacon Press, 1970.
Eisenhower, Dwight D. *The White House Years.* Vol. 1: *Mandate for Change.* Garden City: Doubleday and Co., 1963.

Fountain, Clayton W. *Union Guy*. New York: The Viking Press, 1949.

Gaer, Joseph. *The First Round, the Story of the CIO Political Action Committee*. New York: Duell, Sloan and Pearce, 1944.

Gompers, Samuel. *Seventy Years of Life and Labor*. New York: E. P. Dutton, 1923.

Hartley, Fred A. Jr. *Our New National Labor Policy, the Taft–Hartley Act and the Next Steps*. New York: Funk and Wagnalls Co., 1948.

Hillman, Sidney. *The Reconstruction of Russia and the Task of Labor*. New York: Amalgamated Clothing Workers of America, Education Department, 1922.

Johnson, Walter. *How We Drafted Stevenson*. New York: Alfred A. Knopf, 1955.

Krock, Arthur. *Memoirs: Sixty Years on the Firing Line*. New York: Funk and Wagnalls, 1968.

Labor's Non-Partisan League. *Labor's Non-Partisan League, Its Origins and Growth*. Washington: Labor's Non-Partisan League, 1939.

Labor Union Political Expenditures. Washington: Senate Republican Policy Committee, 1955.

Laski, Harold. *The American Democracy*. New York: The Viking Press, 1948.

McDonald, David J. *Union Man*. New York: E. P. Dutton, 1969.

MacDougall, Curtis D. *Gideon's Army*. New York: Marzani and Munsell, 1965.

Moon, Henry Lee. *Balance of Power: The Negro Vote*. Garden City: Doubleday and Co., 1948.

Moscow, Warren. *The Last of the Big-Time Bosses*. New York: Stein and Day, 1971.

Nelson, Donald M. *Arsenal of Democracy, the Story of American War Production*. New York: Harcourt, Brace and Co., 1946.

Neuberger, Richard L. *Adventures in Politics*. New York: Oxford University Press, 1954.

Nixon, Richard M. *Six Crises*. Garden City: Doubleday and Co., 1962.

Perkins, Frances. *The Roosevelt I Knew*. New York: The Viking Press, 1946.

Rosenman, Samuel. *Working with Roosevelt*. New York: Harper and Brothers, 1952.

Stevenson, Adlai E. *Speeches of Adlai Stevenson*. New York: Random House, 1952.

Truman, Harry S. *Memoirs by Harry S. Truman*. Vol. 2:

Years of Trial and Hope. Garden City: Doubleday and
Co., 1955.

Voorhis, Jerry. *Confessions of a Congressman.* Garden City:
Doubleday and Co. 1947.

Walsh, J. Raymond. *C.I.O., Industrial Unionism in Action.*
New York: W. W. Norton Co., 1937.

Articles

Barkan, Solomon. "Applied Social Science in the American
Trade Union Movement," *Philosophy of Science,* 16 (July
1949), 193–97.

Carey, James. "Labor's Role in Politics: A Non-Partisan
Force," *Common Sense,* 13 (December 1944), 419–20.

——. "Organized Labor in Politics," *Annals of the American Academy of Political and Social Science,* 319 (September 1958), 52–62.

Green, William. "AFL and Politics," *American Federationist,*
48 (December 1940), 19.

Hillman, Sidney. "Is the PAC Beneficial to Labor and to the
Country?" *Reader's Digest,* 45 (November 1944), 77–81.

——. "The Truth about PAC," *New Republic,* 109 (August
21, 1944), 209–11.

Kroll, Jack. "Labor's Stake in Civic Affairs," *National Municipal Review,* 38 (December 1949), 542–45.

——. "You Can Learn a Lot in Ten Years," *American
Federationist,* 64 (December 1956), 428–43.

McDevitt, James L. "Contributions of L.L.P.E.," *American
Federationist,* 57 (November 1951), 13.

Murray, Philip. "Labor's Political Aims," *American Magazine,*
137 (February 1944), 28–29.

Potofsky, Jacob S. "Labor's Views; '54 Election," *Nation,* 178
(May 8, 1954), 403–4.

Watt, R. J. "Labor and Politics," *American Federationist,* 51
(September 1944), 5–7.

Woll, J. A. "High Court Speaks, but Vital Questions Remain
Unanswered," *American Federationist,* 55 (July 1948),
3–4.

Zon, Henry. "Political Education in Labor Unions," *Journal of
Social Issues,* 16 (1960), 21–23.

Union Periodicals

Advance. January, 1943–November, 1954.
American Federationist. December, 1895–December, 1954.
CIO News. March, 1942–December, 1954.

Dispatcher. January, 1943–November, 1954.
Economic Outlook. January, 1954–November, 1954.
NMU Pilot (or *Pilot*). February, 1943–November, 1954.
Packinghouse Worker. February, 1943–November, 1954.
Political Action of the Week. January, 1954–November, 1954.
Report on Congress. February, 1954–September, 1954.
Steel Labor. February, 1943–November, 1954.
Textile Labor. January, 1943–November, 1954.
U.E. News. January 23, 1943–August, 1944.
Union. May, 1943–October, 1954.
United Automobile Worker. December, 1942–November, 1954.
United Rubber Worker. February, 1943–November, 1944.

Secondary Sources

Books

Auerbach, Jerold S. *Labor and Liberty.* Indianapolis: Bobbs–Merrill, 1966.

Bardwell, George, and Seligson, Harry. *Organized Labor and Political Action in Colorado.* Denver: University of Denver College of Business Administration, 1959.

Bartholomew, Paul C. *The Indiana Third Congressional District.* South Bend: University of Notre Dame Press, 1970.

Bean, Louis H. *Influences in the 1954 Mid-Term Elections.* Washington: Public Affairs Institute, 1954.

Bernstein, Barton J., and Matusow, Allen J. *The Truman Administration.* New York: Harper Colophon Books, 1966.

Bernstein, Irving. *Turbulent Years: A History of the American Worker, 1933–1941.* Boston: Houghton Mifflin Co., 1970.

Bornet, Vaughan Davis. *Labor Politics in a Democratic Republic.* Washington: Spartan Books, 1964.

Burns, James M. *Roosevelt: The Lion and the Fox.* New York: Harcourt, Brace and Co., 1956.

———. *Roosevelt: The Soldier of Freedom.* New York: Harcourt Brace Jovanovich, 1970.

Campbell, Angus, and Cooper, Homer. *Group Differences in Attitudes and Votes: A Study of the 1954 Congressional Election.* Ann Arbor: Institute for Social Research, 1956.

Catchpole, Terry. *How to Cope with COPE: The Political Operation of Organized Labor.* New York: Arlington House, 1968.

Cook, Roy. *Leaders of Labor.* New York: J. B. Lippincott Co., 1966.

Cormier, Frank, and Eaton, William J. *Reuther.* Englewood Cliffs: Prentice–Hall, Inc., 1970.

Davis, Kenneth S. *A Prophet in His Own Country*. Garden City: Doubleday and Co., 1957.

Douglass, Paul F. *Six upon the World*. Boston: Little, Brown and Co., 1954.

Epstein, Leon. *Politics in Wisconsin*. Madison: University of Wisconsin Press, 1958.

Ernst, Morris, and Loth, David. *The People Know Best: The Ballots vs. the Polls*. Washington: Public Affairs Press, 1949.

Galenson, Walter. *The CIO Challenge to the AFL*. Cambridge: Harvard University Press, 1960.

Gallup, George. *The Political Almanac, 1952*. New York: B. C. Forbes and Sons, 1952.

Gavett, Thomas. *The Development of the Labor Movement in Milwaukee*. Madison: University of Wisconsin Press, 1965.

Goldman, Eric. *The Crucial Decade and After*. New York: Random House, 1960.

Goodman, Jay S. *The Democrats and Labor in Rhode Island, 1952–1962*. Providence: Brown University Press, 1967.

Greenstone, J. David. *Labor in American Politics*. New York: Alfred A. Knopf, 1969.

Griffith, Robert. *The Politics of Fear: Joseph P. McCarthy and the Senate*. Lexington: University of Kentucky Press, 1970.

Grob, Gerald. *Workers and Utopia*. Evanston: Northwestern University Press, 1961.

Harris, Louis. *Is There a Republican Majority?* New York: Harper and Brothers, 1954.

Hartman, Susan M. *Truman and the 80th Congress*. Columbia: University of Missouri Press, 1971.

Heard, Alexander, and Strong, Douglas S. *Southern Primaries and Elections, 1920–1949*. University: University of Alabama Press, 1955.

Howe, Irving and Coser, Lewis. *The American Communist Party*. Boston: Beacon Press, 1957.

Jacobsen, Julius (ed.). *The Negro and the American Labor Movement*. Garden City: Doubleday and Co., 1968.

Josephson, Matthew. *Sidney Hillman, Statesman of American Labor*. Garden City: Doubleday and Co., 1952.

Karson, Marc. *American Labor Unions and Politics, 1900–1918*. Carbondale: Southern Illinois University Press, 1958.

Kampelman, Max. *The Communist Party Vs. the CIO: A Study in Power Politics*. New York: Frederick A. Praeger, 1957.

Kelly, Richard. *Nine Lives for Labor*. New York: Frederick A. Praeger, 1956.

Kornhauser, Arthur; Sheppard, Harold; and Mayer, Albert. *When Labor Votes: A Study of Auto Workers*. New York: University Books, 1956.

Kornitzer, Bela. *The Real Nixon*. New York: Rand McNally and Co., 1960.

Latham, Earl. *The Communist Controversy in Washington*. Cambridge: Harvard University Press, 1966.

Lee, R. Alton. *Truman and Taft–Hartley*. Lexington: University of Kentucky Press, 1966.

Leggett, John C. *Class, Race, and Labor*. New York: Oxford University Press, 1968.

Lens, Sidney. *Left, Right, and Center*. Hinsdale: H. Regnery and Company, 1949.

———. *Rededication in America*. New York: Thomas Y. Crowell Co., 1969.

Leuchtenburg, William. *Franklin D. Roosevelt and the New Deal*. New York: Harper and Row, 1963.

Logan, Rayford. *The Negro in American Life and Thought*. New York: The Dial Press, 1954.

Lubell, Samuel. *The Future of American Politics*. New York: Harper and Brothers, 1952.

———. *The Revolt of the Moderates*. New York: Harper and Brothers, 1956.

McClure, Arthur F. *The Truman Administration and the Problem of Postwar Labor*. Rutherford: Fairleigh Dickinson University Press, 1969.

McFarland, Charles K. *Roosevelt, Lewis, and the New Deal, 1933–1940*. Fort Worth: Texas Christian University, 1970.

MacKay, Kenneth Campbell. *The Progressive Movement of 1924*. New York: Octagon Books, 1966.

McLaughlin, Doris B. *Michigan Labor: A Brief History from 1818 to the Present*. Ann Arbor: Institute of Labor and Industrial Relations, 1970.

Madison, Charles A. *American Labor Leaders*. New York: Harper and Brothers, 1950.

Mason, Alpheus. *Organized Labor and the Law*. Durham: North Carolina University Press, 1925.

Millis, Harry A., and Brown, Emily Clark. *From the Wagner Act to Taft–Hartley*. Chicago: University of Chicago Press, 1950.

———, and Montgomery, Royal E. *Organized Labor*, Vol. 3. New York: McGraw–Hill Book Co., 1945.

Mills, C. Wright. *The New Men of Power.* New York: Harcourt, Brace and Co., 1948.

Mitau, G. Theodore. *Politics in Minnesota.* Minneapolis: University of Minnesota Press, 1960.

Moos, Malcom. *Politics, Presidents, and Coattails.* Baltimore: John Hopkins University Press, 1952.

Neufeld, Maurice, and Hardman, J. B. S. (eds.). *The House of Labor: Internal Operations of American Unions.* New York: Prentice–Hall, 1951.

Patterson, James T. *Mr. Republican.* Boston: Houghton–Mifflin Co., 1972.

Peterson, Svend. *A Statistical History of the American Presidental Elections.* New York: Frederick Ungar Publishing Co., 1968.

Rehmus, Charles M., and McLaughlin, Doris B. (eds.). *Labor and American Politics.* Ann Arbor: University of Michigan Press, 1967.

Ross, Irwin. *The Loneliest Campaign.* New York: The New American Library, 1968.

Saposs, David. *Communism in American Politics.* Washington: Public Affairs Press, 1960.

————. *Communism in American Unions.* New York: McGraw–Hill Book Co., 1954.

Scammon, Richard. *America Votes.* New York: The Macmillan Co., 1956.

Schaffer, Alan. *Vito Marcantonio, Radical in Congress.* Syracuse: Syracuse University Press, 1966.

Schapsmeier, Edward L., and Schapsmeier, Frederick H. *Prophet in Politics: Henry A. Wallace and the War Years, 1940–1965.* Ames: Iowa State University Press, 1970.

Schlesinger, Arthur M.; Israel, Fred L.; Hansen, William P. *History of American Presidential Elections.* New York: Chelsea House Publishers in association with McGraw-Hill Book Co., 1971.

Schmidt, Karl M., *Henry Wallace: Quixotic Crusade, 1948.* Syracuse: Syracuse University Press, 1960.

Seidman, Joel. *American Labor from Defense to Reconversion.* Chicago: University of Chicago Press, 1953.

Shannon, David. *The Decline of American Communism.* New York: Harcourt, Brace and Co., 1957.

Spanier, John W. *The Truman–MacArthur Controversy and the Korean War.* New York: W. W. Norton and Co., 1965.

Taft, Philip. *The A.F. of L. in the Time of Gompers.* New York: Harper and Brothers, 1957.

————. *Organized Labor in American History*. New York: Harper and Brothers, 1964.

————. *Labor Politics American Style*. Cambridge: Harvard University Press, 1968.

Theoharis, Athan G. *The Yalta Myths: An Issue in U.S. Politics, 1945–1955*. Columbia: University of Missouri Press, 1970.

Teledano, Ralph de. *Nixon*. New York: Henry Holt and Co., 1956.

Turner, Henry A. (ed.). *Politics in the United States: Readings in Political Parties and Pressure Groups*. New York: McGraw–Hill Book Co., 1954.

White, William S. *The Taft Story*. New York: Harper and Brothers, 1954.

Whittemore, L. H. *The Man Who Ran the Subways, the Story of Mike Quill*. New York: Holt, Rinehart and Winston, 1968.

Who's Who in Labor. New York: The Dryden Press, 1946.

Zeiger, Robert H. *Republicans and Labor*. Lexington: University of Kentucky Press, 1969.

Articles

Amidon, Beulah. "Labor in Politics," *Survey Graphic,* 33 (September 1944), 390–93.

Barbash, Jack. "Unions, Government, and Politics," *Industrial and Labor Relations Review,* 1 (October 1947), 66–79.

Berelson, Bernard, and Lazarsfield, Paul F. "Women: A Major Problem for the PAC," *Public Opinion Quarterly,* 9 (1945), 79–82.

Bernstein, Irvin. "John L. Lewis and the Voting Behavior of the CIO," *Public Opinion Quarterly,* 5 (June 1941), 233–49.

"Big Effort Bears Some Fruit," *Business Week,* November 13, 1954, 160–63.

Braunthal, Alfred. "American Labor in Politics and the Possibility of Abandonment of Their Non-Partisan Policy," *Social Research,* 12 (February 1945), 1–21.

"Campaigning for Labor's Votes," *Business Week,* July 17, 1954, pp. 146–47.

Carleton, F. T. "American Labor at the Crossroads," *Sociology and Social Research,* 35 (May 1951), 331–37.

"CIO Studies Political Action, City Budget," *National Municipal Review,* 40 (June 1951), 330.

Cooke, Morris L. "Why Labor Is in Politics," *New Republic,* 111 (October 1944), 454–56.

Crossman, R. H. S. "American Labour in Politics," *New States-man and Nation,* 37 (April 9, 1949), 346–47.

David, Henry. "Labor and Political Teamwork," *Labor and Nation,* January 1948, pp. 20–30.

Destler, Chester M. "Consummation of a Labor–Populist Alliance in Illinois," *Mississippi Valley Historical Review,* 27 (March 1941), 589–602.

Downs, T. "CIO Girds Itself for '44; Joining Forces at the Ballot Box," *Antioch Review,* 3 (September 1943), 448–55.

Fuller, Helen. "Labor and Politics," *New Republic,* 110 (January 24, 1944), 111–13.

Grob, Gerald N. "Origins of the Political Philosophy of the AFL, 1886–1896," *Review of Politics,* 22 (October 1960), 496–518.

Huddle, F. P. "Political Action by Organized Labor," *Editorial Research Reports,* September 16, 1944, 171–83.

Hudson, R. A., and Rosen, H. "Union Political Action: The Member Speaks," *Industrial and Labor Relations Review,* 7 (April 1954), 404–18.

Johnson, Victor H. "The Coming Rebellion of Labor," *New Republic,* 108 (January 21, 1943), 824–25.

Kutler, Stanley I. "Labor, the Clayton Act, and the Supreme Court," *Labor History,* 3 (Winter 1962), 19–38.

LaPalombara, J. G. "Pressure, Propaganda, and Political Action in the Elections of 1950," *Journal of Politics,* 14 (May 1952), 313–21.

Leeds, Morton. "AFL in the 1948 Elections," *Social Research,* 17 (June 1950), 207–18.

Lubell, Samuel. "How Taft Did It," *Saturday Evening Post,* 223 (February 10, 1951), 32–33.

MacKenzie, N. "U.S. Labour and the Elections," *New States-man and Nation,* 40 (November 4, 1950), 399.

"The Meaning of PAC," *New Republic,* 111 (August 14, 1944), 174–75.

Overacker, Louise. "Labor Rides the Political Waves," *Current History,* 7 (December 1944), 468–78.

"PAC–CIO's Political Plunge," *Business Week,* September 23, 1944, p. 22.

Pearl, P. "Political Drive Launched," *American Federationist,* 50 (September 1943), 3.

Pelling, Henry. "Labor and Politics in Chicago," *Political Studies,* 5 (February 1957), 21–35.

Peterson, James. "Trade Unions and the Populist Party," *Science and Society,* 8 (1944), 143–60.

"Picking up the Pieces," *Fortune,* 46 (December 1952), 83–84.

"Planning Labor's Role in 1954," *Business Week,* August 29, 1953, p. 136.

"The Political Aims of Organized Labor," *Annals of the American Academy of Political and Social Science,* September 1948, pp. 144–52.

"Political Trends of American Labor," *Economist,* 155 (August 7, 1948), 226–27.

Pomper, Gerald. "Labor Legislation: The Revision of Taft–Hartley in 1953–1954," *Labor History,* 6 (Spring 1965), 143–58.

Raskin, A. H. "Taft–Hartley and Labor's Perspective," *Commentary,* 4 (November 1947), 435–40.

"Reuther: F.O.B. Detroit," *Fortune,* 32 (December 1945), 149–51.

Rischin, Moses. "From Gompers to Hillman, Labor Goes Middle Class," *Antioch Review,* 13 (June 1953), 191–201.

Rosenfarb, Joseph. "Labor's Role in the Election," *Public Opinion Quarterly,* 8 (Fall 1944), 376–90.

Rovere, Richard. "Labor's Political Machine," *Harpers,* 190 (June 1945), 592–601.

Seidman, Joel, *et al.* "Political Consciousness in a Local Union," *Public Opinion Quarterly,* 15 (1951), 692–702.

Stanley, M. T. "Amalgamation of Collective Bargaining and Political Activity by the UAW," *Industrial and Labor Relations Review,* 10 (October 1956), 40–47.

Stativisky, S. "Labor's Political Plans for '54," *Nations Business,* 42 (April 1954), 25–27.

Stein, Sidney. "The CIO Convention and the Struggle for Labor Unity," *Political Affairs,* December, 1949, pp. 35–45.

Taft, Philip. "Attempts to Radicalize the Labor Movement," *Industrial and Labor Relations Review,* 1 (July 1948), 580–92.

————. "Labor's Changing Political Line," *Journal of Political Economy,* 45 (October 1937), 634–50.

"Union Political Activity Spans 230 Years of U.S. History," *American Federationist,* 67 (May 1960), 6–11.

"Unions Turn to Politics," *Business Week,* October 9, 1954, p. 192.

"Why Labor Is Seeing Democratic," *Business Week,* September 25, 1954, pp. 30–32.

Witte, E. E. "New Federation and Political Action," *Industrial and Labor Relations Review,* 9 (April 1956), 406–18.

○ Zon, Mary. "Labor in Politics," *Law and Contemporary Problems,* 27 (Spring 1962), 234–51.

Unpublished Material

Arnold, Delbert Donald. "The CIO's Role in American Politics, 1936–1948," Ph.D. dissertation, University of Maryland, 1952.

Baisdon, Richard. "Labor Unions in Los Angeles Politics," Ph.D. dissertation, University of Chicago, 1958.

Bender, Ruth. "AFL Political Action in St. Louis, Missouri," M.A. thesis, University of Illinois, 1951.

Carter, Robert Frederick. "Pressure from the Left: The American Labor Party, 1936–1954," Ph.D. dissertation, Syracuse University, 1965.

Feiler, Rita. "Selected Political Attitudes and Opinions of Michigan CIO Secondary Leadership," M.A. thesis, University of Michigan, 1954.

Harris, Avril E. "Organized Labor in Party Politics, 1906–1936," Ph.D. dissertation, University of Iowa, 1937.

Harrison, Selig. "The Political Program of the UAW," B.A. thesis, Harvard University, 1948.

Koistinen, Paul A. C. "The Hammer and the Sword: Labor, the Military, and Industrial Mobilization," Ph.D. dissertation, University of California, 1965.

Kreps, Juanita M. "Developments in the Political and Legislative Policies of Organized Labor," Ph.D. dissertation, Duke University, 1947.

Kuhl, William O. "A Study of the Political Methods of the American Labor Movement since the Eighties," Ph.D. dissertation, University of Wisconsin, 1957.

Leeds, Morton H. "The AFL in National Politics, 1938–1948," Ph.D. dissertation, New School for Social Research, 1950.

Marx, Sue A. "1952 Election Study: Republican Voters in the UAW Membership," M.A. thesis, Wayne State University, 1956.

Mersdorf, Doris Ellen. "Local 222: a Study of Factors Associated with the Willingness of Its Membership to Define Political Action as a Union Function," M.A. thesis, University of Chicago, 1953.

Oshinsky, David Matthew. "Senator Joseph McCarthy and American Labor," M.S. thesis, Cornell University, 1968.

Owen, Homer Leroy. "The Role of CIO–PAC in the 1944 Elections," M.S. thesis, Cornell University, 1952.

Pinola, Rudolph. "Labor and Politics on the Iron Range of

Northern Minnesota," Ph.D. dissertation, University of Wisconsin, 1957.

Pomper, Gerald M. "Organized Labor in Politics, the Campaign to Revise the Taft–Hartley Act," Ph.D. dissertation, Princeton University, 1959.

Rule, Wilma Louise Benta. "Political Discipline in the CIO, 1948–1949," M.A. thesis, University of California, 1950.

Saenger, Martha L. "Labor Political Action at Mid-Twentieth Century, a Case Study of the CIO–PAC Campaign of 1944 and the TWUA," Ph.D. dissertation, Ohio State University, 1959.

Schwartzbach, Irving. "The History of the CIO–Political Action Committee," M.A. thesis, Columbia University, 1957.

Seasholes, Bradbury. "Labor Union Financial Participation in the 1952 Election," M.A. thesis, University of North Carolina, 1958.

Steele, Norbert W. "Political Aspirations of the CIO: an Historical Evaluation of Their Political Action Committee from July, 1943 to July 1953," M.A. thesis, Loyola University.

Tanenhaus, Joseph. "Organized Labor and Freedom of Speech: a study of the Law Governing Picketing and Labor's Political Spending," Ph.D. dissertation, Cornell University, 1953.

Waterfall, Mary. "CIO Political Action, First Year in Operation," M.A. thesis, University of Michigan, 1955.

Wolcott, Roger T. "Opinion Leadership in Union Politics," M.A. thesis, Columbia University, 1955.

Index

A

Abt, John, 24–25
ACTU. *See* Association of Catholic Trade Unionists
ADA. *See* Americans for Democratic Action
Addes, George, 23
AFL. *See* American Federation of Labor
American Federation of Labor: under Gompers, 4–5; and LLPE, 99; and 1954 election, 194; and creation of PAC, 202. *See also* Voluntarism
American Labor party: 7, 15, 35, 96; and 1944 election, 29–32
Americans for Democratic Action: 89; and Philip Murray, 91–93; and Biemiller report, 101–7; and CIO withdrawals, 133–35; and analysis of 1950 election, 152. *See also* Union for Democratic Action
Amlie, Thomas, and advice on 1944 election, 32–36, 41–42, 43, 44
Association of Catholic Trade Unionists, 80, 83–86, 88, 89. *See also* Cort, John; Read, Harry; Rice, Father Charles Owen

B

Baldwin, C. B., 32, 86
Ball-Burton-Hatch bill, 50
Biemiller, Andrew: 95, 125; and analysis of 1947 elections, 101–7. *See also* Americans for Democratic Action
Bill of Grievances, 4. *See also* Gompers, Samuel
Brophy, John: and Cowan-Brophy-Walsh report, 6–8; and CIO Industrial Union councils, 49, 119n; mentioned, 14, 58, 78, 80, 87, 94n
Browder, Earl, 39, 96

Burnside, E. G., 62, 63, 124
Byrnes, James, 46–47, 48

C

Carey, James: analysis of 1942 election, 5, 25–26; and United Electrical Workers, 80–81, 82; and CIO purge, 83–84, 85, 93–94; mentioned, 8, 86, 87, 88
Case bill, 55–56
Chicago Conference of Progressives: and Progressive Citizens of America, 86; mentioned, 65, 68, 75, 90, 96
CIO. *See* Congress of Industrial Organizations
CIO News: and Leonard DeCaux, 87–88; and *United States* vs. *CIO,* 108–9
CIO–PAC. *See* Congress of Industrial Organizations Political Action Committee
Clark, Bennett Champ, 29
"Clear it with Sidney." *See* Krock, Arthur
Clifford, Clark: 69; and Clifford Memorandum, 100–101. *See also* Truman, Harry S., and 1948 election
Committee for a United Labor Party, 31
Congress of Industrial Organizations: and Executive Board, 3, 6, 10, 11–13, 61–62; and Industrial Union councils, 6, 7, 49, 119; and Smith-Connally Act, 10–12; and Committee on Congressional Action, 17, 23; and Taft-Hartley Act, 70–75; and *United States* vs. *CIO,* 108–11. *See also* Congress of Industrial Organizations Political Action Committee; Murray, Philip; Reuther, Walter
Congress of Industrial Organizations Political Action Committee: as a labor party, 9, 13, 203–5; creation of, 13; ideol-

ogy of, 17–21; and 1944 campaign, 36–48; and 1946 campaign, 56, 60–69; and 1947 campaign, 95–99, 105–7; and 1948 campaign, 111–32; and 1950 campaign, 135–54; and 1950s organization, 155–58; and 1952 campaign, 159–75; and 1954 campaign, 177–94; and women voters, 178–81; and the Democratic party, 199–201. *See also* Hillman, Sidney; Kroll, Jack
Cort, John, 84, 85–86
Cowan, Nathan, 6, 7, 87
Cowan-Brophy-Walsh report, 6–10, 13, 21, 90
Cronin, Father John, 84
CULP. *See* Committee for a United Labor Party

D

DeCaux, Leonard: resigns from CIO, 87–88; and PAC as a labor party, 203–5
Democratic National Convention: of 1944, 45–48; of 1948, 114–17; of 1952, 160–62
Democratic party: and CIO in Michigan, 120–22; and PAC options in 1955, 199–201. *See also* Clifford, Clark; Roosevelt, Franklin D.; Truman, Harry S.
Dewey, Thomas, 21, 39, 126–27
Dies, Martin, 28
Douglas, Helen Gahagan: 119, 137; and Richard Nixon, 142–45
Douglas, William O., 115
Dubinsky, David, 29–31, 89, 101. *See also* Americans for Democratic Action, American Labor party

E

Easton, John: and 1944 campaign, 37–39; mentioned, 63, 123
Eisenhower, Dwight David: 114, 155; and 1952 campaign, 162–64, 168; and 1954 elections, 185, 191
Elections: of 1942, 5, 25; of 1944, 39–44; of 1946, 67–70;

of 1948, 126–32; of 1950, 138–54; of 1952, 170–75; of 1954, 189–95
Ervin, Charles, and analysis of 1944 election, 40–41

F

Fish, Hamilton, 35, 36, 41
Fitzgerald, Albert, 13n, 81–82
Frankensteen, Richard T., 59–60
Full Employment bill, 51–52

G

Gaer, Joseph, 18, 21n, 45, 96, 157
General Motors Strike of 1946, 53, 54, 55
Gompers, Samuel, 3–5, 12, 13. *See also* American Federation of Labor; Voluntarism
Green, William, 96, 100–101
Green-Brodie report, 111–12, 126

H

Hannegan, Robert, 45–47
Hartley, Fred, Jr.: and Taft-Hartley Act, 70, 72–74; and *Our New National Labor Policy,* 118, 120. *See also* Hartley bill; Taft, Robert
Hartley bill, 72, 73, 74
Haywood, Alan, 78, 91
Henderson, Leon, 91
Hillman, Sidney: appointed to PAC, 13; and FDR, 22; and Arthur Krock, 45–48; death of, 61; mentioned, 15, 16, 25, 26, 33, 35, 39, 40, 42, 44, 56, 57, 58, 60, 62, 64, 90. *See also* Congress of Industrial Organizations Political Action Committee
Hoffa, James, and Michigan Democratic party, 121
Humphrey, Hubert, 34, 134n, 177; and 1948 Democratic Convention, 116

I

ILGWU. *See* International Ladies Garment Workers' Union

Independent Citizens Committee of the Arts, Sciences, and Professions, 65, 87. *See also* Chicago Conference of Progressives
International Ladies Garment Workers' Union, 29, 31, 89. *See also* Dubinsky, David

J

Jeffries, Edward, 59–60

K

Kefauver, Estes, 104, 160, 177. *See also* Democratic National Convention, of 1952
Kilgore, Harley, 62, 63
Krock, Arthur, and "Clear it with Sidney," 39, 45–48, 202–3
Kroll, Jack: and 1948 Democratic Convention, 114–17; and plans for 1950, 135–38; and Taft purge, 138–42; and Adlai Stevenson, 161; and 1952 campaign, 169–71, 172–74; mentioned, 38, 61, 62, 65, 72, 111, 124. *See also* Congress of Industrial Organizations Political Action Committee

L

Labor's League for Political Education: creation, 99; and 1954, 194; and merger with PAC, 196
Labor's Non-Partisan League, 6–7, 8. *See also* Cowan-Brophy-Walsh report
LaFollette, Robert M., Jr., 67, 198
LaGuardia, Fiorello, 31
Laski, Harold, and PAC as a proto-labor party, 203–4
Lewis, John L.: and LNPL, 6; and Philip Murray, 77, 78, 80; mentioned, 52, 104, 123
LLPE. *See* Labor's League for Political Education
Loeb, James, Jr., 57, 64, 89, 91. *See also* Americans for Democratic Action; Union for Democratic Action
Luce, Clare Booth, 39–40

M

McCarthy, Joseph, 67, 159, 167–68
McDonald, David: and 1948 Democratic National Convention, 115; and Adlai Stevenson, 160–62; mentioned, 117
Mason, Anne, 124, 125
Meany, George, 100–101
Moon, Henry Lee, 27n, 97–98, 157
Morse, Wayne: 189n, 207; and PAC policy, 197–98
Murray, James, 73
Murray, Milton, 66
Murray, Philip: and creation of PAC, 3, 5–6, 12–13; and 79th Congress, 51, 53; and UDA, 57–58; union career of, 76–83; and CIO red scare, 80–83, 86–94; and *US v. CIO*, 109, 110; and Adlai Stevenson, 161; mentioned, 23n, 71, 95, 100, 101, 111, 117. *See also* Congress of Industrial Organizations Political Action Committee

N

National Citizens Political Action Committee: mentioned, 57, 68, 75; creation of, 64, 96; and Chicago Conference of Progressives, 65; and Progressive Citizens of America, 86
National Labor Management Relations Act. *See* Taft-Hartley Act
National Labor Relations Act. *See* Wagner Act
National Labor Relations Board, 10, 72, 74. *See also* Wagner Act
NCPAC. *See* National Citizens Political Action Committee
Nixon, Richard M.: mentioned, 68, 76; and Helen Gahagan Douglas, 143–45; and Nixon fund, 168
NLRB. *See* National Labor Relations Board
Norris, George, 5, 64
Norton bill, 53, 55

P

PAC. *See* Congress of Industrial Organizations Political Action Committee

PCA. *See* Progressive Citizens of America

"'People's Program for 1944," 19–21

Pepper, Claude, 115, 116

Progressive Citizens of America: and Chicago Conference of Progressives, 86; mentioned, 87, 89, 90, 102

R

Randolph, Jennings, 38

Read, Harry, 83–86. *See also* Association of Catholic Trade Unionists

Reisel, Victor, 122

Reuther, Walter: 66, 67; and CIO red scare, 89, 91; and ADA withdrawal, 134; and 1954 elections, 178, 185. *See also* Americans for Democratic Action

Rice, Father Charles Owen, 77, 79, 88, 89n, 90n. *See also* Association of Catholic Trade Unionists

Rieve, Emil: 18, 89, 93, 115; and withdrawal from ADA, 133–34. *See also* Textile Workers Union of America

Right-to-work Laws, 49, 118. *See also* Taft-Hartley Act

Roosevelt, Franklin D.: 17, 19, 30, 49, 100; and Sidney Hillman, 22; and the 1944 campaign, 39, 40, 43; and "Clear it with Sidney," 45, 47

S

Scholle, August, 67, 121–22, 146, 147

Sigler, Kim, 67

Smith, Howard: 10, 29, 71; and CIO investigation, 52–53. *See also* Smith-Connally Act

Smith-Connally Act, 10–12, 24, 52, 64

Speakers Manual for 1944, 36–37

Stevenson, Adlai: and 1952 Democratic Convention, 161–62; and 1952 campaign, 168–69, 170–71

Swim, Allen, 88, 108

T

Taft, Robert: 70–72, 109; and CIO purge of, 137, 138–42

Taft bill, described, 70–73

Taft-Hartley Act: 49, 102, 106; passage of, 70–75; and *US* v. *CIO,* 108–11; and move for revision, 185–86

Textile Workers Union of America, 17–18, 32n

"This Is Your America," 18–19

Thomas, Rolland J., 13, 14, 58, 64, 66, 67

"Toward a New Day," 17–18

Truman, Harry S.: and 1944 nomination, 45–48; and revision of Wagner Act, 54–56, 70; and Clifford Memorandum, 100–101; and 1948 campaign, 102, 117, 126–27, 129; mentioned, 71, 74, 76, 91. *See also* Clifford, Clark; Democratic National Convention, 1948

U

UDA. *See* Union for Democratic Action

Union for Democratic Action: 32, 57, 89, 90; and 1944 nomination, 47; and national liberal coalition, 57–58. *See also* Americans for Democratic Action

United Automobile Workers of America, 53, 59, 66. *See also* General Motors Strike of 1946; Reuther, Walter; Thomas, Rolland J.

United Electrical Workers of America, and CIO purge, 80–83, 93. *See also* Carey, James; Fitzgerald, Albert; Murray, Philip

United States v. *Congress of Industrial Organizations,* 108–11

V

Voluntarism, 3–5, *See also* American Federation of Labor
Voorhis, Jerry, 67, 68

W

Wagner Act, 11, 64
Wagoner, Van, 67
Wallace, Henry: 6, 48, 90, 122, 127; and 1944 Vice Presidential nomination, 46–47. *See also* Progressive Citizens of America
Walsh, J. Raymond, 6. *See also* Cowan-Brophy-Walsh report

War Labor Disputes Act. *See* Smith-Connally Act
Weaver, George L-P, 139
Weber, Paul, 84, 85. *See also* Association of Catholic Trade Unionists
WFTU. *See* World Federation of Trade Unions
Williams, G. Mennen, 121, 122, 147–148
Willkie, Wendell, 21, 78
Wolchok, Samuel, 12, 89
World Federation of Trade Unions, 58, 69, 85, 86

Y

Yalta Conference, 69, 170